THE JOHN HARVARD LIBRARY

Howard Mumford Jones
Editor-in-Chief

AMERICA

A Sketch of Its Political, Social, and
Religious Character

By

PHILIP SCHAFF

Edited by Perry Miller

THE BELKNAP PRESS OF
HARVARD UNIVERSITY PRESS

Cambridge, Massachusetts

1961

Contents

CONTENTS

vi

I

In the first half of the nineteenth century, the solid, learned, civilized ecclesiastics of Europe heard with consternation fantastic rumors about religious life in the new United States. Since the majority of American citizens, for decades after the winning of independence, were reputed to be Protestants, reports of their antics were especially shocking to Protestant congregations in Europe — to English Dissenters no less than to English Churchmen, to Scottish Presbyterians, and to the sedate Dutch churches, Calvinist or Arminian. But no Europeans were more appalled by accounts of America than the German churchmen. There, both in the Catholic Communions and in the Protestant — the latter being either Lutherans or Calvinists — an ideal of scholarship, of courtly relations, of stately acknowledgment of differences, along with a meticulous maintenance of them, and above all, of decorum, had been achieved out of the violence (resolutely relegated to history) of the religious wars.

Still, when historians compelled the burghers of Zürich or Berlin to acknowledge that the wars had really been fought, they had the consolation of remembering that those battles were over majestic issues, of Transubstantiation against Consubstantiation, of Papacy against Principality. States had been champions of churches, and the order which eventually rescued Europe from anarchy proved to be an alliance of a dominant theology with civil power. *Cuius regio, cuius religio* furnished the principle of solidarity, as was demonstrated equally by the Established Church in

England and by the enforced union of Lutherans and Calvinists into the state church of Brandenburg.

From the European point of view, therefore, the American scene loomed as a reversion to bedlam. Its radical separation of church and state seemed to have exterminated every vestige of any concept of authority. There appeared to be a riot of sects, and an unholy competition among them. All this was frightening enough — much more disturbing than any recollection of the bloody but still respectably ideological contentions of Europe — but in addition there were horrendous narratives of the American revivals, wherein hysterical enthusiasts barked like dogs, writhed in sawdust. Every communication augmented the impression of insanity; in the 1830's came, for instance, descriptions of the "new measures" of Charles Grandison Finney, particularly his "anxious bench," upon which troubled souls were seated and then tormented into a desperation which Finney conceived to be regeneration. In Germany there had been, of course, pietistic revivals, and in England a preaching to vast throngs in the fields by Whitefield; but these had not been maniacal convulsions. In the settled opinion of Germany, America was a religious chaos, and so the source of a plague that threatened to spread around the world, despite the efforts of German scholars, working sixteen hours a day in their libraries, to protect the Fatherland by erecting the thick walls of their erudite tomes. That these bulwarks of print were at best readable only by the fraternity of the universities, and were utterly incomprehensible to the frontiersmen of Kentucky who shouted and fainted at Cane Ridge, was not in the least a consideration of theirs. Not one of the *Geheimrats* would have ventured into the American pandemonium. Occupying chairs of theology which they had won in fumigated academic struggles, secure in their tenure, their salary insured by the state, they could produce their surveys of systematic theology, of dogma, and of church history, showing meanwhile a shuddering apprehension of the distant but ever haunting apparition of America.

In the summer of 1843 there suddenly appeared amid the groves of German Protestant academia two emissaries out of this wilderness. But they were not red Indians, nor were they Finney revivalists. Instead they bore such indisputably German names as Benjamin S. Schneck and Theodore L. Hoffeditz; they constituted a committee from the Pennsylvania Synod of the German Reformed Church. Though coming from an immense distance, and despite many difficulties in even gaining access to German publications, they were worshippers of German scholarship. Their humble mission was to secure, if possible, a "Doktor" for the professorship of historical and exegetical theology in their pioneer seminary in the forests around Mercersburg. They had absurd hopes of securing Dr. Frederick Krummacher, of Elberfeld in Prussia; soon they realized that the then foremost preacher in Protestant Germany would hardly consider extinguishing himself in the wastes of America, or that, had he been inclined to listen, the King of Prussia would never permit him to depart. Thus rudely instructed as to the connection of state and church in Brandenburg, the ambassadors begged the pundits of the kingdom to suggest a candidate, one who might adequately represent Teutonic scholarship but be still young enough, not yet established enough, and adventurous enough in spirit, to risk the call, and whom the state would let go. The professors solemnly caucused — among them the majestic Neander — and recommended Philip Schaff, a *Privatdocent* in the University of Berlin, aged twenty-four, who had become a Doktor only two years previously, but who had studied under almost all the outstanding teachers of Germany, who already exhibited a capacity for an unlimited acquisition of facts, who in addition was born in Switzerland and might therefore, in the opinion of the Prussian Sanhedrin, be more acceptable to a republican society. The emissaries returned to a meeting of the synod in Winchester, reported that Schaff was the best they could find, and on October 12, 1843, got a consent to their motion from a German brotherhood thankful to receive anybody who would bring the aroma of August Neander and Friedrich Tholuck into the raw corridors of Mercersburg.

Dr. Schaff would never tire of relating (as in the present volume) that Germans began to emigrate to America in the seventeenth century and so could claim almost as ancient a lineage as the Virginians and the New Englanders. But the big wave of settlers swelled in the early eighteenth century. The Reformed peoples came mostly from the Palatinate, and generally located in groups rather than ranging as individuals like the Scotch-Irish. They had a profound respect for learning and strove under even the most penurious of frontier conditions to maintain elementary schools. As soon as possible they organized their churches in synods and strove to import educated ministers from Europe. They subscribed to the Heidelberg Catechism, which is substantially Calvinist but omits reference to an eternal decree of reprobation. The churches were inevitably caught up in the excitement of the Great Awakening and in the evangelical movements at the end of the century; several internal conflicts developed, but in general the Reformed congregations resisted revivalism and Methodism, and maintained a "sound" theological position against pietistic tendencies. Their retention of the German language helped to insulate them against the disruptive influences of American society. But after the Revolution, when they found their connections with Germany extenuated and so were thrown abruptly upon their own resources, they perceived that they would have to establish a seminary to train native-born ministers in both the language and the theology of their forbears, in order to maintain their individuality.

After several abortive attempts and much self-sacrificing labor, in 1837 an institution was set up in Mercersburg. The first president, Frederick Augustus Rauch, had studied at several German universities, chiefly Heidelberg, and was aware of the new ideas emerging from the intense theological as well as philosophical ferment over there. Under his leadership the synod made a bold move in 1840 by calling to a professorship a Presbyterian who was not a German and who had been educated at Union College and at Princeton Seminary. John Williamson Nevin had already shown himself to be a character of strength and had become a resolute opponent of the "new measures" sweeping back and forth through the revivals continually ravaging the country. The synod and the seminary took a large risk in joining together in the faculty two such prime donne as Nevin and Schaff; but despite the vast differences of their backgrounds, they proved to be intellectually so congenial that their relations were ideally cordial.

The synod sought for a man in Germany because, except for Nevin, there was no competent scholar available in America. Although Nevin was a prodigious worker and read German fluently, he received communications from abroad without possessing that intimate knowledge of their nuances which only one who had actually studied under Tholuck and Neander could appreciate. And, as the event proved, in Philip Schaff the synod found the ideal man for its assignment. The conclave of professors in Berlin who recommended him to the delegates performed a great service for the German Reformed Church and also for the Presbyterian Churches in America, but more importantly they rendered an inestimable service to the cause of American scholarship in general. Schaff became the main channel through which the riches of German Protestant theology (as distinguished from, if it can be really separated from, the literature of German Romanticism) flowed to the New World.

II

Schaff was born in 1819 at Chur in Switzerland. (He would delight in asserting, "I am a Swiss by birth, a German by education, and an American by choice.") His father was a carpenter, the family undistinguished and miserably poor. About the only wealth his parents could transmit to him was a splendid physical constitution which permitted him to devote hour after hour to concentrated study without the slightest flagging. He later contended that from the free air of Switzerland he imbibed a republican, if not quite a democratic, predilection, and so could see the United States as a sort of extended Switzerland. "On my arrival here," he would recollect, "I found it much easier to fall in with American institutions and to feel at home in this country than the emigrants from imperial Germany." The latter, he characteristically added, upon being exposed to the whirlwind of America, were apt either to retreat the more fanatically into authoritarianism or else "to run into an excess of democracy, especially on the Sunday question." The point of this last remark may be lost on the youth of today: Schaff means that the German population, Reformed as well as Lutheran, as they became numerous and vocal, agitated increasingly for music-halls and beer against the still dominant formula of the "Puritan" Sabbath. In this issue, as in many others, the Swiss-German Schaff was on the side of purity. This is one reason why he was able to become a powerful instrument for instructing and warning American Protestantism about the "dangerous" sophistications of the Germanic temper.

The poverty of Schaff's boyhood was, by any account we can gather, grinding. The wonder is how he made his way out of it, and entered upon a long pilgrimage from university to university, in the manner of the wandering scholars of the middle ages. The still greater wonder is that the struggle left no marks of bitterness upon his enormously genial spirit. He commenced his journey at the age of fifteen, carrying all his earthly possessions in a knapsack and travelling alone and on foot to Württemberg. Just how he managed to earn enough for food and tuition is a bit obscure, at least in his own reminiscences, but evidently he did a fair amount of tutoring or else bodily labor. In the midst of these exertions he acquired a thorough grounding in Latin and Greek, though as he subsequently acknowledged, he learned little or nothing of the natural sciences.

In the years from 1837 to 1840 he attended Tübingen, Halle, and Berlin. In each he attracted the attention of the most distinguished professors. When one considers how remote these Olympian deities were (and their successors try to be) from the plebeian students, one sees how remarkable a scholar Schaff must have been to break through their barriers. To list his teachers, many of whom became his friends, is to recite the names of the giants in that epoch of earthshaking controversy: Baur, Schmid, Tholuck, Müller, Twesten, Hengstenberg, and above all August Neander of Berlin, who impressed upon him the importance of correct historical methods and imparted to him the ironic spirit for which he later suffered in America but which he laboriously vindicated in his adopted country.

Schaff's sense for the grand stream of Christian history was undoubtedly strengthened by the opportunity given him to enjoy an early and vivid acquaintance with Italy. He had been tutoring the son of a wealthy Prussian baroness; in 1841 she took both the pupil and the tutor on a leisurely fourteen-month tour of Italy, where Schaff systematically (in the authentic German spirit) went through the museums, worked over every ruin, and conscientiously studied all manifestations of Roman Catholicism. His stalwart Protestantism was never in the slightest endangered, but he did acquire a deep respect for Catholic piety. He even had an audience with Pope Gregory XVI, a fact which would count against him among American Protestants, who believed that one could not touch pitch without being defiled. He left the city of Rome with a sad heart, reflecting that in it "we find from youth up an intellectual home, an inexhaustible fountain of study and moral counsel, of wisdom and experience." He stubbornly refused ever to surrender this central insight into forms of Christian fragmentation, and eventually it so informed his masterpiece, the *History of the Christian Church* (best consulted in the fifth edition, seven volumes, 1882–1892), that the work remains, even though many additions have been made by modern research, a stupendous achievement of comprehension.

In Rome, and upon the return journey through Switzerland and Germany, Schaff commenced what was to become his life-long habit, calling on the leading religious figures of the several communities. He always won attention, by his knowledge, his amenability, his interest in local problems. This talent further enlarged his sensitivity to the whole situation of Christianity, Catholic or Protestant, orthodox or heterodox, and strengthened his ability to transcend sectarianism. Out of these multiple experiences he acquired that faith in the essential unity of the Church which informs all his writings, and which supremely enabled him, as this volume demonstrates, to look benevolently upon the incoherence of America, where all of his compatriots, Swiss or German, could behold only a repellant vulgarity.

Back in Berlin, as *Privatdocent* in 1842, he was besieged by an American who announced himself as Dr. Edwards Park, coming from some weird institution known as the Andover Theological Seminary. The name of Jonathan Edwards at that time meant nothing to Schaff. Park requested instruction in the system of Schleiermacher, but Schaff's English was not up to the task of communication.

He turned Park over to a colleague, who found Park's questioning of everything German so intolerable that he exclaimed to Schaff, "God forgive Christopher Columbus for having discovered America!" This was the attitude that generally prevailed among the cultivated of Berlin, most of whom by then sadly concluded that the German churches of America had fallen into the American pit and were unreclaimable. In the atmosphere of this conviction Schneck and Hoffeditz emerged out of the mist with an invitation that *Privatdocent* Schaff become a full professor in a place called, implausibly, Mercersburg.

III

The motives that determined Schaff to accept this call deserve serious scrutiny. The mass of Germans who since the early eighteenth century clawed their way out of the Fatherland had done so under cruel compulsion, with heavy hearts and no grandiose expectations. They were indeed what Oscar Handlin terms "uprooted." Schaff was subject to no such pressures. He was assured of his promotion at the University of Berlin — and in the German academic hierarchy this was no slight consideration. Also, he was being considered for a chair at Zürich; had he decided to take this, he would have been enthroned among the scholars of central Europe in a principality of his own, an equal of Tholuck and Neander.

Perhaps, however, there were a few external influences. German hierophants regularly lamented that the Germans in America had become spiritually destitute, but few of them proposed to do anything about the tragedy except to lament. These joined fervently in hoping that Schaff would act in their stead. It illuminates the mental world Schaff left behind him to realize that Professor Dorner, who would never have thought of leaving Tübingen for a wigwam in Pennsylvania, urged Schaff to go in exactly these terms:

Especially do I think it exceedingly important that German theological scholarship be represented there. Only through that channel can the Germans be expected to make that full contribution which they are able to make, and the German-American Church will only then show its peculiar strength when it yields to theological science her rightful place.

Such a letter could have been written, in 1843, only in Germany. Yet we perceive more closely what Herr Professor Dorner was driving at when he continues with the observation that sooner or later questions will arise in the United States which are of decisive "national" importance — "questions touching the relations of the state to religion which can only be answered by such scholarly culture." Professor Dorner had not read, or if he had, did not comprehend, the First Amendment to the American Constitution. Neither, presumably, had Philip Schaff. But Dorner's exhortation does illuminate the reasons for a professorial eagerness that Schaff should become the sacrificial lamb: America was a threat to German (and European) hard-won religious serenity. In this light it is further instructive to learn that King Frederick William IV, relieved that he could suppress any inclination in Dr. Krummacher to escape the enclosure, gave his blessing to Schaff's migration, called the emissaries in for a discussion, and contributed 1500 thalers to the seminary at Mercersburg.

Schaff himself was fully aware of these inducements toward cultural imperialism, and was in no sense a rebel against the German complex of state, church, and university. Though he was always to think of himself at least as partially cast in the rôle to which Dorner consigned him, he seemed at the beginning not to have assumed the obligation entirely in the imposed terms. This is possibly the best explanation for his ample career in the wilderness and for the astonishing freedom displayed in this book, his first report to the Germany of Dorner. At the end of 1843 he communed with himself upon what he had decided; the passage must be given in full if we are to comprehend the passions which, artfully but not entirely concealed in the delivery, make his *America* one of the most searching analyses of the national character composed in his century.

I am to go to another part of the earth, to teach German theology in a land with a great creative activity before it, which breathes the fresh air of spring and where every tendency can develop itself unhampered from without. My call should be a summons to a connection to be equally blessed to both parties, the mother churches in Germany and the brethren who have emigrated abroad and who, unless help be soon extended to them, are in danger of sinking into irreligion or of falling into the Roman Catholic Church, which is very active on the other side of the ocean, or of being swallowed up by the numberless sects.

Here, as seen from Germany, was the challenge of America, and to this the youth replied. Quite fittingly, he concluded, "Lord, imbue me with wisdom and love that I may worthily respond to this call which by Thy grace has come to me."

As though Schaff were about to be sent down into an arena to be mauled by wolves, Protestant Germany, both Reformed and Lutheran, gave him a round of send-off parties. The most impressive was his ordination in the Reformed church of Elberfeld where Dr. Krummacher delivered the charge. The words of Krummacher are worth recording — if, that is, we wish to understand the special aspect under which these Germans conceived the meaning, or rather the contamination, of American religion:

You are called to transport German theology in its thoroughness and depth and its strong, free life together with the various branches of learning that stand related to it as a family of full-grown daughters. The many-headed monster of pantheism and atheism, issuing from the sphere of German speculation, as it has there become flesh and broken forth into actual life, in concrete form, spreading desolation and terror, you are called to meet in the armor of the shepherd boy of Bethlehem and to smite with incurable wounds.

We may smile at the notion that Jacksonian democracy or even New England Transcendentalism could be contorted by German theologians into a demonic eruption of the evil forces they had withstood, so far successfully, in their own land. But the fact is, this is how they did interpret what little information they had. So they sent Schaff to Mercersburg as a David against the Philistines.

It needs to be emphasized that on his trip to America Schaff stopped for six weeks in England, and there promptly acquired the Anglophilism which was to be a passion with him for the rest of his existence and to gain him access to all degrees and complexions of English and Scottish religious life. Here again he exercised his genius for being an engaging guest, but in this case he was the more welcome because of what henceforth would be his pious admiration of the British compromise between an established order and a genuine toleration of dissent. He made friends among nonconformists as well as among bishops, and – as was to be cited against him – displayed a lively curiosity about the Oxford Movement. He conversed freely with Dr. Pusey, and exhibited no dismay over Newman's conversion. From England he sailed in June of 1844, and upon his first sight of Staten Island recorded, with some amazement, "The evidences of civilization are here, as in the land we left."

IV

Schaff was not an original mind, in the sense of having any marked aptitude for speculation or abstract thinking. Though he came of age in a Germany where thought was an intoxication, he was an absorber and recorder rather than a participant, and throughout his work proved an expert expositor of other men's ideas. Yet out of the tumult of this intellectual ecstasy he extracted one of the more substantial conceptions, to which he clung tenaciously. He was introduced to it by Baur, whom he admired but against whom he revolted; he later described it as the idea "of historical development or of a constant and progressive flow of thought in the successive ages of the church." The full implications of the idea were unfolded to him by Neander. (Nevin had painfully been working his way through Neander before Schaff arrived, and this allegiance formed a bond between them.) The major conclusion of Neander's philosophy was, to oversimplify, that "church history" is no bare compilation of dates and events but an organic part of systematic theology, showing how in the growth of Christian thought the deeper, and then the still deeper, meanings of the Gospel have successively emerged. In this view, ecclesiastical and theological narratives, though seemingly constructed on a chronological pattern, would become — or should become — dramatizations of the evolving doctrine, with the obvious lesson that at any one time still more remained to be unfolded.

To one who knew the situation, as did Schaff, obviously this presentation owed much to Schelling and even more to Hegel, but to Schaff it was a Christian appropriation of the pagan apparatus. It spiked Hegel's guns with Hegelian metal. It was a liberation from the tyranny of Hegel's "absolute knowledge." But certainly one deduction from this restatement of Hegel was that such divisions within Christendom as the Reformation — indeed, this above all — were not violent shatterings of the community or of history, but phases in a process of development which, seen through the philosophical eye, appeared as rational, even as smooth, stages in a cosmic plan. Hence came Schaff's lack of anti-Catholic fervor, and also his interest in the Oxford Movement, though he could never have gone along with it. Hence also came his instinctive hostility to revivalism, which taught a sudden and violent conversion that by thunderings and torments endeavored to slice a deep chasm between the serious growth of an individual's religious consciousness and the moment of cataclysm. Here he and Nevin again saw eye to eye.

However, in America there was virtually no public, not even among the German churches, that had heard enough of Hegel — hardly even the name — to understand the premise of Schaff's doctrine of church history. There prevailed in these churches, as among all the evangelical groups in the nation, a deep-seated, an angry, a blind hatred for Catholicism. They cherished this antagonism as the most precious heritage of the Reformation; and for them it was being daily exacerbated by the increase of the numbers and power of the Church through the augmenting flood of immigration. And though the German Reformed Church had in the main resisted the revival, and adhered fairly steadily to its ancient ideals of ecclesiastical decorum, still it could not help secretly yearning for a few of the satisfactions of the upheaval.

Schaff contrived, out of an innocence that was pathetically absolute, to outrage all three of these indigenous passions — belief in the revolutionary character of the Reformation, hatred of Rome, and a hankering for revivalism. Fifty years afterwards he mused that he had flung out a firebrand, but "I did it unintentionally." In the First Reformed Church of Reading, Pennsylvania, he delivered his inaugural, on October 25, 1844. He spoke in German; the address was published in that language, and early in 1845 in English under the title, *The Principle of Protestantism as related to the Present State of the Church*, with a preface by Nevin in the form of a sermon on catholic unity. In Germany, Schaff's masters, Krummacher and Tholuck, nodded in sage agreement; Lutherans also joined in approval, noting in the speech a "fearless candor and a devotion to Christianity which rises superior to all denominations." In the United States a few professional theologians in the Presbyterian or Dutch Reformed Churches recognized its importance. But to majorities in all the communions which looked to Calvin as their source, and to the others which venerated Luther, and particularly to many in the German Reformed brotherhood, all this novel Germanic mystagogue said, as far as they could understand it, was downright pernicious. Dr. Schaff was given a rude awakening as to just how perilous was the mission he had undertaken. Indeed, for a time it appeared to him that he had failed before he had started, and he meditated a retreat to Berlin.

He had spoken only what had long before become a conventional wisdom among the disciples of Neander. Asserting himself to be a Protestant, Schaff categorically denied that the Reformation was an abrupt overthrow of the Catholic system or that it was a restoration of the primitive church. Protestantism was an organic growth out of the previous centuries, and Luther had been no iconoclast. All historical development becomes a cumulative apprehension of Christ, an ever increasing appropriation of the spirit of the Apostles. Not realizing that this was shocking enough for most American Protestants, Schaff serenely continued, in the best Germanic vein of insensitivity, to enumerate the "diseases" of Protestantism, which he said were rationalism and sectarianism. Since his hearers were firmly convinced that rationalism — or what they took it to be — was a foul contagion brewed in Europe, and primarily in Germany, that had been smuggled into America by seedy characters like Tom Paine, they emphatically rejected the suggestion that Protestantism could be called responsible for it. As for sectarianism, in America they had become not only reconciled to it but proud of it, and had learned to behold in the "voluntary principle" an ultimate solution of the ecclesiastical problem, which America was providentially assigned to teach a distracted Europe.

Schaff then compounded his offense by discussing "Puseyism," which he declared to be no cure for rationalism and sectarianism, but which he treated sympathetically as a viable remedy for these Protestant diseases. He concluded with an eloquent plea for, and prediction of, church unity — not, he said, in a single organization but in a living intercommunication among all Christian churches. In short, the theory of historical progress afforded the only true principle of fraternity.

The story of the consternation Schaff created need not here be recounted in detail. He refers to it discreetly on pages 92 and 93 of this volume; though he was not a man to cherish grudges, there is no doubt that the ordeal was a bitter one. In Philadelphia the German Reformed classis, aided and abetted by Presbyterians, accused the address of being Puseyite and "crypto-Catholic." Resolutions were passed, sermons were preached, which declared the Papacy the mystery of iniquity, the mother of abominations, which denounced every notion of organic development as a subversion of Protestantism. Frenetic articles appeared in religious periodicals denouncing "the Protestantism of Mercersburg" as contrasted with "the Protestantism of the Bible."

Schaff was called upon to stand trial on the charge of heresy, levelled by the Philadelphia classis, before the Synod of Pennsylvania at York in October 1845. He was vindicated by a vote of thirty-seven to three. But during the examination his character and his ideas were attacked with a ferocity that left him anguished and bewildered, and with a horrified realization that America might not after all have retained much of European culture, that even amid his beloved Germans he had fallen into the hands of savages.

V

Philip Schaff was the sort of man — the sort of German of his generation — who, when criticized, did not immediately slash back but who courteously listened to the charges and conscientiously examined himself to discover whether these might after all be true. He had been in America only a few months, but a glimmering of a suspicion already dawned upon him that possibly he had ignorantly accepted as axiomatic a rather too doctrinaire condemnation of sectarianism. In America, he commenced to comprehend, diversity of denominations was quite another matter from what it appeared to be in Europe. He was, of course, pleased that his former colleagues wrote from Germany in amazement that any American organization, least of all a German Reformed Synod, should find the slightest taint of heresy in his address. But he was perplexed when one of them smugly commiserated with him thus: "I appreciate what an important mission is before you in Mercersburg, especially in view of the labyrinth and great evil of the sections and factions of which here in Germany we can form no adequate conception." That was how it looked from a distance, but Schaff was already so committed that he could only object to an obtuse wiping of America off the account. Might it be that here the principle of historical development had a grander scene to encompass than Germany could dream of? His American critics had indeed shown themselves provincial Calvinists — "Puritans" — but conceivably the German intellectuals, in their pompous assurance that the jarring sects of America showed nothing but the disintegration of Christianity, were really the provincials.

At any rate, for the next ten years Schaff devoted himself with all his titanic energy to his professorship at Mercersburg. He and Nevin propounded what was known as the "Mercersburg Theology," chiefly through the medium of a

journal, *The Mercersburg Review*, which was as sophisti-
cated a work as America could then boast. Schaff and Nevin
constituted the entire faculty of the seminary, and the number of students each year was no more than twenty-five.
It is an astounding fact that Mercersburg in this period
could be such a driving force in American religious thought.

Unhappily, the fact became more and more evident that
the Church, in settling upon Mercersburg as the site of the
seminary, had been beguiled by the naïve American assumption that small towns in the forests were as suitable for the
life of the mind as large cities. Schaff was increasingly
hampered by the remoteness of the place, by the inadequate
library, by the lack of intellectual companionship beyond
Nevin and his own students. He advocated removal to Lancaster, and was again attacked for being a crypto-Catholic.
In 1845 he married an American girl, of German ancestry,
and commenced to speak English in his home. Thereafter
he led the movement within the Church to convert to English, and once more was accused of being Puseyite. He kept
up a vigorous correspondence with his German friends,
wherein he revealed his steady appreciation of the American
point of view. For instance, by 1847 he informed a no doubt
amazed Frau Heusser that Protestantism in Germany, Switzerland, and England had made a terrible mistake in binding
itself so closely to the worldly power; to her he proudly
declared, "An American cannot submit to the theory of
dependence in which the church stands to the state in
Europe." The people of America, he went on, further out-
raging the good woman, are "more capable of spreading
Christianity in spite of the separation of church and state."

Restricted by Mercersburg's isolation, Schaff nevertheless
bought or borrowed books, and worked interminably in his
study. The first volume of what eventually became his seven-
volume *History of the Christian Church* was published in
German in 1851 and in English in 1853, so that the founda-

tions of his scholarly reputation were securely laid throughout the Western world. In the United States he resolutely refused to be confined within German circles and made friends in Princeton, Andover, St. Louis — in fact in just about every theological center except Harvard.

By 1853 even his robust constitution was tired; his eyes were failing, his voice almost gone. The Synod graciously, "in view of the arduous labors he had been rendering the church," gave him a year's leave of absence. Schaff was thereafter to become a steady traveller back to Europe and England and to resume his cultivation of theological friendships over all the Continent. But this first return was the crucial visit. The story of his encounter with the wilderness and with bigotry and sectarianism was everywhere known. What he would say about the jungle was eagerly awaited, with mingled feelings. Here would be no snobbish Mrs. Trollope looking down her nose at the pig butchers of Cincinnati, no theoretical Tocqueville fitting facts into preconceptions, but a German of the comprehensive school, who had worked and lived for ten years with all sorts and conditions of men, but who could be trusted not to have lost sight, amid the American disorder, of the sober standards of Germanic Protestantism. In Berlin the theological faculty voted him an honorary Doctor of Divinity, and then invited him to explain his adopted country in two lectures within the hallowed rooms of the Evangelical Verein. He spoke there on March 20 and 30, 1854, the result being the first two sections of the present volume, published in Berlin as *Amerika*. Edward D. Yeomans volunteered to translate it. As Schaff gave a later address at Frankfort, which reviewed some of the same ground he covered in the Berlin lectures, but which brought out other reflections, and since this too was translated, he put the three together to make *America*, published by Scribner in New York in 1855. A Dutch version was printed at Rotterdam in the same year.

Only a summary of Schaff's later career is here called for, though it was so full of activity and utterance that a flat summary does him grave injustice. His bibliography is staggering. By 1863 he could no longer stand the rusticity of Mercersburg and removed to New York. In 1869 he became a professor at Union Theological Seminary. He died on October 20, 1893. By then his fame as a scholar was world-wide, and he was regarded as the dean of ecclesiastical historians. The faith he held in youth he kept to the end. A year before his death he wrote:

The true theory of development is that of a constant growth of the church in Christ the head, or a progressive understanding and application of Christianity, until Christ shall be all in all. The end will only be the complete unfolding of the beginning. All other theories of development which teach a progress of humanity beyond Christ and beyond Christianity are false and pernicious.

Shortly after his death historians of the churches in America noted that in his revision of the *History of the Christian Church* Schaff had excised his polemical assertions of the theory of historical development. One commentator in 1895 remarked that when Schaff arrived in the United States he had been assailed as a "Romanizer," but was happy to conclude, "His heresy has become almost a commonplace now." Looking back from the second half of the twentieth century, we may not be altogether sure that his was a heresy or not, and certainly not all of us are persuaded that it is any longer a commonplace. Schaff was so situated in the nineteenth century and was so alert to the central currents of ideas that he appears to us as possessing, only half-knowing what he had, a Janus-like capacity for looking both backwards and forwards. Wherefore his report concerning America on the eve of the Civil War, delivered to respectful but highly sceptical audiences in Berlin and Frankfort in 1854, is valuable not as a piece of antiquarianism but as an astute read-/ing of the American destiny.

VI

Philip Schaff's *America* is a unique book in several respects, and therefore is of several uses to the modern reader.

First of all, it is the preëminent accounting to the home country by an immigrant of the early nineteenth century as to what translation to the New World means. It is not a letter to the old country telling of opportunities and wages, but an exposition of the fundamental character of the American civilization as seen and absorbed by one who was, before his removal, an expert on cultures. In the history of that mysterious process called "Americanization" it is a document of primary importance.

Yet much more eloquently, it is an analysis of America presented by a mind that could cope with the ambiguities of language as used in Europe and in the United States. As a testimony, for instance, to the varying connotations of such smashing words as "liberal" and "conservative," Schaff's well-mannered discourse illuminates the problems of the dialogue between Europe and America, even when conducted by members of the same confession, in a way that is as instructive today as on the day Scribner published the book.

For in several senses of the word, Schaff is a conservative. He believes in "The Church," in the Heidelberg Catechism, in dignified order, in intellectual probity. He is opposed to the rationalism and deism of the eighteenth century, he condemns the noise of revivals, he sets orthodox German theology, even when romanticized, against the vagaries of German literary romanticism. The very existence of diver-/gent religious denominations is a pain to him, and the increase of them in the nineteenth century, and especially in

America, is for him a nightly torment. He believes in the intellectual supremacy of Germany and admires the stately homes and cathedrals of England. He considers all the revolutionary demonstrations of 1848 — Frankfort, Paris, Rome — utterly reprehensible. He thinks the achieved stabilizations of religious differences in Germany an ideal arrangement, and the ceremonials of German universities the summit of modern civilization.

And yet, plummeted into the American disorder, he has to argue by the very lights of his German conservatism that in the contentions and stupidities of America something is taking shape which Europe fails to understand, and that Europe fails at its own peril. Schaff needed immense tact to say these difficult things in Berlin, but he needed even more a solid courage. He had both at his command, and this book, even though fragmentary and often repetitious, is a testimony to his integrity.

Schaff found himself obliged to argue — even though with reluctance — and further to demonstrate by his biography and his manner of speaking, that what in Europe had been a decent, self-respecting conservatism was bound to become in America a destructive liberalism. It was bound to be thus transformed, but not into rationalism, or into deism or godless transcendentalism, but into diversity, fragmentation, even revivalism. And having accepted all these horrors — or so they would appear when retailed in Germany — the truly conservative spirit must recognize that in the voluntaryism of America lies the promise of stability. As against an obstinate adherence by Europeans, even in Switzerland, to the moribund ties between state and church, the American anarchy, so-called, is the guarantee of a pervasive order. Who in Europe, having no experience of America, could grasp this paradox? Who among them, even with the lesson of 1848 writ clear before their eyes, could admit what an Americanized Schaff told them in 1854, that

"Europe rests upon a volcano, which can at any moment break out into a new eruption, and no bayonets, no political wisdom is able to stand security for the present order of things for the space of two years to come" (pp. 228–229)?

The volcano did not erupt within the next two years, yet we know that eventually something did. Meanwhile, Schaff hammered hard on one point which even today can turn the most courtly of European academic officials into angry denunciators of American callousness. Schaff could say it because he was a European academician, and could state the case gently, as he does here, for instance, on pages 79 and 80. It is simply that when professors of theology are appointed to the faculties of state-supported universities, they may just as easily be scholars of no religious conviction as actual Christians. Schaff, indeed, felt it a crushing argument for the effectiveness of the voluntary system that in the colleges of the United States, most of which were offsprings of churches, such men as Straus or Baur (with their "higher criticism") would simply never get appointments, no matter how vast their scientific qualifications! Schaff never tired of lecturing his European colleagues on this matter, and often caused them considerable discomfort. One of them in 1890 finally blurted out that "the farther theology and the church keep apart, the better," to which Schaff answered that the "American sentiment" was exactly opposite, that theology is the daughter of the church and must not rebel against the mother. We perceive how far he had travelled from his academic origins as he continues:

In a German university a theological professor is appointed by the state, supported by the state, responsible to no creed, and expected to teach and promote science. The state looks only at theoretical qualifications, and cares little or nothing about the orthodoxy and piety of the candidate. The church, as such, has nothing to say in the matter. The result is that a professor may teach doctrines which are utterly subversive to the church, and disqualify the student for his future work. This is an unnatural state of things. It may be favorable to the freest development of theological science and speculation, but very dangerous to the healthful and vigorous development of church life.

Schaff was here taking part in a grave controversy, which still endures. The Europeans asserted that they were the free ones, while the "free" system of America bound theologians to parochial views, dictated what they should teach, and held them over the constant threat of a trial for heresy. Schaff, by putting the emancipated life of the church ahead of the concern for mere scholastic rigor, shows that he had come over entirely to the then prevailing American position. Of course, just about the time of his death the issue was shaping up within America itself, precisely at his Union Seminary. As the universities have become increasingly secularized, the problem of whether the obligation of the professor of theology is to theology itself or to his church becomes with us more aggravated. We owe Schaff thanks for having posed it so early in our intellectual adventure.

Thus Schaff found himself as the European intellectual in America obliged to revaluate the fundamental terms of European social discourse, and yet could not abandon those terms entirely either, because no others existed, or because new-coined ones would have been incomprehensible to his European audiences. Yet in aid of his endeavor came a strong insistence which had suddenly sprung up among American Protestants just prior to his arrival. In social reality, this argument ran, despite all previous liberal theorizing, the system of separation of church and state, combined with the widest possible diversity of sects and a casting of each of them upon the generosity of its members for financial support, instead of making for chaos, made for sobriety, for a regulation of society by the religious spirit all the more powerful for being vaguely but generally diffused. Outsiders were deceived by the surface appearances of violence in the revivals, by the energy of the competition among revivalists for converts, into supposing that the central core of unanimity was destroyed. Indeed, not only were foreigners thus blinded, but enemies of the revival close to home — Unitarians, Catholics, Old School Presbyterians — were equally misled. Schaff very likely had in mind, when trying to reach the comprehensions of Germans, a book he is said to have admired, Robert Baird's *Religion in America*, published the year Schaff ventured across the Atlantic, 1844. Baird was a Presbyterian, a Princeton man, who had served as emissary of his church to the Protestants of France, and there encountered the same rooted preconceptions Schaff found upon his return to Germany. One might say that in some respects Baird provided the model for Schaff, and his book is also one of the strangely neglected classics of American social history. Yet Baird was native to the forest, and seems, despite his years of residence in France, not quite to have grasped how the mysterious American solution, or lack of solution, still made no sense abroad. Furthermore, he was untrained in the metaphysics of Germany, and so could present his case only in the empirical terms of American experience, which had few or no counterparts in the European intelligence.

Baird offered the voluntary principle as the one and only "great alternative" to all European history, which to him was bloody, tragic, and inconclusive. Having none of Schaff's scruples, he boldly asked, "Upon what, then, must Religion rely?" and confidently answered, "Only, under God, upon the efforts of its friends." While vainly endeavoring to plead that the success of the principle had not depended upon the peculiarly American conditions, he nevertheless admitted that it did so by linking it with the energy and self-reliance of emigrants who left the luxuries of civilization "for a life in the woods, amid wild beasts, pestilential marshes, and privations and innumerable difficulties." Such a people quickly learned to disregard superfluous trappings — a state church, for example. Thus, Baird concluded, separation of church and state is not merely a negative device, it is a way of enabling religion to stand upon its own positive assertions. It provides a chance — as Baird was certain no Old World society ever had — for a church to act *"spontaneously*, if the word may be allowed."

The key to Baird's presentation is this often repeated adverb. Hence, we must give Schaff full credit for working his way out of the metaphysics of Neander's historicism — wherein advances occurred under decipherable rules of philosophical progression — to this leap into the American dark. The respect public men show to religion, Baird asserted, is the more interesting "as it can only flow from the spontaneous feelings of the heart." If Baird ever suspected that some politicians put on a pious mien in order to gain votes, he lived on too lofty a plain to notice the hypocrisy. Schaff was more politically astute, but he also found a proof of the American pudding in the lofty moralism of the American orators, above all in the God-like, the "sublime," Daniel Webster (page 69). As for the dependence of American clergy and professors upon the financial support of their laity, and so their sacrifice of freedom — Baird would have none of that accusation; the people "most esteem that one who fearlessly and impartially declares the whole counsel of God, and presents the depravity of man and the threatenings of the Divine Word as faithfully as he does the comforting promises." Schaff again was more guarded, and recognized the frequent abuses, but he was, considering his situation, as defiant as Baird in telling the Germans (page 80) that an American minister impartially declares the whole counsel of God to those who pay his wages.

The consequence of the line of defense Baird erected in France, which was imitated by his colleagues in the Protestant churches at home, was to devise a dream of logic out of illogicality. It sought to prove that the liberalism of

American ecclesiastical confusion became somehow a "conservative" order. There may have been an element of anti-Jacksonianism in this mixture; yet ardent Jacksonian churchmen could add their portion to it, in order to demonstrate that the Democratic Party was neither irreligious nor anarchic. At either rate, a student can find thousands of utterances such as this (it happens to be by the Reverend Hiram Ketchum in 1840):

> There is no gentleman here who will deny that the Christian religion is the great conservative principle of the community. And how is that best promoted and advanced? By being let alone; by giving every denomination a fair chance; by leaving religion to voluntary support. It is best for religion itself that it should be let alone to extend its own boundries.

So, one has to say again, and with deepening admiration, that it was a feat of intellectual generosity for Schaff to make the gesture of appropriating this wisdom, and then of daring to display it in Berlin. Some may sneer that he would be more deserving of praise had he come out of autocratic Prussia into such a religious radicalism as that of Theodore Parker's. Had he done so, he would figure as another among the pack of German radicals who played indeed an important part in such domestic movements as Abolition, Socialism, and the labor unions, but he would not then have occupied the special, even if sometimes equivocal, place he does in American intellectual history. Undoubtedly he could make his adjustment because he found, with the help of such Americans as Ketchum and Baird, a method, however devious, for defining the American manner as fundamentally "conservative." Though by the standards of a calcified Europe, it was revolutionary, he could contend that it worked out as a "conservative" power. It was not (page 37) the "purely negative" destructiveness of European radicalism. It was not an escape from religion but rather a more subtle and more effective method for subduing the whole society to piety than could be any governmental administration. In short the riddle and the glory of America was that it was *both* liberal and conservative (page 47). It united what Europe had long ago decided were irreconcilables, the impulse to freedom and the sense of law and order.

Schaff in his first decade as an immigrant — he being both a historian and an acute observer — noted as many of the unpleasant facts which contradict the American version of its religious triumph as any modern researchers can adduce — the squabbles between pastors and people, the heresy trials, the crudities of denominational rivalry, and the spasms of anti-Catholicism. But he had the largeness of vision to perceive that, even so, the mass of the major Protestant churches honestly and rightly believed that in the revelation of voluntaryism (not worrying their practical heads about the theological intricacies of voluntarism), they had solved the historic dilemma of the Christian past. They neither submitted the church to a civil authority nor summoned the saints to resist magistrates in the name of the Spirit. And behold the magnificent result! Not only was the state forever relieved from the terrible burden of supressing dissent, but the churches so prospered that there was virtually no real heresy in the country (except for the "vagrant" Mormons), while dissent only subserved a greater unanimity. Out of this conjunction, too complex for any dialectical mind to have devised in advance of the actual experience, the sects found the soul of a nation and a revivification of the Christian life.

By the time the English version of his three lectures was ready for the New York press, Schaff, along with thousands of other Americans, feared that the nation was breaking apart, that in spite of all the signs it had exhibited of providential guidance, it had proved rotten before it had a chance to become ripe. He suffered from such apprehensions even as he spoke in Berlin, for he was by then aware of the portent of the Kansas-Nebraska Bill. Yet he spoke boldly, and he published resolutely, and he did not for a minute blur a line of his portrait. It is a measured, judicious, intelligent analysis, which by its objectivity and affectionate power is as fine a tribute to America as any immigrant has ever paid.

PERRY MILLER

Cambridge, Massachusetts
September 1960

AMERICA.

A SKETCH OF THE

Political, Social, and Religious Character

OF THE

UNITED STATES OF NORTH AMERICA,

IN TWO LECTURES,

*Delivered at Berlin, with a Report read before the German Church Diet
at Frankfort-on-the-Maine, Sept., 1854.*

BY DR. PHILIP SCHAFF.

Translated from the German.

NEW YORK:
C. SCRIBNER, 145 NASSAU STREET.
1855.

PREFACE

THE present work has grown out of two discourses, which I delivered, by request during a visit to the capital of Prussia, on the 20th and 30th of March 1854, before a select assembly of ladies and gentlemen, as part of the course of weekly lectures held there on various topics by Drs. Hoffman, Nitzsch, Stahl, Hengstenberg, Tholuck, Müller, Schmieder, Ritter, and other distinguished scholars for the benefit of the Berlin Evangelical Society for inner missions, in the Oranien Strasse, N. 106.

I had at first not the most distant thought of their publication, and so made no written preparation except a general outline. But they were received by the highly respectable and accomplished audience, which the King of Prussia and other members of the royal family occasionally honor with their presence, with an interest to me altogether unexpected, although some of the most intelligent hearers considered them — perhaps not without reason — too favorable to the land of my adoption. And as a number of eminent divines and professors of the University, such as the venerable Dr. C. Ritter, the acknowledged standard authority in all that relates to the earth and its inhabitants, earnestly solicited their publication, I felt it a duty to yield to such honorable requests; the more, since the other addresses, delivered in behalf of the Inner Mission at Berlin during the last two winters, have also been given to the press.

So I wrote the discourses, as nearly as I could remember them; the first, in Berlin and at a neighboring country-seat; the second partly in Potsdam under the hospitable roof of my honored friend, the Court-preacher, Dr. Krummacher (who was once called to the same professorship in Pennsyl-

3

vania, which I have now held for ten years), and partly in Carlsbad, and Vienna. The views and the train of thought remain the same; but I have taken the liberty, especially in the second address, to add and expand in many places for further illustration, as I would have done in the delivery, if time had permitted.

But instead of treating the German churches of America, as I did in Berlin, as briefly as the symmetry of the discourse required, my publisher thought it more to the purpose to devote to these a separate part. Accordingly, after an interruption of several weeks and a tour through Italy and Tyrol, I composed the third part on my native mountains of Switzerland. Since little is as yet authentically known in Germany on the subject there treated, I hope this part will be to many readers a welcome addition. For there I had the special advantage of moving in the field of my own immediate experience and observation, and I think I have depicted light and shade with as much impartiality as elsewhere.*

Thus, contrary to the original calculation, the two addresses have grown to a little book, which bears, perhaps only too plainly, the marks of its fragmentary and almost planless construction without the help of a library and amidst the distractions of an extensive journey. After all it is only an outline miniature of a country, on which many volumes have already been written, and many more might be. Had I composed the work at home, with the aid of my library and the manuscripts, which I have collected on American church history and statistics, it would have been, no doubt, more symmetrical, cautious, accurate, and thorough, but probably also much more prolix and less interesting, at least for the general public. Miniature pictures, at any rate, are as well authorized as full-size portraits; and

---

* In the present edition the discourses are restored to their original form by inserting an abridgment of the above mentioned Third Part in the proper place in Part II. [All footnotes included in the John Harvard Library edition appeared in the 1855 edition here reprinted.]

in the present burdensome profusion of literature, one must really be grateful to every author, who uses as few words as possible. Then again, this kind of composition, with all its inconvenience, has the advantage of suggesting all sorts of interesting comparisons between Europe and America, not expressly made indeed in my representation, but implied by manifold allusions, which will be readily understood by the reflecting reader.

I have now within the last eight or nine months conversed with intelligent and excellent men of different ranks, and with many celebrated scholars and statesmen in Scotland, England, France, Germany, Austria, Italy, and Switzerland, on the subject of America; and I have heard the most favorable and the most unfavorable opinions. By both I have been in general only confirmed in the views already publicly expressed in Berlin. It might not be out of place, however, to add here a few remarks on these opposite views, with the wish and design to adjust the contradictory judgments of Europe respecting this remarkable country, which is increasingly engaging the interest of the Old World. For I would appear neither as the unqualified eulogist of the Americans, nor as an unsparing censor of them, especially behind their backs.

There are respectable men, professedly of the highest culture, especially in despotic Austria, who have a real antipathy to America, speak of it with the greatest contempt or indignation, and see in it nothing but a grand bedlam, a rendezvous of European scamps and vagabonds. Even in a north-German city, where there is otherwise so much intelligence respecting the whole world, a lady of the first rank asked me in good earnest, if I could think of returning to such a barbarian country, where the mob ruled supreme, and where neither person nor property is safe. Such notions it is unnecessary to refute.

Not so the charges of slavery, materialism, radicalism, and sectarianism. These features of the country are almost universally censured in the most intelligent circles of Europe, and set down as the chief deformities of the United States, and as the rocks, on which they must ultimately suffer shipwreck, unless they take in time a different course. Unquestionably these are the sorest places and most dangerous infirmities of the country; and under them it would have to fall, had it not soundness and vitality enough to react against the morbid matter. But soundness and vitality it has; and this cannot be overlooked without the greatest injustice.

SLAVERY is, without question, the political and social canker, the *tendo-Achilles*, in the otherwise vigorous system of the United States, and contradicts alike its own republican symbol and the spirit of Christianity and philanthropy. It may yet divide the Union, in spite of all compromise measures, and may even produce the horrors of a civil war, which God in mercy prevent. Quite recently, the passage of the Kansas-Nebraska bill and the overthrow of the Missouri Compromise have roused the deepest indignation in the North, which is bound in self-respect and by still higher considerations to resist with all constitutional means the further extension of the curse of slavery on the soil of freedom. The best men of the Southern states themselves cannot wish it, if they prize the union of their beloved country, the cause of freedom and humanity. It is idle to set against it the "white slavery," which is bad enough, to be sure, especially in the manufacturing towns and mineral regions of Europe; for one sin can never justify another. The appeal to the fact, that humanity and Christianity everywhere mitigate the evil; that the slaves are in many cases far better off than the free negroes in the north; and that monsters, like Mrs. Stowe's Legree, are rare exceptions; — does not amount to an exculpation; for we have here to do with a principle and a legal institution.

6

But to those, who see only the writings of Theodore Parker, recently translated, and the literature of the Garrisonian Abolitionists, which are unsound, fanatical, and extremely radical in all political and social questions, and infidel in religion, and who so pass an unsparing and unqualified condemnation on the United States as a whole, I would suggest the following considerations, which may at least modify their judgments. In the first place, the Americans are not responsible for the introduction of the evil, but only for the continuation of it; the introduction of it is due to the Spaniards, Portuguese, French, Dutch, and English. Secondly, thousands and millions not only in New England, where abolitionism prevails, but also in the middle and western, and indeed even in the southern states, as thoroughly abhor this institution, as any European philanthropist does; though they differ about the way and the time of abolishing it. Thirdly, this interest has already lost the preponderance in the Union, and must in time die out, as it did in the Northern states, where it formerly existed; for since the acquisition of California the fifteen slave states have against them sixteen free states with incomparably better prospects of growth and thrift. Fourthly, there is here involved an almost irreconcilable difference of races, and that not in distant colonies, as was the case with England, and is still the case with Spain, but in the heart of the country itself and in the closest connection with the material interests of the South. Fifthly, the condition of the negroes in the American slave states is a great advance on the heathen barbarism of their brethren in Africa. And finally, since the founding of the American Colonization Society, which is engaging a growing interest even in the Southern states, while a part of the Abolitionists fanatically oppose it, the tragical mystery of the negro race promises to unfold itself in a truly providential way, and the gloom of slavery begins to break into the dawn of the Christianization and civilization of Africa by her own unfortunate children once violently torn from her and now peacefully sent back to the Republic of Liberia.

MATERIALISM, the race for earthly gain and the worship of the "almighty dollar," finds unquestionably vast encouragement in the inexhaustible physical resources of the country and the rapid accumulation of wealth. But it fortunately has a strong and wholesome counterpoise in the zeal for liberal education, the enthusiastic spirit of philanthropy, and the munificent liberality of the people; and above all, in Christianity, which points thousands and millions among them away from the vain glories of time to the imperishable riches of heaven, and fosters all the higher interests of the mind and heart. The Americans, indeed, have better opportunity to get rich, and so are under greater temptations in this view, than most other nations. But in general they also make very good use of their gains. This is incontrovertibly proved by the numberless churches, schools, scientific and benevolent institutions of all sorts, which owe their origin purely to voluntary contributions. The Americans, like the English and Scotch, are more avaricious, but also more liberal, than, for example, the Germans, who keep much more closely what they once get, and are thus more inclined both to the virtue of economy and the corresponding vice of niggardliness. I speak, of course, of the rule, admitting a thousand exceptions. As there are extremely benevolent and self-sacrificing Germans, so there are most niggardly and covetous Anglo-Saxons. Of the correctness of our general assertion one may assure himself daily and hourly in America by comparing the German and English churches. Further testimony is furnished by the annual reports of the Bible and Missionary Societies, which show that England alone contributes more money for the distribution of the Bible and the conversion of the heathen, than the whole continent of Europe. I would not make light of the vast danger, which threatens America from her position and her outward prosperity. Only it must be remembered, that ungodly, worldly philosophy, pantheistic self-deification, and the most refined pleasure-seeking, are the infirmities of all modern civilization, and are much more deeply rooted and widely spread in Europe than in Puritanic America, as a comparison of Boston with Petersburg, New York with Hamburg or Paris, Philadelphia with Berlin or Vienna, especially on a Sunday, would very soon show.

RADICALISM finds in republican America full play for its wild, wanton revelings, its reckless efforts to uproot all that is established, and to lift the world off its hinges. There is a great deal of political atheism in that country, which practically denies the divine origin of civil government altogether, and makes the sovereign people not only the medium and instrumental cause but the ultimate source of all power. And this kind of democracy is generally only a decent name for social despotism, or downright mobocracy. There have occurred lately in the most respectable cities of the Union — Philadelphia, New York, Cincinnati, and even Boston — most disgraceful scenes of rowdyism, which, at first sight, might justify the worst fears concerning the future of that country. Happily, however, these wild outbreaks are not the true expression of the sentiment of the people, and even the legislatures and the Congress represent by no means the heart of American society. There is unquestionably in the Anglo-Saxon race a strong conservatism and a deeply-rooted reverence for the divine law and order; and even in the midst of the storms of political agitation it listens over and anon to the voice of reason and sober reflection. It should never be forgotten, too, that when in 1848 all the thrones on the continent of Europe trembled, and the foundations of social life were shaken, England and North America stood firm. This fact alone proves more than whole volumes of argument. Despotism and abuse of the power of government make revolution; while moderate constitutional liberalism forms the safest barrier against it. Radicalism, therefore, can never have such a meaning, and do so much harm in England and America, as in countries where it is wantonly provoked to revolutionary reaction. It continually breaks on the free institutions of the country and the sound sense of order in the people. Some hundred unarmed constables keep the two-million city of the Anglo-Saxons in order; while whole armies cannot preserve Paris from revolutionary outbreaks. All depends, of course, at last upon the character of the nation. Liberal and even republican institutions of themselves are no guarantee to the freedom and order of the people, unless it be fully prepared, by the power of self-government, to turn them to proper account. This is sufficiently clear from the example of Mexico and the other South American republics, where revolutions and social disorders follow each other in rapid succession.

Finally, the SECT SYSTEM is certainly a great evil. It contradicts the idea of the unity of the church; which we can no more give up, than the unity of God, the unity of Christ, the unity and inward harmony of truth. But, in the first place, so long as confessional controversies are unsettled, it is an inevitable consequence of the universal freedom of religion and worship, which seems to be making progress even in the public opinion of Europe, and the advantages of which on the whole outweigh the disadvantages of a police force and dead uniformity. For religion is the deepest and holiest interest of man, and thrives best in the atmospherc of freedom. It is, in fact, itself the highest freedom, the liberation of the spirit from the bonds of sin and the merely natural life. "Faith," says Luther, "is a free thing, which can be forced upon no one." Compulsion in this sphere only produces hypocrisy and infidelity. It is a fact, that the civil equality of all churches and sects in America, and the voluntary system inseparable from it, have aroused and are sustaining a great mass of individual activity and self-denial for religious purposes, and an uncommon rivalry. The editor of a celebrated political journal in Austria who has lived several years in America (an Israelite, I believe, and therefore, an impartial witness), lately said to me: "The United States are by far the most religious and Christian country in the world; and that, just because religion is there most free." This is the opinion of many others, who take an unprejudiced view of the country. Thus God can bless even the sectarian division of the church, to the advancement of Christianity, as he used the papacy in the Middle Age for the discipline of the Germanic and Romanic nations. This justifies neither the former nor the latter in itself. There may still be something Antichristian in both.

The abstract separation of Church and State, I cannot regard as the perfect and ultimate condition of things; for Christianity aims to leaven and sanctify all spheres of human life, as well as all the powers of the soul. But the union hitherto subsisting in Europe is equally far from the truth, and rests in part on grand illusions, as the year 1848, for example, must show to the blindest. And where is the European power, which, in the present Eastern conflict, would put Christian interests foremost, or even allow them a preponderance over political? Catholic France and Protestant England professedly declared war against a Christian power for the integrity of Turkey, which can not be separated, as it now stands, from Mahometanism, the inveterate foe of Christendom. Russia, indeed, seems to plant the standard of the cross against the crescent, but the love for territorial aggrandizement is, in fact, the principal cause of her aggression upon Turkey; and even if her profession were perfectly sincere, it would be only the Greek cross, which is no longer a blooming tree of life, as in the days of the Apostles, martyrs, and church fathers, but a dead idol and a despotic sword, intolerable alike to the Latin crucifix, and the evangelical preaching of the Crucified. Of course the connection be-

tween the temporal and spiritual power, where it exists,
ought not to be arbitrarily dissolved in a revolutionary spirit;
nor was it so abolished in America; things took their present
shape there, in this respect, by an entirely natural growth.
Christianity proceeds in an altogether conservative spirit
and with the tenderest regard for all existing institutions.
With many disadvantages, union has, in fact, great advantages; not the least of which is, that it brings all the
children of the state under religious instruction — and the
spiritual guardianship of the church. A Christian government can be made an infinite blessing to a people; and to
have such a government must be matter of joy. But in the
first place, the freedom and independence of the church is,
after all, a precious boon. In the second place, it is very
hazardous for the church to expect too much of that union,
and to put her trust in the temporal arm, especially in our
days, when truly Christian princes and statesmen have become much more rare than in the times of the Reformation.
And in the last place, the Church will do well to hold herself in readiness for the possible event of a violent rupture
of that venerable bond, if not for a formal persecution by the
temporal powers, if they should fall again, by some unexpected turn, into Red Republican hands. In America, as
well as in the Free Church of Scotland and of Vaud, she
already has the practical proof (indeed, the first three centuries are proof enough), that the Church can live and thrive
without the support of the secular arm.

Furthermore, sectarianism, as we have endeavored to
show in the second discourse, is really not an infirmity of
America only, but, if you please, of all Protestantism. It is
the natural result of the centrifugal tendencies of a one-
sided religious subjectivity, and would reveal itself also in
Germany, the moment universal religious freedom were
conceded. The theoretical germs of it are all here. Even as
matters now stand, Europe shows not everywhere the same

evangelical church; England and Scotland have their established churches with a great number of dissenting communions, which are likewise Protestant, but have no connection with the establishment or with one another; in Germany and Switzerland there is a multitude of Lutheran United, and Reformed national and cantonal churches, each of which has its own constitution, hymn-book, and liturgy, and presents in the pulpit and the professorial chair the most various theological tendencies, from the stiffest orthodoxy to the boldest rationalism and pantheism. For even the question concerning the authority of the Protestant creed is as yet confessedly nowhere fully settled. Only in free conferences of ministers, on the largest scale at the German Church Diet and the Swiss Ministerial Association, does that inward unity of spirit plainly appear, which, blessed be God, still exists among all true believers. But these conferences are not the church in the proper sense of the word. They only represent a part of it. They have no official and legislative power. They pass pious resolutions, but not binding decrees; and they can be regarded only as a preparation for the one evangelical church of the German tongue. The difference between European and American Protestantism in this respect is, therefore, not so great as would at first sight appear; and the reproach of want of unity, which Roman Catholic divines are continually casting up to us, falls as much on Europe as on America. Indeed Bellarmine and Bossuet used the argument of dissent and perpetual variation against the Reformers and their immediate successors; and Melanchthon himself died of grief over the distraction of the evangelical church in the sixteenth century. Not to give up, therefore, the good cause of the Reformation and bow to the yoke of Roman uniformity, preferring the repose of the church-yard to the struggle of life, we must regard the present distraction and fermentings of Protestantism as the necessary transition state to a far higher and better condition, to a free unity in spirit and in truth, embracing the greatest variety of Christian life. But first the religious subjectivity and individuality of the sect system, with all the accompanying infirmities, must freely and fully develop themselves; just as a full unfolding of the principle of Catholicism, in both the good form of authority and the bad form of tyranny had to precede the purifying and emancipating struggle of the Reformation. Now America tends towards this consistent carrying out of the religious and political principle of Protestantism; that is, the practical application of the universal priesthood and kingship of Christians.

These are the leading charges against America. I would not extenuate them by what I have now said. For I grant, I myself very painfully feel them, especially the misery and confusion of the present condition of the church. I only wish to modify them, and by pointing to kindred evils in Europe, to forestall an immoderate condemnation of America.

But then on the other hand, I have heard it said in various quarters, and by most intelligent men too, even by those who really have no sympathy with the peculiar genius and the present condition of the United States, that the future lies with this country. This is ascribing to it a vast importance. Even one of the most experienced and celebrated absolutist statesmen of Austria, whom I will not name here, conceded this, though he thought, that America would have to undergo radical changes, and become a monarchy, before it could accomplish its great mission. Many others, among them able writers and former Hegelians, are of opinion, that old and declining Europe must gradually exhaust herself by a series of revolutions and convulsions, which only temporarily failed in 1848, and will repeat themselves on a larger and larger scale; and that she must sink into Asiatic stagnation, that America may be an improved continuation of Europe; that is, provided a new age of humanity and the church is to be expected at all. The Romanic nations,

14

say they, have already outlived themselves, and nothing great is any longer to be expected from Greece, Italy, and Spain. France is a volcano, which may break out again at any moment and set all Europe on fire. Even in obstinate, conservative England the ancient Christian institutions are gradually giving way, and must sooner or later make room not only for a change of dynasties, as in 1688, but for a formal social revolution. Germany has done her work for the history of the world by the production of the Romano Germanic empire and by the Reformation, in the results and after-workings of which she still lives; and she will gradually die away, as did Judaism after the birth of the Messiah. From Russia little is to be expected except perhaps an overthrow of the civilization of western Europe by a new irruption of barbarism, without much prospect of a new creation on the ruins of the old. For the Sclaves are not fresh children of nature as were the Germans at the threshold of the middle ages, but are already too old, and have taken up the very worst elements of European civilization, as for example, the most refined voluptuousness. The only alternative therefore is either to believe in the speedy destruction of the world, or to look hopefully to the western hemisphere as the land of promise, to which in fact the massive emigration from all parts of Europe seems to point.

To Americans of the common stamp, especially the Nativists and Know-Nothings (as the anti-foreigners call themselves), this would be water for their mill, and a capital text for Fourth-of-July speeches, which usually overflow with the most disgusting self-glorification at the expense of the Old World. I must confess, I cannot adopt so comfortless a view of the prospects of Europe. At worst, I would hope for a resurrection of this quarter of the world from its grave. For if Asia may be regenerated by Europe, as it now seems probable, and as the Eastern question seems to indicate, so that Palestine and Syria, the sacred birth-place of Chris-

15

tianity, shall bloom again, and East India and China join with them in praising the triune God; why may not Europe, if she should ever decay, be likewise regenerated by America? As the setting sun throws back his golden beams to the eastern horizon, as the pledge of his return in the east; so history shows likewise its reacting influences. But at all events, Europe still stands on the summit of Christian civilization, and will certainly yet long remain there in spite of all threatening storms, and long continue to furnish her youthful, vigorous daughter beyond the ocean with the richest nourishment of her spiritual life.

But whatever may become of her venerable mother, Europe, America is, without question, emphatically a land of the future. This is no merit of the Americans; for, of course, they are in themselves not a whit better than the Europeans. It is the favor of Providence; and it should not make them vain and haughty, but earnest and humble, that they may faithfully and conscientiously fulfill their mission. So surely as the sun goes from east to west, only to rise again in the east, so truly "Westward the star of empire takes its way." Of this I have only been more firmly convinced by my present tour in Europe. This visit will always be to me, indeed, one of the most delightful memories of my life. For everything beautiful and good, which I have seen and heard, especially for stimulating and profitable interchange of ideas and cordial intercourse with many dear friends, old and new, in Germany and Switzerland, I feel most deeply thankful to God, the Giver of every good gift. Yet I return with an elevated sense of the vast importance of America for the destiny of mankind.

While Europe is now in the ripest age of manhood, America is as yet an unripe youth, not seldom wanton and adventurous, but fresh, vigorous, and promising; a giant youth, already stretching out his arms over land and sea, east and west, even to Africa and Japan. As to particulars, he is justly open, almost indefinitely, to censure and reproach; but on the whole, and especially in perspective, he is truly sublime in his proportions, like the Niagara Falls, the Mississippi River, and the Rocky Mountains of his majestic fatherland. He has already turned over a new leaf of the history of the world and of the church, and will assuredly write it full of great deeds. All is in a ferment there as yet, in the first formation state; but looks to the grandest future. A process of amalgamation is now going on there, like that among the Germanic, Romanic, and Celtic races at the migration of the nations, and that in England after the Norman invasion; but on a far broader foundation, on a much larger scale, and under much more favorable conditions. In the United States all nations, all churches and sects, all the good and evil powers of the old world, meet without blows or bloodshed; and while Europe began with paganism and barbarism, America begins with the results of Europe's two thousand years' course of civilization, and has vigor, energy, enterprise, and ambition enough to put out this enormous capital at the most profitable interest for the general good of mankind.

It is, of course, not my design to mingle in European strifes, or indirectly to favor this or that political or ecclesiastical party. This would be, indeed, for a stranger, a beginning as immodest and unskillful as it would be unprofitable. I very well know that Germany has an entirely different work from America, and that it would be altogether unhistorical and unnatural to transfer the institutions of the one country abruptly to the other. Every country must develop itself from within by a natural growth. But this process does not exclude the beneficial co-operation of foreign elements. The German, for example, will never become, and should never become, an Englishman, nor the Englishman a German or Frenchman. Nevertheless each may learn very much from the other. For instance, the real ism and the practical church activity of the Englishman and Anglo-American may stimulate and improve the German, as much as the idealism and science of the German may improve the American. But to do this mutual service they must first become better acquainted with each other, and drop their mutual prejudices. I would that the following sketch of the actual condition of America might help them to do so. There certainly is a great deal in the political and religious life of the New World which may both stimulate and warn Germany; and the sight of zealous activity and fresh energy in others rouses and improves ourselves, even though our work may be of an altogether different kind.

The great thing now is, to collect and concentrate all the better powers of the mental and moral world. Europe and America ought to link themselves together, not only by steamships and commerce, but by the far closer bond of intellectual and religious intercourse, that they may learn more and more to understand, esteem, love, and advance each other in the common work of extending the kingdom of God and Christian civilization throughout the length and breadth of the world.

THE AUTHOR.

ST. MAURICE, IN ENGADIN, SWITZERLAND,
August 10, 1854.

TO THE AMERICAN READER

In committing this volume to the American public, in a faithful translation by the hand of an esteemed friend, who thought it worth while to assume the task, the author would respectfully ask the reader to keep in mind, that, with the exception of the notes, it was written in Germany and for Germany, in view of false impressions and strong prejudices, which are widely spread in the higher circles of Europe, concerning the United States. The address delivered by appointment before the Evangelical Church Diet at Frankfort-on-the-Maine, in September last, is no part of the original work; but as it treats on the same subject under a different and more practical aspect, it was translated by another and equally skillful hand from the published proceedings of that large assembly, and forms now the third part in the place of a separate chapter on the German churches, which has been greatly abridged by the translator with the consent of the author.

Since the publication of the original in Berlin, many things have happened in America in rapid succession in the departments of both national and state politics, of finance, and of municipal government, which seem to contradict the highly favorable views of this book on the present condition and future prospects of our country, and to justify the fear, that it is rotting before it is ripe, and will yet add another proof to the sad reflection of the poet of Childe Harold:
"There is a moral of all human tales;
  'Tis but the same rehearsal of the past;
First freedom, and then glory — when that fails,
  Wealth, vice, corruption — barbarism at last."
In view of the history of the past and present year, we

have no reason to boast and to look down upon any nation of the Old World. Still I would not on this account retract any sentiment publicly expressed at Berlin and at Frankfort, and several other cities of Europe. The manifold appearances of corruption, I hope, are only the scum on the surface; diseases of the skin, and not of the heart. They may darken our immediate prospects, but they cannot affect our ultimate destiny.

Providence has evidently prepared this country and nation for the greatest work, and no power on earth can arrest its progress and prosperity, if we are true to our calling, if we fear God and love righteousness, mindful of the maxim — "No liberty without virtue; no virtue without religion; no religion without Christianity; Christianity, the safeguard of our republic and hope of the world."

P. S.

Mercersburg, Pa., Aug. 1, 1855.

PART I

Importance, Political System, National Character,
Culture, and Religion of the United States

THE
UNITED STATES OF NORTH AMERICA

THEIR IMPORTANCE, POLITICAL SYSTEM, NATIONAL CHARACTER, CULTURE, LITERATURE, AND RELIGION

IT is not without embarrassment, and an urgent request for your kind indulgence, that I appear in this metropolis of German science and of the highest intellectual culture, to give you a miniature picture of the political, social, and religious life of the United States of North America. The few days since my arrival, the distracting excitements of a visit to my beloved German fatherland, and the daily greeting of so many dear friends after a ten years' separation, have prevented my making a preparation at all worthy of my theme. But though I cannot do anything like justice either to such an assembly, as I have the honor to see before me, or to myself, or to my comprehensive subject, I have at least the no small advantage of being able to speak not merely from books, but from life; not as a distant spectator, but from immediate observation and personal experience, respecting a land, which the providence of God, without at all weakening my attachment for Switzerland and Germany, my bodily and spiritual fatherland, has made a second dear home to me.

America! — I feel that the sound of that word leaves none of my hearers indifferent. In every one, not confined to the narrow circle of his own personal existence and of his particular country, but interested, as every man of intelligence and cultivation should be, in the future history of the world and the church, the name of America awakens either sympathies or as deep antipathies, joyful hopes, or desponding fears, or perhaps a strange mixture of bright anticipations and dark forebodings. And this is increasingly so every year, the nearer America and Europe are brought together by the modern space-mocking means of communication, and the more strongly and decisively they act and react on each other. For, as the eastern hemisphere sends its innumerable thousands and millions in swelling tide across the Atlantic; so the new world, on its part, is perceptibly gaining influence, be it for good or for evil, over the old. This is especially true of the great North American confederacy, which we here have particularly in view, and the free citizens of which call themselves, and are everywhere called, simply Americans; as if anticipating their destiny to be the lords of the new world. Already have the United States undeniably become a power in modern history, not only by their commerce, but also by the rise of an independent literature, by the weight of their public sentiment, and above all by the example of their political and religious institutions; and their influence is felt more and more every year in the movements of Europe. Nay; they have already, through the promising republic of Liberia, put their hand to the civilizing and christianizing of Africa; and, through evangelical missions in the East and commercial relations with East India, China, and Japan, to the regeneration of Asia.

To this general interest, which all educated men must feel in America, add the personal concern of thousands in all parts of Europe for sons and daughters, brothers and sisters, kinsmen and friends, who have exchanged the old world for the new, and form through individuals, so many connecting links between the two.

But where shall I begin, and where shall I end? The older a man grows, the more he feels the difficulty and risk of passing general opinions on whole nations and countries. Every vigorous nation is a microcosm, representing all the various tendencies and diversities of our whole race; and an advance in wisdom and experience is also an advance in caution and modesty of judgment. This is very peculiarly true of my present theme, which has elicited the most contradictory opinions, according as this or that subordinate point has been made the criterion. I would remind you especially, that a complete picture of the condition and circumstances of America properly includes a view of all Europe, which transmits both good and evil forces thither from all her countries. In the time allotted to me you can expect, of course, only a very imperfect sketch; and I will confine myself to points, which appear to have special interest for my hearers, and seem fitted to remove, or at least to soften, certain widespread prejudices, which I have already had frequent occasion to notice during my short visit here.

Allow me to speak, first, of the size and growth of the United States of North America; secondly, of their political condition; thirdly, of their social state; fourthly, of their civilization and literature; and lastly, of their morals and religion.

I. SIZE AND GROWTH

If any one fact of modern history marks an epoch, it is the discovery, or rather the re-discovery of America by Columbus. This, with the invention of the art of printing about half a century before, opened an illimitable perspective into the future. But both these events derived their chief importance from the vast spiritual and intellectual movement of the Reformation. They were its forerunners; as now the great inventions of the steam-engine, the railroad, and the magnetic telegraph seem to be again undesignedly preparing a new epoch in the history of the world and the church, a general union of the nations in one brotherhood by the bonds of civilization and of the everlasting Gospel. The States of Central and South America, settled by Roman Catholic Spain and Portugal, have remained stationary or gone backwards. But North America, which is essentially German or Teutonic in nationality and Protestant in religion, has developed itself with unexampled rapidity, and will become in fifty years more of such progress, nay, is already, one of the largest and most powerful nations of the earth.

The United States date their independent national existence, as is well known, from the Declaration of Independence in 1776. They are accordingly not yet a century old. At that time there were thirteen colonies; now there are already thirty-one well organized states, besides a number of territories, either not at all or at best very thinly inhabited, which will easily make a dozen new states, each as large as a German kingdom. The whole area of the United States, since the late acquisition of Texas, California, and New Mexico, amounts to more than three million English square miles (3,221,595), — almost as much as the whole continent of Europe (3,807,195), and fifteen times larger than France (197,400); while in variety of soil, climate, productions, and natural facilities for commerce, it surpasses any other equal extent of country on the globe.

The population has increased in like proportion. About the end of the last century the Union had hardly three millions of inhabitants; now it numbers already five and twenty millions, the natural increase of which is very much favored by the general prosperity and early marriage. The growth of many American cities is almost fabulous. It exceeds European experience ten if not a hundred fold. Vienna is now nearly two thousand years old, and has not as many inhabitants as New York or Philadelphia, which have existed hardly two centuries. Chicago in Illinois was commenced in

1831, and already numbers over 60,000 souls. I have seen it stated that forty years ago the whole ground, on which the city stands, might have been bought for $500, while now every foot almost is worth more. Before 1788 there was hardly a white man seen on the banks of the Ohio, where now the "Queen of the West," the city of Cincinnati, stands with a population little less than 150,000, while the whole State of Ohio numbers upwards of two millions.

Such an unparalleled growth of states and cities rising from the ground as at the stroke of the enchanter's wand, can only be accounted for, of course, by the swelling tide of immigration. Hundreds of thousands now annually leave the various countries of Europe, especially England, Ireland, and Germany, for America; and latterly an emigration has begun in an opposite quarter, in far off China, which, allured by the gold-diggings of California, is sending from the bosom of her three hundred and sixty millions an increasing number across the Pacific to the marts of San Francisco and the banks of the Sacramento.

We have before us here one of the most remarkable and important facts of modern times. This tide of emigration may be called with perfect justice a migration of nations, — proceeding, however, in the most peaceful way, without sword or bloodshed. It has no warlike spirit like the advance of the Germanic tribes on the threshold of the Middle Ages; it is not the work of religious enthusiasm like the crusades; it is chiefly the result of individual and domestic want and discontent, of national oppression and misery as regards Ireland, and of the desire for freedom, and for outward and inward improvement. With the Germans there is superadded that "Heimweh nach dem All," that cosmopolitan trait, which may be called both their intellectual strength and their political weakness. But in this vast march of nations from east to west, and from west to east we must recognize above all the progress of history itself and the hand of an over-ruling, allwise Providence, who is here breaking new paths, as he did two thousand years ago in Europe, and opening new and boundless prospects for the further development of humanity and of the kingdom of God.

The basis of the population of North America is the English and Scotch emigration. For some time past that of Ireland has been greater than that of all the other European countries put together; so as already to be spoken of as a formal exodus, threatening even the extinction of the Celtic race and of Romanism in Ireland. Now, however, the German emigration exceeds the Irish, and will do so probably for many years to come. Of late years more than one hundred thousand Germans have landed annually at the port of New York alone; and this year, I have been told on reliable authority, the German emigration, on account of the gathering storm of a general European war (which God graciously avert!) in addition to the usual causes, might reach at least between two and three hundred thousand, mostly to America.*

Bid them God speed, and give them at least your blessing and your prayers. The American bids them all welcome; the good especially; but even the bad he does not reject, hoping that in the new world they will become new men, and not confirm the old adage: "Cœlum non animum mutant, trans mare qui currunt." They all, and many millions more, can find room and employment in vast and still uncultivated tracts of the most fertile soil; in inexhaustible mines of coal

---

* The number of German immigrants at the port of New York alone for the year 1854, was 179,648. The whole number of immigrants to America for 1854, according to the reports laid before Congress, was:

To the United States . . .	460,474
To Canada	53,803

Of these it is supposed, 225,000 were Germans;

118,000	"	Irish;
61,000	"	English and Scotch;
13,000	"	French;
13,000	"	Chinese (to California)

and iron, of which Pennsylvania alone is supposed to contain more than the whole continent of Europe; on numberless canals, steamboats, and railroads; in the building of villages and cities, which shoot up as in a dream, so that names fail, and old ones have to be repeated often to confusion; in the most flourishing commerce and business of all sorts; and in the bosom of a nation full of the boldest enterprise and the most untiring energy.

The Atlantic coast, which is the most populous part of North America, and has thus far been the chief theatre of its history, and already has cities of half a million inhabitants and more, is yet very thinly settled in comparison with the countries of Europe. The Pacific coast — Oregon and California — has hardly yet risen into the view of the world, and has room for whole kingdoms. And the Mississippi valley, the immensely rich river tract between the Alleghany and Rocky Mountains, which forms the proper body of the United States, and contains now hardly ten million inhabitants, will itself, it is thought, conveniently support a population of more than a hundred millions.

Only one thing must we say to emigrants: Prepare for all sorts of privations; trust not to fortune and circumstances, but to God and to unwearied industry. If you wish a calm and cheerful life, better stay at home. The good old advice: Pray and work, is nowhere more to the point than in the United States. The genuine American despises nothing more than idleness and stagnation; he regards not enjoyment, but labor, not comfortable repose, but busy unrest, as the proper earthly lot of man; and this has unspeakable importance for him, and upon the whole a most salutary influence on the moral life of the nation. The New York merchant is vexed, if stopped with a question on the street; because he loses a couple of minutes. The same zeal, the same parsimony of time, is employed by the minister, the missionary, the colporteur, the tract and bible societies, for higher ends. Even the business man, if in any degree religiously disposed, considers his pecuniary gain only a means "to do good" — as he expresses it; and though the Americans are not unjustly reproached with avarice and covetousness, yet they are entitled, on the other hand, to the praise of a noble liberality towards all sorts of benevolent objects, — a liberality unrivalled in modern history save by the extraordinary offerings of the Free Church of Scotland in the glow of her first love.

In view of the extent and growth of the United States, thus briefly sketched, — a growth absolutely without parallel in history; — in view of their inexhaustible resources for agriculture, commerce, and all kinds of industry, for culture and science, and all the arts of peace; and in view of this modern European migration to the land of the west, — nothing but stupidity can be indifferent, and nothing but narrow-mindedness can deny these states a future.

Even geographically, America stands as in some sense the "Middle Kingdom." The people of the United States, these Americans in the emphatic sense of the term, have control of a whole continent and of two oceans, one arm outstretched towards Europe, the other towards Asia; and they possess ambition and energy enough to turn the advantages of their position and relations to the very best account. Unless a higher hand suddenly stop the wheel of universal history, they have — even in the possible though not probable case of a separation into four republics, northern, southern, eastern, western — a tremendous problem to solve; and no friend of humanity and of the kingdom of God can behold without the deepest interest the further development of this land of freedom and of promise.

II. POLITICAL CONDITION

In their political constitution the United States actually present the picture of a new world. In Europe all civil institutions rest more or less on the feudal system of the Middle Ages, as these again rest on the patriarchal relations of Asia. The further west, the stronger the tendency to individual and national freedom and independence. This is especially the case in the Germanic tribes; and of these, most of all in the Anglo-Saxon. Favored by its insular segregation, moulded by Christianity and by Protestantism, England has most fully developed the principle of self-government as the foundation of national strength and greatness for all nations, and now presents the sublime spectacle of an organic union of freedom and deeply-rooted loyalty; of manly independence and faithful conservatism; of a well-organized constitutional monarchy, not artificial on paper, but of perfectly natural historical growth, joined with a civil and commercial power, which reaches off to Canada, Australia, and East India, and carries into all the colonies the spirit of law-abiding freedom and the seed of the Gospel and of Christian civilization.

In North America the last traces of medieval feudalism disappear, except in the slavery of the southern states. You see there no king; no nobility; no privileged class; no aristocracy, except that — unavoidable even in a republic — of character, talent, and wealth; no orders nor titles, except the professional, which rest upon personal attainments; no entailed estates; no standing army; no established church. Instead of these you find universal civil and religious liberty and equality; unrestricted freedom of speech and of the press; the sovereignty of the people; the election of almost all officers by the majority; the highest stations, even the presidential chair, accessible to the poorest and humblest citizen, on the single condition of personal capacity and merit: and yet, with all this apparent excess of freedom, a universal respect for right and law; deep reverence for Christianity; a conservative spirit; well-ordered government; perfect security of person and property; and great independence, too, towards other nations, as was shown by the Mexican war, where glowing patriotism and national pride supplied in a few weeks the want of a standing army, threw hosts of volunteers into the heart of their hostile neighbors' country, achieved victory after victory over the Spaniards, and planted the star-spangled banner of the Union on the palace of Montezuma.

To those who are wedded to a particular theory of politics, who apply the same measure to all countries and all constitutions, and who fail to see, that history is not a dead uniformity, but a living scene of change and variety, and that every nation has its peculiar calling, — to such all this must be very incongruous and disagreeable fact. But fact it is, and with facts and an actual state of things we here have to do. Though a Swiss by birth and an American by adoption, I have yet lived too long under monarchies to be at all insensible to their historical necessity and great advantages. I have no sympathy whatever with the narrow, fanatical republicanism of "Young America" and the radical propagandism of the "manifest destiny" men, who see no salvation for Europe but in the universal spread of republican institutions, and are therefore disposed to welcome — though certainly in ignorance — even the worst revolutions, coming from the very spirit of darkness. But unhistorical, useless, nay, absurd as it would be to transplant American institutions bodily to European soil, I think, on the other hand, that for the United States themselves only one form of government is reasonable and proper: and that is, the republican. In fact, no other would be possible under present circumstances. It has there all traditions and sympathies in its favor. It grows out of the whole history and the present mission of the country. Under it the nation has become large and strong; under it she can best develop her physical and moral resources; under it she feels contented and happy. Whence, indeed, could a king for America come? Certainly not from Europe; for on the east and west the republic has an ocean-barrier against any successful invasion; and from north or south she is made impregnable by her own inward force. No monarch could arise, except as a military despot and usurper, like Napoleon, out of bloody civil wars, and from such a one Christianity and good sense we hope will save us.

But though the American constitution rests on a groundwork wholly different from all European systems, and thus forms an entirely new phenomenon in the history of the world; yet it did not come into life by any means abruptly and without preparation. It stands in the closest historical connection with England. *The American revolution of 1776, which gave birth to the independent confederacy, was entirely different in principle, character, and tendency from all the revolutions of the European continent since* 1789; and it is of the greatest importance to keep this difference steadily in view, if we would duly understand and appreciate that country and its prevailing idea of freedom. The American revolution has far more affinity with the rising of the German nation against the usurpation of Napoleon, and of the Greeks against the tyranny of the Turks. Properly speaking, it was no revolution at all, in the sense of insurrection and radical overthrow of all social relations. It was strictly and only an emancipation — forcible, indeed, but historically necessary — of colonies which had arrived at the age of self-government from the guardianship of the mother country, which had become unnecessary and oppressive. Language, customs, religion, laws, and institutions remained substantially the same, and were changed only in form and so far as the new state of things required. The English common law and the whole judicial process is retained to this day as before the revolution. In the place of the hereditary monarch came a president, chosen, it is true, every four years by the people, but clothed with proportionally as much power and influence as the queen of England, and in some respects with more. In the place of Parliament came Congress, with its two branches, the Senate, — corresponding to the House of Lords, and representing in general the conservative principle, — and the House of Representatives, answering to the English House of Commons, and more progressive in its reigning spirit.

The fathers and leaders of the American struggle for freedom — excepting Tom Paine, the English Voltaire, who, however, by his infidelity, vices, and vulgar habits soon lost all influence, and was thrust out of all decent American society — were anything but radical reformers or wild destructionists, like the heroes of the French and German revolutions. They were men of sound practical judgment, of decidedly liberal, and yet sober, conservative, and constitutional views, and of the most honorable, moral, and in some instances even decidedly religious character. From the first settling of the country, especially among the Puritanic New Englanders, a very strong practical religious spirit maintained itself, and prevented the national progress from running into the wild extravagances of radicalism. George Washington, the noblest embodiment of the American revolution — or rather secession from England, — the "father of his country," "first in war, first in peace, and first in the hearts of his countrymen," revered from Maine to Florida, from New York to San Francisco, as a sort of national god, — was a perfectly disinterested patriot, a mild, noble-minded, plain, modest man, of irreproachable and symmetrical character, not of very profound knowledge of religion, but sincerely reverencing the holy word and law of God; a worthy and consistent communicant of the Protestant Episcopal church, holding private devotion daily in his library, kneeling and praying over the Bible. His successors in the presidency, down to Pierce, who regularly attends public worship — a practice, which in the United States is almost inseparable from moral and social respectability, — need not fear comparison in a moral and religious point of view with any dynasty of Europe. The greatest American statesmen and orators have on various occasions thrown the weight of their voice into the scale of virtue and piety, and have repeatedly and emphatically declared that Christianity is the groundwork of their republic, and that the obliteration of the church must involve the annihilation of all freedom, and the ruin of the land. You seldom hear in the halls of Congress, however badly it may occasionally behave in other respects, a word of disrespect to religion; and whenever one it uttered, it is commonly repelled with indignation. But you may sometimes hear there an open confession of the fundamental truths of revelation. Every session of the Senate and House of Representatives is opened with prayer; while a proposition for the same arrangement in the Frankfoil parliament of 1848 was rejected with scorn. No wonder the Scripture was there verified: "Except the Lord build the house, they labor in vain that build it." The renowned statesman and orator, Henry Clay, on his death-bed in 1852, confessed that he had tried the glories of earth and found them all vanity, and that he sought peace and salvation only in Christ crucified. His great rival, Daniel Webster, the American Demosthenes who in the grand simplicity of his style betrays the study of the Bible, found in his last hours the greatest comfort in the 23rd Psalm of David, the "rod and the staff" of the good shepherd, died in 1852, with a prayer for forgiveness on his lips, and ordered for his epitaph the words of Scripture: "Lord, I believe; help thou my unbelief!" Such testimonies from such mouths, have in America the weight of a mighty sermon, and of a sacred legacy to the whole nation.

Such things explain the well-known fact, that the modern European heroes of liberty, or rather of licentiousness — too many of whom have unfortunately been sent adrift upon us

by the abortive revolutions of 1848 — become mightily un-
deceived in America, and begin at once, in beer-houses and
infidel journals, to scoff at the intolerable tedium of the
Jewish Sabbath, the pharisaical church-going, the tyrannical
priestcraft, and whatever else they may call the pious habits
and institutions of the United States. They find themselves
exceedingly uncomfortable, and would fain come back again
to kindle revolutions in Europe, which they cannot kindle in
America. Most of these radicals, who a few years ago made
such a noise in France, Italy, and Germany, have there sunk
to mere cyphers, or have become at best, common citizens,
who earn their livelihood with their own hands, and have
first to build up a character, before they can claim any influence or importance.

The only revolutionary character, who really made a great
stir, was Kossuth. During his half-year's residence in America, as the "guest of the nation," he delivered several hundred
English and some German addresses; and by his rare gift of
agitation, and his certainly most remarkable eloquence, even
in a foreign tongue, he won the admiration of thousands.
But the history of his meteorlike rhetorical campaign through
the States of the Union may be told in the few words: "He
rose like a rocket and fell down like a stick." When he came
back to New York, where he had been received a few months
before with frantic enthusiasm, he attracted no attention;
and unnoticed, and even under the *alias* of Alexander Smith,
he returned to England to retire into a private house in one
of the suburbs of London. The best proof of the total failure
of his mission, is the fact, that the American government
still adheres as firmly as ever to the wise policy, previously
observed, and so earnestly recommended by Washington
and the dying Clay, of non-intervention in the broils of the
European powers; though Kossuth expended the most brilliant efforts of his inexhaustible forensic oratory, to turn
this policy to an active interference in favor of all European

revolutions, especially of a new insurrection against the house of Hapsburg in Hungary, which he predicted as near at hand; and in this neutral course the government will persevere, though at this moment the Russo-Turkish question affords the most favorable of all occasions for departing from it and for asserting the influence of America in the councils of the great powers of Europe. The general government at Washington, which manages our international affairs, rightly prefers to stand on a friendly footing with all European states; to offer all a free asylum for their overflowing or oppressed population; and to operate upon the old world, not by the rude power of arms and gratuitous intermeddling, but solely by the silent, though far deeper and worthier moral power of example.*

The whole Anglo-American conception of freedom is specifically different from the purely negative notion which prevails amongst the radicals and revolutionists on the continent of Europe. With the American, freedom is anything but a mere absence of restraint, an arbitrary, licentious indulgence, every one following his natural impulse, as the revolutionists would have it. It is a rational, moral self-determination, hand in hand with law, order, and authority. True national freedom, in the American view, rests upon a

---

* The appointment of Saunders as consul for London, and of Soulé as ambassador to Madrid, can hardly be adduced as indication of a foreign-intervention policy and an aggressive revolutionary propagandism. For the first was expressly rejected by the Senate, and the second, although confirmed by that body, met the decided disapprobation of public opinion and was freely condemned as an unprovoked insult upon Spain, and an impolitic measure of the Administration. It is well known that the fiery advocate of Cuban Fillibusterism, after the failure of his efforts to buy or to steal the Pearl of the Antilles, resigned at the end of last year and is already replaced by the Hon. Cæsar Augustus Hannibal Dodge, who will not prove as formidable as his name sounds. It would be the greatest injustice to judge the United States by their diplomatic representatives abroad. While some of them by their intelligence and dignity challenge the esteem of foreign nations, not a few others bring only disgrace or ridicule upon our good name. It were best either to send such men to European courts as are really fit for the station and will mind their proper business, or to give up the diplomatic intercourse altogether.

moral groundwork, upon the virtue of self-possession and self-control in individual citizens. He alone is worthy of this great blessing and capable of enjoying it, who holds his passions in check; is master of his sensual nature; obeys natural laws, not under pressure from without, but from inward impulse, cheerfully and joyfully. But the negative and hollow liberalism, or rather the radicalism, which undermines the authority of law and sets itself against Christianity and the church, necessarily dissolves all social ties, and ends in anarchy; which then passes very easily into the worst and most dangerous form of despotism.

These sound views of freedom, in connection with the moral earnestness and the Christian character of the nation, form the basis of the North American republic, and can alone secure its permanence. We also find there, indeed, beyond all question, utterly unsound and dangerous radical tendencies; in the political elections all wild passions, falsehood, calumny, bribery, and wickedness of all sorts, are let loose; and even the halls of the legislatures and of Congress are frequently disgraced by the misconduct of unprincipled demagogues, so that multitudes of the best citizens, disgusted with the wire-pulling and mean selfishness of self-styled friends of the people, shrink from any active participation in politics, or discharge their duty as citizens by nothing more, at most, than their vote at the ballot-box. But on the whole, there prevails undeniably among the people a sound conservative tone, which exerts a constant influence in favor of right and order; and it is an imposing spectacle, when immediately after the election of a president or governor, a universal calm at once succeeds the furious storm of party strife, and the conquered party patiently submits to the result, never dreaming of such a thing as asserting its real or supposed rights in any violent way. Any dissatisfaction — for such certainly has place there as well as elsewhere — reaches never to the republican form of government, but only to the manner of its exercise, not to the constitution of the land, but only to the measures of the dominant party; and it seeks redress of its wrongs always in a lawful, constitutional way. So far as this goes, it may well be asserted, that the North American Union, with all the fluctuation and insecurity of its affairs in particular instances — which is to be expected in so new a country — stands in general more firmly on its feet, and is safer from violent revolutions, than any country on the continent of Europe.

A very characteristic proof of our assertion, that American freedom is different in principle from radicalism and licentiousness, and rests entirely on the basis of self-control and self-restraint, is presented in the really sublime temperance movement, particularly in the "Maine liquor law," as it is called. This law wholly forbids, not directly the drinking — for this would be an infringement of personal liberty, — but the manufacture and sale of all intoxicating drinks, including even wine and beer, except for medicinal, mechanical, and sacramental purposes. This law was first introduced a few years ago in the predominantly Puritanical, New England State of Maine, and has since been extended to several other states by a popular majority; and even in the great States of New York, Pennsylvania, and Ohio, the most zealous efforts are now making by public addresses, by tracts and periodicals, and other means of agitation, to secure the election of legislators favorable to the temperance cause, who will strike at the root of the terrible evil, and remove even the temptation to drunkenness.* Even last fall, shortly before the election, I was personal witness of the zeal and earnestness, with which the agents of the temperance so-

* Since the above was written the Maine law has even passed the Legislatures of New York and Pennsylvania (in April, 1855), and is to go into effect on the fourth of July of this year. Think of the law as you please. This is one of the greatest marvels of self-restraining popular legislation, and we would admire it still more, had it not been mixed up with politics, which in its present state seems to spoil whatever it touches, whether men or things.

39

ciety, ministers and laymen, canvassed the counties of Pennsylvania, and spreading their tent under the open heaven, after a solemn introduction by singing and prayer, eloquently described the horrible consequences, temporal and eternal, of intemperance, and demonstrated to the people by the most convincing arguments, the duty of using their elective franchise in a way demanded by the public weal, in the consciousness of their high responsibility to God and the world.

It must be granted that this Maine temperance law, *in itself considered*, goes too far, and is to be ranked with radical legislation. It contradicts the letter of the Bible; for it is a fact, that Christ himself turned water into wine, drank wine according to the general custom of the time, used it for the illustration of the most sacred things, and consecrated it in the holy Supper, as the symbolical vehicle of his atoning blood. But on the other hand what St. Paul says of abstinence from meat, is equally applicable to beverage: "If wine make my brother offend, I will drink no wine while the world standeth, lest I make my brother to offend." The moderate American temperance men take the position not of abstract right in the case, but of present expediency and moral necessity under existing circumstances. For it must be considered, that the United States have hardly begun to produce their own wine, and that most of what is there sold under this name, is more or less adulterated and fully as injurious as brandy. Yet, think of the "Maine liquor law" as we may, — and we would here neither advocate nor condemn it, — we must admire the moral energy and self-denial of a free people, which would rather renounce an enjoyment in itself lawful, than see it drive thousands of weak persons to bodily and spiritual ruin.

To those, who see in America only the land of unbridled radicalism and of the wildest fanaticism for freedom, I take the liberty to put the modest question: In what European state would the government have the courage to enact such a prohibition of the traffic in all intoxicating drinks, and the people the self-denial to submit to it? I am sure, that in Bavaria at least the prohibition of bier would produce a bloody revolution; for "der schrecklichste der Schrecken, das ist der Bayer ohne Bier."

Time, of course, does not permit me to enter into a more detailed analysis of the American constitution; the relation of the central government in Washington to the rights and governments of the several states; the composition of congress and of the legislatures; the duties of the president and the organization of his cabinet; the differences of the two parties, Whigs and Democrats, into which the great nation has heretofore been divided, and the principles of the new party of Know-Nothings which is just now sweeping over the country like a whirlwind; the nature of the popular elections; the courts; juridical and parliamentary eloquence; &c. But on one point I must add at least a few words; viz., on slavery. This prevails, indeed, only in the Southern States, but, by the union of these States with the Northern in one confederacy, it is made a national matter; and latterly, especially through the unparalleled circulation of "Uncle Tom's cabin," which gives substantially a tolerably true picture of life in the slave States, it has engaged also in a high degree the attention of Europe.

Slavery is unquestionably the greatest political and social difficulty of the Union. It keeps up a constant agitation; throws the apple of discord, year after year, into Congress and even into whole churches; and in 1850 brought us to the brink of a formal division of the Republic. The leaders of the two great political parties — Clay and Webster among the Whigs, Cass and Buchanan among the Democrats — at that time exerted all the power of their eloquence and statesmanship to secure the passage of the "Compromise Measures," as they are called, and thus save the Union. But the agitation on this subject still continues in state and church; has broken out anew this winter in the stormy debate in Congress on the Nebraska bill; and will only be abated with the abatement of the evil itself. That there are in the United States over three millions of negro slaves, who may be bought and sold as common merchandize, is certainly in most palpable contradiction to the first principle of that government, that all men are born free and equal; or, as it should be more properly expressed, are born or destined for freedom. What an anomaly, that the freest country in the world should maintain and defend a relic of barbarism and heathenism, which humanity and Christianity, reason and revelation, and all the civilized nations of Europe condemn with one voice! But when and how this social evil, not introduced by the national American government itself, but inherited from the colonial period, rooted in the heart of the land, and interwoven with all the material interests of the South, is to be done away, is one of the most difficult questions, which statesmanship has ever had to solve.

On the subject of slavery the Union is divided into three principal parties:

(1.) The Abolitionists of the North, especially of New England, who regard slavery as sin *per se*, and insist on its immediate abolition. These, however, fall again into two very different branches; some proceeding on Christian principles, while others run into the most radical excesses, even in other matters; "women's rights," for example, and open infidelity, — and thus do the cause more harm than good.

(2.) The Secessionists of the South, especially of South Carolina, who, embittered by the unsparing attacks of the Abolitionists, threatened Congress in 1850 with secession from the Confederacy, and the formation of a southern republic of their own. Many of these advocate slavery as a necessary social counterpoise to the democracy of the North, as a conservative element; appealing to the ineffaceable difference between the African and the Caucasian races, the miserable condition of the freed negroes, and even to the Holy scriptures of the Old Testament, and to the Epistle of Paul to Philemon.

(3.) The Union party in North and South. This is by far the most numerous, made up of both whigs and democrats. These, from motives of patriotism and interest, would maintain the Union at all hazards, and leave slavery to the legislation of the slave states themselves, and to its fate. Most of them believe that slavery will gradually die out of itself, and that, in any case, a sudden emancipation, without previous education of the slaves, would be rather an injury than a benefit to them.

Die out it assuredly will in time, as it has done in all the northern states; and perhaps it would have already disappeared in Maryland and Kentucky, but for the abolition agitation, which has called forth a violent reaction against the unsparing condemnation of slave-holders. Thus much, however, seems to me clear, from the philanthropic and Christian point of view; that the state and the church ought, in a quiet way, and without infringement of the right of property, to provide for a gradual emancipation of the slaves, by training them to the rational use of freedom, and by laws for the liberation of the new generation at a certain age.

But even in case of a general abolition of slavery, it is still a question of great difficulty, whether the African race can at all stand by the side of the Caucasian in full equality, amalgamate with it, and enter fully into its destiny. Even in the free states there is confessedly an impassable gulf between the whites and the free blacks, and even the most zealous abolitionist, after all his talk about the absolute equality of all men, would never, for any price, consent to marry a negress. I doubt whether an Englishman or a German would. The condition of the free negroes in America is in general more pitiable, and not seldom worse than that of their brethren in bondage at the south, at least where these are carefully provided for by Christian masters — of whom, thank God, there are not a few — and are so kindly treated, that in many cases they will not accept freedom when it is offered. It seems to me, therefore, that duty as much requires the northern states to improve by wise laws and charitable institutions the social condition of the free negroes, and to raise them to the dignity of genuine humanity, as it demands of the southern states the gradual emancipation of the slaves.

Thus far, I see but one luminous point in the tragic gloom of slavery; and that is the American Colonization Society, and its offspring, the negro republic of Liberia, on the west coast of Africa. In this colony, which has thus far made altogether unexpected progress, and which has its warmest and most liberal patrons in the southern states, and among the slave-holders themselves, there is at least, the beginning of a radical improvement in the condition of the negroes, and at the same time the groundwork of a general Christian civilization for the wild negro tribes around, in a land whose climate the Caucasian race cannot bear, any more than the negroes amongst the whites can, to all appearance, sustain an equal social importance and dignity with them. Thus God seems here also to be giving a new proof of his wonderful wisdom, which can bring good even out of evil. By Christian and civilized negroes he is kindling in the heart of that *terra incognita* the light of the everlasting Gospel, and is thus turning the dreadful curse of American slavery — that griev· ous crime of European and American christendom (for it was under Spanish, French, Danish, and English rule that slavery came into the New world) — into an incalculable blessing to the pagan savages of Africa.

III. NATIONAL CHARACTER AND SOCIAL LIFE

The United States present, in the first place, a wonderful mixture of all nations under heaven. A tour through them is in some sense a tour through the world, and therefore one of the most interesting and instructive journeys one can make, who would see the confused motions of the living present, rather than the rich treasures of the dead past; though of the latter, Italy, for example, that flower-crowned mausoleum of history, affords infinitely more. In America, English, Scotch, Irish, Germans of all provinces, Swiss, Dutch, French, Spaniards, Italians, Swedes, Norwegians, Poles, Magyars, with their well-known national virtues and weaknesses, have peaceably settled down together in political and social equality. And to these representatives of European nations are added the red aborigines of the country, who are constantly retreating further into the forests and prairies of the West, and, in spite of all attempts to Christianize and civilize them, are steadily approaching the tragical fate of self-extermination by intestine wars, contagious diseases, and the poison of rum. Then the black sons of Africa, rejoicing in the childlike cheerfulness of their nature, and even in freedom bowing instinctively before the superiority of the whites. Lastly, the yellow immigrants from the Celestial Empire, attracted by the gold of California, and bringing with them their oblong eyes, their quiet disposition and mechanical culture, their industry, avarice, and filthy habits.

Thus we have in America an ethnographic panorama, which one may see pass before him in a few hours on a walk through Broadway in New York, or Chestnut street in Philadelphia, or along the markets of San Francisco.

Not only the nationalities of the Old World, however, but even national peculiarities of condition, manners, and habits, obsolete in their native lands, there perpetuate themselves

45

to this day in many instances with remarkable tenacity. In Virginia you meet the English gentleman of the age of Elizabeth and the later Stuarts; in Philadelphia, the Quaker of the days of George Fox and William Penn; in East Pennsylvania, the Palatine and the Swabian of the beginning of the last century; in New England, the Puritan of the times of Cromwell and Baxter; on the banks of the Hudson and in New Jersey, the genuine Hollander; on the shores of the Northern lakes hundreds of Scotch, so that a traveller from the country of Burns "at the Kirk on Sabbath would hardly ken he were frae hame;" in South Carolina, the Huguenot and French nobleman of the seventeenth century, or at least very striking traces of their character, which in Europe are even far more obliterated. This fact itself shows, how cautiously one must receive the accounts of so many European tourists, which take some single element by itself, and make it the standard for the whole; thus producing the most contradictory representations.

But now what is most remarkable is, that over this confused diversity there broods after all a higher unity, and that in this chaos of peoples the traces of a specifically American national character may be discerned. Those, who find in the United States only the faint echo of European nationalities, and so feel obliged to deny that country an independent future in history, are very much mistaken. Whoever treads the soil of the New World with open eyes, perceives at once a thoroughly fresh and energetic national life, which instantly takes up and assimilates all foreign elements, excepting only the African and the Chinese. The American's digestive power is really astonishing. How many thousands and millions of Europeans has his stomach already received! and yet he has only grown firmer and healthier thereby.

The basis of the American nationality is undoubtedly English, though unquestionably a peculiar modification of

46

it, possessing much greater capacity than the original for
receiving and working up foreign material. To gain a clear
conception of the Anglo-Saxon race, one must travel to
England, Scotland, and North America. If he sees the Englishman only abroad, he meets him in the most unfavorable
circumstances. An Englishman on the continent is like a
fish out of water. He commonly retains his well-known
spleen, and by his stiff awkwardness and his obstinate adherence to his peculiar insular notions and habits, even down
to his favorite tea-kettle, beaf-steak, and plum-pudding, presents without question a ludicrous aspect, so that a spectator
must wonder, how this strange John Bull could obtain the
dominion of the seas. The like is true, though not so strikingly, of the American. But what seems their weakness
abroad — seems, I say, for with all their stiffness and strange-
ness one cannot help respecting and admiring them on other
accounts — that very thing is their strength at home. The
Anglo-Saxon and Anglo-American, of all modern races, possess the strongest national character and the one best fitted
for universal dominion, and that, too, not a dominion of
despotism but one, which makes its subjects free citizens.
For they are at once liberal and conservative. In them — and
this is the secret of their national greatness and importance
— the impulse towards freedom and the sense of law and
order are inseparably united, and both rest on a moral basis.
Conscience and the sense of duty are very strongly marked
in them, and I doubt whether the moral influence of Christianity and of Protestantism has more deeply and widely
affected any nation, than it has the Anglo-Saxon. It is characteristic, that the word "glory," which occurs in almost
every sentence of Napoleon's proclamations and bulletins,
never appears in the despatches of Wellington, but gives
place to the term "duty." *Gloire* is the motto of the Frenchman; *duty*, of the Englishman. Napoleon, at the battle of the
Pyramids, fired the ambition of his soldiers with the cry:

"Centuries look down upon you!" Nelson at Trafalgar simply reminded his seamen: "England expects every man to do his duty to-day!"

Mental energy and solidity the Anglo-Saxons have in common with the Germans; both being in fact off-shoots from the same Teutonic root. But whilst in the latter this mental power turns inward, and occupies itself with thought and theory, in the former it is rather directed outward, concerning itself in a practical way with will and action. The one has the deeper mind, and can take up and comprehend everything in himself; the other has the stronger character, and can shape and organize everything out of himself. The German excels in the facility of transferring himself into all circumstances and adapting himself to all, and thus very often loses himself in foreign nationalities; the Anglo-Saxon is stiff and unyielding, but makes everything, as of itself, serve him. The former is the most cordial and good-natured man of the world, giving free play to his warm, hearty feelings and impulses; the latter has a heart indeed, but it beats under a marble cover; he has perfect self-command, and is therefore best fitted to rule others. True, he puts no hindrance in the way of the stranger; he gives him perfect freedom, within the wholesome limits of the law. Yet he exerts upon him a vast power and an attractive force, which cannot be ultimately resisted.

The American has the same organizing talent, the same self-control, the same practical energy, the same business faculty, as the Englishman. His spirit of enterprise is still stronger, and not rarely degenerates even into fool-hardiness and the most reckless disregard of human life, fearfully manifest in the countless conflagrations in cities, and disasters on steamboats and railroads.

The American, I grant, has less solidity than the much older Englishman. But he makes up for this in vivacity, elasticity, and capacity for improvement. The Englishman, too, is shut up on his island; the American moves on a great continent and between two oceans. The former has not yet been able to assimilate to itself the Celtic Irishman in his immediate neighborhood, nor thoroughly to redress his grievances; the latter, at once infuses into the immigrant the common feeling of the American.

But though the main features of the American national character may be already quite plainly discerned, and reveal themselves as predominantly Anglo-Saxon; yet it is only in its formation state; and the more it developes, the more sensibility do the un-English elements, favored by the increasing emigration from the continental countries of Europe, modify the whole. In New York the Hollanders — the first settlers — in Louisiana the French, can never be wholly obliterated. Least of all, the Germans, who, with their descendants, must already number four millions and upwards. Even now, the middle and western States, in which most of the Germans have settled, differ very perceptibly in character, from New England and the southern States. As they lie between the two geographically, so they hold a middle place also in a natural and social point of view. Pennsylvania, for example — the Keystone State, as it is called, which binds together the giant structure of the Union —is neither purely English nor purely German, but Anglo-German; and will become more and more so. Even where the German language is swallowed up by the English, the German disposition and German ways still maintain themselves under the new dress, and from the ashes of the old German Adam rises not rarely an American gentleman, who unites the excellencies of the German and the Englishman in beautiful harmony. Beyond all question the German has a great work to do in the New World, though he is as yet hardly aware of it. He will not fully meet the demand, however, if he coldly and stiffly shuts himself out from the Anglo-Americans, and thinks to form a state within a state.

This would be the most unwise policy, and would unavoidably end in a failure. He must rather, by his native cosmopolitan, universal spirit, boldly and energetically master the Anglo-American, appropriate its virtues, and then breathe into it, as far as it may be desirable, the breath of his own spirit and life. In this way he will work in a larger and richer field; whereas by selfish seclusion, he robs himself of all influence on the central stream of the American life. If the land of the Reformation has furnished the ideal part, the heart's blood, of the modern European history of the world and the church, its literature and better class of emigrants have a similar mission also for the United States of America.

Then let the oddities and weaknesses — in a word, the whole long cue of the raw German — the cue in front, too, which seems to have become fashionable since 1848 — let all these go, if only his virtues, his depth of mind and of heart, may remain, and be enriched and quickened with the undeniable energy and practical turn of the Anglo-American. The German and English, too, mix much easier than other nations. They are both, in fact, essentially Germanic or Teutonic. They have, in common, a certain simplicity and honesty of character, a deep-rooted respect for woman, love for home and the family life, especially moral earnestness and a religious turn; and even the ecclesiastical life has taken a like course in them, the two being the chief supports of the ideas and institutions of evangelical Christianity, and holding in their hands the theoretical and practical mission of Protestantism for the world. Their duty, therefore, where they are brought by Providence into immediate contact, and meet in all the relations of social life, cannot possibly be to hate and fight one another; it must be to esteem, and love, and learn from one another, and contribute to each other's perfection.

The English national character itself is, like the English language, confessedly the result of an organic combination of the British-Celtic, the Anglo-Saxon, or Germanic, and the Norman-French nationalities; the Anglo-Saxon, however, plainly forming the proper stem, upon which the Norman was grafted in the twelfth century; as, in fact, the fundamental elements of the English language, all the words for the most essential relations of human life, are of German origin.

A similar process of national amalgamation is now also going on before our eyes in America; but peacefully, under more favorable conditions, and on a far grander scale than ever before in the history of the world America is *the grave of all European nationalities*; but a *Phenix grave*, from which they shall rise to new life and new activity in a new and essentially Anglo-Germanic form.

The English influence, of course, predominates in America, not only in language, but also in the whole social life; but it is greatly modified, partly by influences from continental Europe, partly by the political institutions of America itself. The further west, and the newer the country, the more unformed and changeable is the state of society; and on the frontiers, and in uncultivated regions, the rudest state of nature sometimes appears. In California, for example, with all its gold, I would not live for any price. Every thing there is still in chaotic confusion; though even in this State the indestructible Anglo-American sense of law and order already shows itself energetically among the people. Lately, for example, the authorities being too cowardly to do their duty, the people took the punishment of certain offenders into their own hands, and executed "Lynch law" upon them. In the larger States of the west, however, and especially in the east and south, we find well-ordered, respectable, and cultivated society. The interior arrangements of a house commonly afford every thing that the Englishman denotes by the untranslatable word "comfort" — carpets in the rooms, on the stairs, and in the hall; a parlor, with sofas, piano,

cushioned rocking-chairs, a centre-table, covered with illustrated works, the latest ladies' journals, &c. After the English
plan, each family occupies a house by itself, which, at least
in the smaller cities and towns, has generally a garden
attached. Many of the larger cities even, as New Haven and
Cleveland, are charmingly arranged, almost every house
having an inclosed green in front, planted with trees and
flowers, so that the streets present the delightful aspect of
a garden promenade. The smaller towns are, in general,
much handsomer, the streets wider and straighter, the houses
more inviting and convenient, than in Europe. And in the
principal cities, New York, Philadelphia, Boston, Baltimore,
Washington, Cincinnati, New Orleans, all European luxury
is making only too rapid and perilous progress. Had not
New York so many churches and Christian societies, and so
strictly kept Sundays, it might already be called a second
Paris, which it will soon be also in point of population.

In the lead of this luxury stand sometimes the most disgusting forms of a mushroom aristocracy, which rests upon
nothing but the dust of gold. These American fops and
quack-aristocrats, who, void of all true nobility, have no
sense for any thing but outward show, are not rarely met,
to our shame, in European capitals and watering-places,
striving to outdo the polite world in vanity and folly. I heard
but yesterday, for example, that the son of a New York
merchant-prince in the Berne Highlands, where everybody
goes on foot, if possible, to enjoy and admire, *con amore*,
the sublimity of the mountain scenery, was driving around
everywhere with two horses, to show the English lords and
Russian nobles right visibly his pecuniary superiority. It is
characteristic that the two largest and most princely mansions
in New York and Philadelphia were built by quacks (Dr.
Townsend and Dr. Jayne) out of the proceeds of their sarsa-
parilla. Whether the enormous increases of luxury, and
worldly pomp, and splendor, will gradually undermine the

Republic, whose proper foundation is the patriarchal style of simplicity and honesty, time must tell. At any rate the flourishing commerce and growing wealth of the country involves great danger of a bottomless materialism and worldliness; and I see in Christianity alone the powerful corrective, which has thus far saved the higher intellectual and moral interests, and which will secure to them in future the predominance over the "almighty dollar." It is a remarkable fact, however, that wealth hardly every continues to the third generation in the States, and that all this artificial aristocracy soon runs out. The middle classes are there, more than in any other country, the proper bone and sinew of society, and always restore the equilibrium.

Social life in America is in some respects freer, in others stiffer, than in Europe. Much, that is not at all offensive there, is rudeness to the European; and the American, in turn, is greatly scandalized with things which in the Old World are innocent customs. It were unjust and pedantic to make such mere externals the standard of judgment respecting the people. The old proverb here holds true: So many countries, so many customs. So highly and liberally cultivated society, as is found for instance here in Berlin, where, to speak without flattery, one may spend every evening in the most stimulating and agreeable conversation, with ladies as well as with gentlemen, on matters of science and art and all the higher affairs of life, is, I grant, very rarely met with in America. Female education especially is, in general, very superficial there, valued more for outward show than for inward solidity; and in many companies of which, judging from appearance, one would expect better things, you sometimes hear for a whole evening, hardly anything but the flattest and most insufferable gossip about the weather, the fashions, and the latest projects of marriage. On the other hand, however, there is more of a kind of medium cultivation than in Europe, where accomplishment is aristocratic, or confined to certain classes. The United States is the country for average intelligence, average morality, and average piety. Republican institutions, as may even be observed to some extent in Switzerland, tend to level away social distinctions. In America, while there are not so many towering heights of culture, there is, on the other hand, no such wide-spread and degrading ignorance as in the masses of Europe. There almost every one tries to become a gentleman or a lady; that is, to attain the English ideal of outward and inward intellectual and moral culture, so far as his circumstances and position allow. Almost every man has some routine, at least outwardly; he can represent something; he reads gazettes and newspapers; knows how to talk sensibly about the general affairs of his country; and can, if necessary, make a speech, and generally turn his knowledge to good practical account.

The Yankee especially — that is, the New Englander — has a natural business genius, and can undertake anything. He can begin and make a fortune easier with one idea, than a German can with ten. His mottoes are: "Help yourself," and "Go ahead." He early becomes independent, and even in youth learns to push through all possible difficulties. Hence the Jews hardly play any part in America; they find their masters in the Yankees. It must not be thought, however, that these descendants of the old Puritans are made only of shrewd, selfish calculation. It would be the greatest injustice to take the famous Barnum, the prince of humbug, as the only type of the "universal Yankee nation." They are generally liberal, conscientious, temperate, strictly moral, religiously-inclined, friends of liberal education, and ardent philanthropists. The six north-eastern States, included under the name of New England, especially Massachusetts and Connecticut, are still, in regard to culture and Christianity, the garden of America.

Domestic life in the United States may be described as,

on an average, well regulated and happy. The number of illegitimate births is perhaps proportionally less than in any other country. Divorces are very rare, and are made by the laws far more difficult than, for example, in Prussia. This is the good effect of the laws of old England, which has practically made divorce almost impossible, by requiring for it an act of Parliament, and therefore an enormous outlay of money. True, the American family life is not characterized by so much deep good-nature, and warm, overflowing heartiness, as the German. But instead of this the element of mutual respect predominates. Husband and wife, parents and children, stand more independently towards one another, in a respectful dignity, and thus avoid many collisions. When the partners speak of each other in the third person, it is not commonly by the familiar names: My husband, My wife, but by the family name with Mr. or Mrs. prefixed, or by the official title. In fact, even in direct address the wife not unfrequently gives her husband his title of Doctor, Professor, &c., particularly in company.

The American's profound respect for the female sex is well known. This old Germanic trait, celebrated so early as by Tacitus, has most fully developed itself in the Anglo-Saxon race under the influence of Christianity, and is very favorable to domestic and public morality. Whoever is acquainted with family life in England, knows how high and dignified a position woman holds there, and how much is comprehended in the term *lady*. America goes yet a step further. It is sometimes called woman's paradise. I take it, indeed, that this earthly life is a paradise neither for ladies nor for gentlemen, but for both a purgatory, to purify them for heaven. It is a fact, however, that in the United States woman is exempt from all hard labor (except perhaps among the immigrants, who keep their foreign customs, and in new settlements, say in Texas, or Wisconsin, or Oregon, where circumstances demand the strength of all hands);

that she can travel unattended, from one end of the vast country to another, without being molested in the least; that in the steamboats, the great hotels, and public places, she finds her own saloons, sometimes extremely elegant, and all possible conveniences, and has the precedence in every company. It is characteristic, also, that in America one must address a mixed audience, not as "Gentlemen and Ladies," as in all other languages, but in the reverse order, as "Ladies and Gentlemen." Of course this respect for woman requires monogamy as its indispensable groundwork; and it is one main reason why the Mormons, who are charged, you are aware, with polygamy, are so hated there, and have been banished even by force from the territory of the organized States. They will never make many proselytes among the Americans, and they are accordingly now directing their missionary efforts almost entirely abroad.

The crown of the American family life, and one of the strongest proofs of the power of Christianity over the people, is table-prayer, which is almost universal; and daily family worship, which is the rule at least in religious circles, and is proportionally more frequent there, than in any other country, except perhaps England and Scotland. The ultimate effects of this pious custom on children and children's children are incalculable; and it must go well with a people, where the father feels it his duty and his joy to gather the members of his household every morning around the Holy Scriptures, as their daily bread of life, and to bow with them before the throne of the Almighty, and implore His blessing on the labors of the day.

IV. SCIENCE AND LITERATURE

It were extremely unfair and unreasonable, to demand of a country so young as America the same degree of scientific and aesthetic culture, as of those countries of the Old World, which have risen through a history of thousands of years to the height of modern civilization. Rather must one greatly wonder, that in two hundred years since the settlement of New England, with which the history of North America began, that country has even advanced so far in this respect. We should never ungratefully forget, indeed, that it had an enormous capital to rest upon and start with, in the results of the two thousand years development of Europe. Yet there remains reason enough for amazement at the uncommon energy, activity, and assiduity displayed by the Americans even in the sphere of science and literature. It is ignorance or calumny, which pictures them so often as a purely materialistic race, estimating a man only by his money. They have, on the contrary, the liveliest interest in all branches of higher intellectual culture, and show it sometimes by a truly princely liberality. There are instances in New England of single individuals giving of their own accord hundreds of thousands to establish scientific institutions. Were this noble liberality to be found among the Germans of America, we should long ago have had in Pennsylvania a complete German university, which would compare, not indeed in its faculties — for these require time — but in outward resources, with the venerable scien tific foundations of Europe.

The general tendency in America is to the widest possible diffusion of education and the multiplication of institutions. This is in keeping with the republican system of liberty and equality. Hence the large and rapidly increasing number of colleges, seminaries, academies, and literary associations. Every little synod, or even every little town, must have its own little seminary or other little quasi scientific institution. Of course, then, these are often accordingly. Depth and thoroughness by no means go hand in hand with extension. Even among the professors in the higher institutions there is a surprising amount of superficiality, joined commonly with learned vanity and magniloquence. For superficial knowledge puffs up, while thorough knowledge humbles. Profound scientific culture must necessarily always be the property of the few. A world of only scholars could never stand a day. Nevertheless that tendency to the widest possible diffusion of a certain grade of education cannot be restrained in such a country as America, and it has, after all, its favorable aspect.

I will speak first of the institutions and appliances of education.

1. Elementary education has now been in great part taken charge of by the several States; still leaving parents, however, a perfect right to send their children to private schools. All New England, New York, Pennsylvania, Ohio, and other States, have adopted a general free-school system, partly after the much admired Prussian model, which offers even to the poorest and meanest the rudiments of knowledge. In fact, you will very rarely find one in New England, who cannot read and write, and who does not besides know something of the public affairs of the country. A peculiar phenomenon is the great number of female teachers. Among these are particularly distinguished the "Yankee girls," who know how to make their way right successfully everywhere as teachers; as in Europe the governess from French Switzerland.

Latterly, the Roman clergy in New York and other States have been making a systematic effort to overthrow the State schools, because the Protestant influence which prevails in them imperceptibly draws away the youth from their church. But the agitation has miscarried; it has only made Romanism more unpopular, and confirmed the old charge against her of hostility to general education.

These public schools, however, as now constituted, have assuredly their great defects. Though commonly opened with singing and the reading of the Bible, yet they do not duly provide for the proper moral and religious education of the children, without which secular culture can do little good. True, there are everywhere, along with the State schools, Sunday schools, as they are called, where the children receive gratuitous instruction in Bible history and the catechism, from male and female members of the church, who give themselves to this useful labor of love in disinterested zeal for the good cause. Yet, after all, invaluable as these are, and benignly as they have operated, they do not seem wholly to supply the need. Hence prominent men, in Protestant confessions, have likewise taken a stand against these public elementary schools, and are working for the establishment of parochial schools, in direct connection with the church, to train youth not only for time, but also for eternity.

2. The higher education is begun in academies, as they are called — i.e. classical schools — and continued in colleges. The latter answer, in some cases, to the higher classes in the German gymnasium and lyceum; in others, they, at the same time, correspond, in some degree, to a university, not only requiring a classical preparation, and embracing almost everything that does not pertain to some special department, but also have from the State legislatures power to confer all academic degrees. The age of college students varies from sixteen to thirty years. A university, in the full German sense of the word, America properly as yet has not. The idea of one has lately been suggested by very influential men, and will perhaps in time be carried out. Such an institution there, however, would probably have to be without a theological faculty, on account of the rivalship among so many churches and sects; and a university without theology — that *regina scientiarum* — is without its animating soul and its ruling head. The nearest approach to a proper university is in the colleges at Cambridge, Mass. (Harvard University), New Haven, Conn. (Yale College), and the University of

Virginia. In these institutions schools of theology, law, and medicine, are connected with the literary department. But a philosophical faculty is still wanting. All the philosophy taught in them is embraced in the proper collegiate or gymnasial course. But while philological, historical, and metaphysical studies are not carried so high and deep as in Germany, the natural and practical sciences receive greater attention. Several colleges have within a few years past added a special department under the name of scientific schools, which correspond somewhat to the polytechnic institutions of Europe. They embrace several distinct branches, such as agricultural and practical chemistry, geology, and mineralogy, botany, zoology, mathematics, and astronomy, engineering, physiology, and mechanics.

The American colleges proper are organized on the old English model, with four classes: Freshmen, Sophomores, Juniors, and Seniors. The students commonly lodge together in one building, under the eye of tutors or assistant-teachers. The day's studies are opened and closed with Divine service. Drunkenness, and other excesses, are punished with a fine, public censure, and suspension, and repeated offenses with expulsion. Such unlimited freedom as prevails in the German universities, would be considered dangerous and impracticable in America. It is thought, that youth must be kept under discipline, in order to a rational use and enjoyment of freedom in manhood. At the end of their four years' course the students have to pass an examination before the faculty, and deliver public orations, at what is called the Commencement, which is generally very largely attended by ladies as well as gentlemen, far and near, and forms a great holiday for all the neighboring population. On that occasion, the graduating students receive from the president, in form, before the crowded assembly, the diploma of *baccalureus artium*, and usually three years afterwards the diploma of *magister artium*. An address from the president, music, and prayer close the festival. On such an occasion honorary degrees also are commonly conferred; and indeed so lavishly that they must at last entirely lose their significance, unless a reaction take place. There are American doctors of divinity, who, however distinguished they may be as men and as preachers, have not done science the least service, and can hardly read the New Testament in the original text.

The number of colleges is already very considerable, and is increasing almost every year. Of course, not a few are very feeble, and do science no honor. Most have been founded by churches, primarily as schools preparatory to theological seminaries, and by voluntary contribution. Others, as the Universities of Harvard, Michigan, Virginia, are State foundations, and have no particular denominational character. Still others owe their origin to the liberality of an individual; as Girard College, in Philadelphia, with its sumptuous buildings of pure marble. The education afforded by these institutions is not so thorough as in Germany, but better adapted to public, practical life. The students divide themselves into two rival literary societies, which are almost as important for their mental development, as the recitations and lectures. In the weekly meetings of these societies they practice declamation and debate, and learn also the management of public assemblies, and the whole parliamentary order; a matter of great importance in the political and social life of a republic. It is remarkable what *esprit de corps* already reigns in the students' societies. They are as completely organized as the great political parties of the country.

3. Faculty Studies. — As in England, so also in America, very many take a college course, who do not devote themselves to any learned profession, but become merchants, land-owners, politicians, and statesmen, wishing at the same time, however, to be educated gentlemen. Yet, the proper faculty studies are already better attended to in the United States than at the English Universities of Oxford and Cam-

bridge, where they are almost entirely eclipsed by the general college studies. Jurisprudence is usually pursued, indeed, privately with a practising attorney, and deals far less in the abstract theories of law, and its historical development, than in the concrete forms of the old English laws and the American Constitution. Yet Harvard University, for example, and Yale College have formal law-schools. Far more numerous are Medical Colleges for the education of physicians — in Philadelphia alone there are three, and, in fact, a fourth for female doctors! — and Theological Seminaries for educating preachers.

Formerly it was customary for students to prepare for the ministry under some experienced clergyman, and some do so still; but since the beginning of the present century it has been found desirable to erect special institutions for this purpose, mostly in connection with a college. Now, almost every respectable denomination and sect has one such seminary or more of its own; and the tendency to multiply them is, in truth, only too strong. For when the public interest becomes so much divided, it is almost impossible for any one institution to be duly sustained. Thus, for example, the various branches of the German Church of America have already almost a dozen such schools, most of which are still in their infancy, with insufficient faculties, few students, small libraries, and still obliged to struggle for their material existence; so that the honor of a theological professor there is not very enviable. Sometimes he is even sent out as an agent to collect the money for his own support. Humbling as this business is, it sometimes seems unavoidable; and the self-denial and energy of the men who undertake it are worthy of all recognition, when they spring from sincere interest in the church. And when it is remembered that the State, being in fact separate from the church, does nothing for institutions of this kind — that they must be established and maintained, therefore, wholly by the voluntary contributions of the church — the wonder will be, that so much has been done in this line in so short a time. Many of the older seminaries, as that of the Congregationalists at Andover, and that of the Presbyterians at Princeton, are not only permanently endowed, and furnished each with four or five professors, fine libraries, large buildings for teachers and students, but have also already displayed no insignificant literary energy. Scientific theology has, I think, a more genial soil, and in the last twenty years has accomplished proportionally more in America than in England and Scotland. Certainly very much in this department is to be expected from America in the future. And then these American theological seminaries have, at all events, this advantage, that the students devote themselves to theology, not for their bread, as is so often the case in the State Churches of Europe, but from religious impulse, and hence are, so far as fallible man can judge, all converted young men; and that they always combine practical preparation for the holy office with their scientific pursuits. Very often a seminary proves the mother of a college, as a preparatory school, which from the first maintains a more or less ecclesiastical and denominational character.

4. We now have also in America an institution somewhat corresponding to an Academy of Sciences — the Smithsonian Institution, at Washington, the seat of the General Government. It was founded by a wealthy Englishman, whose name it bears, "for the increase and diffusion of knowledge among men," under the supervision of Congress, and the immediate control of three secretaries.

A large part of the interest which had accumulated for many years, before it went into actual operation, was applied to the erection of a magnificent Gothic building, and the establishment of a library. Thus far it has devoted itself almost exclusively to the natural sciences, though it has already done much towards elucidating Indian languages and antiquities, and sends its superbly illustrated publications to almost all institutions and societies of learning at home and abroad.

Besides this, there are in almost all the older States smaller scientific associations, historical societies, &c.

✓ 5. Libraries are already very numerous in the United States, though none have yet reached a hundred thousand volumes. The most considerable are at Cambridge, Boston, New York, Philadelphia, and Washington. Every scientific institution has a larger or smaller collection of books. The richest colleges send agents from time to time to Europe to purchase valuable works in all branches of literature. Not rarely, whole libraries are bought. Neander's library, for example, is now in a Baptist Seminary at Rochester, N. Y., and that of the late Dr. Thilo, of Halle, will go in a few weeks to Yale College, New Haven, for which it has just been purchased by one of its professors, now present in Berlin. Some years ago, John Jacob Astor, of New York, the richest man in America, a German by birth, left nearly half a million of dollars for the establishment of a public library in the city of New York. This has lately been opened, with forty thousand volumes, in an admirably arranged building in Astor Place. He might as well have founded, with a part of his eighteen millions, a full German university, at least for his countrymen, if he had a right interest in them.

✓ 6. Literature. — The American receives his education not only in scientific institutions, but almost as much from public life, and from the enormous mass of periodical and other literature which circulates through the land.

The United States are the classic soil of newspapers. Every political party, every religious sect, every theological school, every literary and philanthropic association, nay, every village, has its periodical organ, by which it seeks to form public opinion in its favor. The number of quarterly reviews, and monthly, weekly, and daily papers, is therefore, legion.

The reading of the political and religious periodicals has become as indispensable as breakfast. Every respectable man takes, at least, one, not rarely half a dozen, newspapers, which are commonly *in omnibus aliquid*, though very often also *in toto nihil*. Such reading tends, unquestionably, to diffuse a kind of culture among all classes of the people; but it equally tends to superficiality — kills taste for the study of solid books, and dissipates the mind almost as much as novel reading, in the place of which, to a great extent, it there comes. An earnest and worthy professor, of New England, said to me lately: "The religious newspapers, which often live only on flat gossip and party wrangling, are the curse of our country." They are, however, at worst, a *necessary* evil; and it is the task of all good men, not to restrict the public press, which is now absolutely impossible, but to labor to make it more and more the vehicle and lever of truth and virtue. The circulation of many of these sheets is without a parallel in Europe. Several political newspapers of New York number over 100,000. "Harper's Magazine," an illustrated monthly, for the fashionable world, about 150,-000 subscribers.* The monthly organ of the American Tract Society has a still larger circulation. This may be owing to its extraordinary cheapness and its catholic character. But even denominational organs far exceed the circulation of German and French church gazettes. The "New York Ob-

---

* The "New York Tribune," whose chief editor is the well-known Horace Greeley, called the Napoleon of the American press, and which is devoted to the interests of Whig politics, abolitionism, temperance, and socialism, has now a total circulation (daily, semi-weekly, and weekly) of 178,000. See Number for May 24, 1855. As far as I know, no French newspaper strikes off 100,000 copies, unless it be the "Moniteur." The "London Times" has, no doubt, more readers, and deserves them too, than any American newspaper, but hardly as many subscribers as the "New York Tribune." According to the census reports of 1850, there were in that year printed in New York city alone 106 newspapers proper (exclusive of other periodical sheets), with an average circulation of 82,368,473 sheets; 14 of which appeared daily, 58 weekly, and 14 monthly. The daily circulation amounted to 153,621; the weekly to 425,200; the monthly to 401,200 copies.

server," for instance, one of the oldest and best known religious papers, professing Presbyterian principles, as far, at least, as it suits its very conservative policy, and containing, after the general American fashion, a great variety of religious, political, and other news, devotional pieces, foreign and domestic correspondence, advertisements, etc., sends out nearly 20,000 copies every week. The "New York Evangelist," the best organ of New School Presbyterianism, and the "Independent," which pleads in very able and very radical style the cause of progressive Puritanism and Abolitionism, are not yet so long established as their neighbors of the "Observer," but will, probably, ere long, reach the same circulation. Besides, in the absence of an international copyright, all the more important English and Scottish quarterlies, the "Edinburgh," "London Quarterly," "Westminster" and "North British Reviews," "Blackwood's Magazine," "Chamber's Journal," "Dicken's Household Words," &c., are reprinted either bodily or by extracts, and sold far cheaper than the original edition.

And the number of other works is in proportion. All books of any account, which appear in Great Britain, are reprinted in America, and sold at never more than half the price. The greatest establishment of the kind, and perhaps the largest publishing house in the world, is that of the Brothers Harper, in New York. It was burnt last December (1853), but with true American energy immediately put in operation again in another street, and with the aid of presses in Philadelphia, Boston, Andover, &c., as if nothing had happened. Intelligent men have expressed to me the positive expectation, that New York will soon be the greatest book market in the world. The American Tract Society vies with the secular press, and multiplies copies of the classical English works on practical religion, the ascetic writings of Baxter, Flavel, Owen, Howe, Bunyan, Chalmers; Merle D'Aubigné's "History of the Reformation," Krummacher's "Elijah," &c., by thousands, and circulates them by its agents, at a nominal price, in the humblest cottages of the Far West.

One might think, that this enormous republication of foreign works must destroy the country's own productive power, and choke the growth of an original literature. But this is not the case. True, America has as yet produced no genius of the first magnitude in science and art, and scarcely one in twenty of its literary productions is of any real worth, the others falling still-born from the press. But we may already observe there at least the promising beginnings of an independent American literature; and Europe herself, formerly disposed to make sport of it, now does it homage. How many American books have, within the last twenty or thirty years, been reprinted in England and Scotland, and translated into German, French, Italian, and all the cultivated languages! The names of Cooper, Channing, Washington Irving, Longfellow, Bryant, Dana, Hawthorne, Poe, Willis; and of the authoresses, Stowe, Wetherell, Fanny Fern, &c., already have a literary reputation far beyond their native country. How often during this visit have I seen "The Wide Wide World" and "Queechy" on the tables of Berlin! What immense celebrity, and one may say almost unexampled circulation, has "Uncle Tom's Cabin" attained in a few weeks, not only in England, but also on the whole continent! The Pope himself, in spite of public opinion, has felt it necessary to place it with Humboldt's "Cosmos" and Macauley's "History of England," on the list of forbidden books. As if such works were more dangerous than Boccaccio's "Decamerone," to be found in almost every Italian family, and the text-books of Jesuitical casuistry and refined immorality.

But America can show something far better and more permanent, than mere romance; though even in this we must commend a kind of moral earnestness and a religious turn, which give it a clear advantage over the frivolous novel literature of the French. Prescott, Bancroft, Washington Irving, and Sparks, take a very honorable rank among historians; Story, Kent, and Marshall, among jurists; Benjamin Franklin, Agassiz (who, however, like his friend and associate, Guyot, brought his reputation with him from his native Switzerland), Silliman, Morse, Henry, Maury, Hitchcock, among naturalists; Jonathan Edwards, Stuart, Park, Stowe, Barnes, Hodge, the Alexanders (father and sons), Nevin, Smith, are all learned and able divines; Robinson and Lynch have opened a new path in the investigation of the localities and antiquities of the Holy Land, and are acknowledged authorities in this department even in Europe. The natural sciences particularly, on account of their practical utility and their influence on the development of the material resources of the country, have there been carried to a high degree of perfection, and will probably lead yet to many new discoveries and inventions.

The liberal cultivation of forensic, parliamentary, and sacred eloquence, which only thrives in the atmosphere of freedom, is particularly favored by the political institutions and the synodical self-government of the churches in America. The great struggle for independence in the last century called forth some of the noblest specimens of eloquence in a noble cause. When the strongest passions were excited, when the dearest interests were at stake, when the question was to "sink or swim, live or die, survive or perish," then "patriotism was eloquent, then self-devotion was eloquent." But the succession of Patrick Henry, the "forest-born Demosthenes;" of Otis, Adams, Hancock, Warren, and Ames is not yet extinguished. I doubt whether any country, not even England excepted, can show, in proportion to its population, so great a number of good public speakers, debaters, and preachers, as the Anglo-Saxon Republic. Nor is she deficient in talents and geniuses, which rise far above the level of ordinary respectability. Webster, Clay, Calhoun, Everett,

Choate, Seward, and Sumner, stand, at least, not far behind
the brilliant and unrivalled rhetorical galaxy of the British
Parliament, from the elder Pitt and Burke down to Sir Robert
Peel and Lord Brougham.

Several of Daniel Webster's speeches, on the Dartmouth
College cause (especially the peroration); on the landing
of the Pilgrim Fathers; on the laying of the corner-stone,
and also on the final dedication of the Bunker Hill Monument; on the death of John Adams and Thomas Jefferson;
against the nullification doctrine of Judge Hayne (think of
the inimitable encomium upon his native State, Massachusetts!) and of Calhoun, of South Carolina; and for the
Constitution and the Union, in March, 1850, will be read
and admired for their strength of logic, simple grandeur,
and classic finish, as long as the Anglo- Saxon tongue is spoken,
and some passages in them fully answer his own definition
of genuine patriotic eloquence, which "comes like the out-
breaking of a fountain from the earth, or the bursting forth
of volcanic fires, with spontaneous, original, native force,"
that eloquence which combines "the clear conception, out-
running the deductions of logic, the high purpose, the firm
resolve, the dauntless spirit, speaking on the tongue, beam-
ing from the eye, informing every feature, and urging the
whole man onward, right onward to his object;" that eloquence, which is "something greater and higher than all
eloquence, which is action, noble, sublime, god-like action."

In the Fine Arts the Americans are certainly still far behind; especially in the arts of design, the cultivation of which
has been more or less hindered by the reigning Puritanic
prejudices. Yet poetry, that highest, most spiritual, and most
versatile of the liberal arts, already has respectable representatives, as the names above-mentioned prove. For Music
the Americans have, to say the least, more susceptibility than
the English; Jenny Lind was received in 1850 with frantic
enthusiasm, and her tour through the States was a real tri-

umphal progress. Architectural taste is rapidly improving, and in the larger cities there have arisen within a few years, magnificent churches in the Grecian, Byzantine, Norman, and Gothic styles. Benjamin West and Leutze, the distinguished painters, are Americans; and Powers and Crawford rank high amongst the sculptors of the present day. In the mechanical or useful arts, especially in the building of railroads, steam and sailing vessels, and machinery of all sorts, the Americans already equal, and in some cases even surpass, the English.

I cannot close this section without referring to the growing influence, which, in spite of all the prevailing prejudices, German science and literature have exerted in the United States for some years past, especially in philology, history, philosophy, and theology. No important Latin, Greek, or Hebrew grammar and dictionary, no edition or commentary of an old classic, has appeared there, not based on the works of Zumpt, Buttmann, Kühner, Winer, Freund, Passow, Gesenius, Böckh, Jacobs, &c. Coleridge, the English Schelling, began the transfer and assimilation of the ideas of German philosophy. His profound and stimulating works have as many readers and friends in America as in England. The most important productions of the modern German theology; the historical works of Neander, Gieseler, and Ranke; the dogmatic productions of Knapp, Nitzsch, J. Müller; the exegetical writings of Olshausen, Hengstenberg, Tholuck, and Lücke; are widely circulated in more or less successful translations. Almost every number of the "Bibliotheca Sacra," of Andover, the "Biblical Repertory," of Princeton, the "New Englander," of New Haven, the "Methodist Quarterly Review," of New York, the "Christian Review," of the Baptists, the "Mercersburg Review," of the German Reformed, the "Evangelical Review," of the Lutherans, presents translations or reviews of the latest theological productions of Germany. In the most respectable colleges and seminaries of the Congregationalists, Presbyterians, Baptists, &c., some acquaintance, at least, with German literature, were it only for the sake of opposing it, is now almost the rule.

The German book trade has accordingly very much increased in consequence of native American demand as well as the increase of immigration. I well remember, when I landed in America, ten years ago, how hard it was to procure German books and periodicals with any thing like regularity. Now, there are in New York alone four respectable German book-stores, as many in Philadelphia, and two in Cincinnati, which lay before us the latest works, especially in theology, within a few weeks after their appearance.

Many Americans, particularly from New England, visit German universities, to finish their scientific education. There are said to be now in Berlin alone more than twenty engaged in various studies. With the increased facilities of communication, the tour to Europe becomes more and more frequent, and even the visit to the far East, especially to the holy places, which the Saviour trod, and to which this people of the far West look back with singular interest. Once across the ocean, the American is not afraid of distances of hundreds and thousands of miles; and from the remotest regions of the earth he gathers new knowledge and new views, and returns with elevated love and enthusiasm of his native land, to work them up for the advancement of American culture.

In short, America, favored by the most extensive emigration from all other countries, will become more and more the receptacle of all the elements of the old world's good and evil, which will there wildly ferment together, and from the most fertile soil bring forth fruit for the weal or woe of generations to come.

71

V. RELIGION AND THE CHURCH

I come now to the point most important in my own view, and, doubtless, most interesting to this assembly. But want of time obliges me to confine myself to some general remarks, which may, at least, help to pilot you through the mazes of American church history.

It is a vast advantage to that country itself, and one may say to the whole world, that the United States were first settled in great part from religious motives; that the first emigrants left the homes of their fathers for faith and conscience' sake, and thus at the outset stamped upon their new home the impress of positive Christianity, which now exerts a wholesome influence even on those later emigrants, who have no religion at all.

The ecclesiastical character of America, however, is certainly very different from that of the Old World. Two points in particular require notice.

The first is this. While in Europe ecclesiastical institutions appear in historical connection with Catholicism, and even in evangelical countries, most of the city and village churches, the universities, and religious foundations, point to a mediaeval origin; in North America, on the contrary, every thing had a Protestant beginning, and the Catholic Church has come in afterwards as one sect among the others, and has always remained subordinate. In Europe, Protestantism has, so to speak, fallen heir to Catholicism; in America, Catholicism under the wing of Protestant toleration and freedom of conscience, has found an adopted home, and is everywhere surrounded by purely Protestant institutions. True, the colony of Maryland, planted by the Catholic Lord Baltimore, was one of the earliest settlements of North America. But, in the first place, even this was by no means specifically Roman. It was founded expressly on the thoroughly anti-Roman, and essentially Protestant, principles of

72

religious toleration. And then, again, it never had any specific influence on the character of the country; for even the prominent position of the city of Baltimore, as the American metropolis of the Roman Church, is of much later date. Far more important and influential were the settlements of the Puritans in New England, the Episcopalians in Virginia, the Quakers in Pennsylvania, the Dutch in New York, in the course of the seventeenth century, the Presbyterians from Scotland and North Ireland, and the German Lutherans and Reformed from the Palatinate, in the first half of the eighteenth. These have given the country its spirit and character. Its past course and present condition are unquestionably due mainly to the influence of Protestant principles. The Roman Church has attained social and political importance in the eastern and western States only within the last twenty years, chiefly in consequence of the vast Irish emigration; but it will never be able to control the doctrines of the New World, though it should increase a hundred fold.

Another peculiarity in the ecclesiastical condition of North America, connected with the Protestant origin and character of the country, is the separation of church and state. The infidel reproach, that had it not been for the power of the state, Christianity would have long ago died out; and the argument of Roman controversialists, that Protestantism could not stand without the support of princes and civil governments, both are practically refuted and utterly annihilated in the United States. The president and governors, the congress at Washington, and the state legislatures, have, as such, nothing to do with the church, and are by the Constitution expressly forbidden to interfere in its affairs. State officers have no other rights in the church, than their personal rights as members of particular denominations. The church, indeed, everywhere enjoys the protection of the laws for its property, and the exercise of its functions; but it manages its own affairs independently, and has also to depend for its resources entirely on voluntary contributions. As the state commits itself to no particular form of Christianity, there is of course also no civil requisition of baptism, confirmation, and communion. Religion is left to the free will of each individual, and the church has none but moral means of influencing the world.

This separation was by no means a sudden, abrupt event, occasioned, say, by the Revolution. The first settlers, indeed, had certainly no idea of such a thing; they proceeded rather on Old Testament theocratic principles, like Calvin, John Knox, the Scottish Presbyterians, and the English Puritans of the seventeenth century; regarding state and church as the two arms of one and the same divine will. In the colony of Massachusetts, the Puritans, in fact, founded a rigid Calvinistic state-church system. They made the civil franchise depend on membership in the church; and punished not only blasphemy and open infidelity, but even every departure from the publicly acknowledged code of Christian faith and practice as a political offense. In Boston, in the seventeenth century, even the Quakers, who certainly acted there in a very fanatical and grossly indecent way, were formally persecuted, publicly scourged, imprisoned, and banished; and, in Salem, of the same State, witches were burnt as accomplices of the devil. The last traces of this state-church system in New England were not obliterated till long after the American Revolution, and even to this day most of the States have laws for the observance of the Sabbath, monogamy, and other specifically Christian institutions. Thus the separation of the temporal and spiritual powers is by no means absolute. While New England had Congregationalism for its established religion, New York also had at first the Dutch Reformed, and afterwards the English Episcopal church, and Virginia, and some other Southern States, also the English Episcopal, for their establishments. With these the other forms of Christianity were tolerated either not at all, or under serious restrictions, as formerly the Dissenters were in England.

But on the other hand, there prevailed in other North American colonies from their foundation, therefore long before the Revolution of 1776, entire freedom of faith and conscience; as in Rhode Island, founded by the Baptist, Roger Williams, who was banished from Massachusetts for heresy, and thus set by bitter experience against religious intolerance; in Pennsylvania, which the quaker, William Penn, originally designed as an asylum for his brethren in faith, but to which he soon invited also German Reformed and Lutherans from the Palatinate, guaranteeing equal rights to all, and leaving each to the guidance of the "inward light;" and, finally, in Maryland, founded by Lord Baltimore on the same basis of universal religious toleration.

After the American Revolution this posture of the State gradually became general. First, the legislature of Virginia, after the colony had separated from the mother-country, annulled the rights and privileges of the Episcopal establishment, and placed all the dissenting bodies on a perfectly equal footing with it in the eye of the law.* Her example was followed by the other colonies, which had established churches. When Congress was organized at the close of the war, an article was placed in the Constitution, forbidding the enactment of laws about religion; ‡ and similar prohibitions are found in the constitutions of the several States.

We would by no means vindicate this separation of church and state as the perfect and final relation between the two. The kingdom of Christ is to penetrate and transform like leaven, all the relations of individual and national life. We much prefer this separation, however, to the territorial sys-

---

* The result is owing to the combined influence of the oppressed dissenters, the liberal amongst the Episcopalians, and the infidels of the school of Jefferson, who was then almighty in the political circles of Virginia.

‡ "Congress shall make no laws respecting an establishment of religion, or prohibiting the free exercise thereof."

tem and a police guardianship of the church, the Bride of the God-man, the free-born daughter of heaven; and we regard it as adapted to the present wants of America, and favorable to her religious interests. For it is by no means to be thought, that the separation of church and state there is a renunciation of Christianity by the nation; like the separation of the state and the school from the church, and the civil equality of Atheism with Christianity, which some members of the abortive Frankfurt Parliament were for introducing in Germany. It is not an annihilation of one factor, but only an amicable separation of the two in their spheres of outward operation; and thus equally the church's declaration of independence towards the state, and an emancipation of the state from bondage to a particular confession. The nation, therefore, is still Christian, though it refuses to be governed in this deepest concern of the mind and heart by the temporal power. In fact, under such circumstances, Christianity, as the free expression of personal conviction and of the national character, has even greater power over the mind, than when enjoined by civil laws and upheld by police regulations.

This appears practically in the strict observance of the Sabbath, the countless churches and religious schools, the zealous support of Bible and Tract societies, of domestic and foreign missions, the numerous revivals, the general attendance on divine worship, and the custom of family devotion — all expressions of the general Christian character of the people, in which the Americans are already in advance of most of the old Christian nations of Europe.

In fact, even the state, as such, to some extent officially recognizes Christianity. Congress appoints chaplains (mostly from the Episcopal, sometimes from the Presbyterian and the Methodist clergy) for itself, the army, and the navy. It opens every day's session with prayer, and holds public worship on the Sabbath in the Senate Chamber at Washington. The laws of the several States also contain strict prohibitions of blasphemy, atheism, Sabbath-breaking, polygamy, and other gross violations of general Christian morality.

Thus the separation is not fully carried out in practice, on account of the influence of Christianity on the popular mind. It is even quite possible that the two powers may still come into collision. The tolerance of the Americans has its limits and counterpoise in that religious fanaticism, to which they are much inclined. This may be seen in the expulsion of the Mormons, who so grossly offended the religious and moral sense of the people. Great political difficulties may arise, especially from the growth of the Roman church, which has been latterly aiming everywhere at political influence, and thus rousing the jealousy and opposition of the great Protestant majority. The Puritanic Americans see in Catholicism an ecclesiastical despotism, from which they fear also political despotism, so that its sway in the United States must be the death of Republican freedom. Thus the Catholic question has already come to be regarded by many as at the same time a political question, involving the existence of the Republic; and a religious war between Catholics and Protestants, though in the highest degree improbable, is still by no means an absolute impossibility; as, in fact, slight skirmishes have already occurred in the street fight between the two parties in Philadelphia in 1844, and the violent demolition of a Roman convent at Charlestown, Mass. The secret political party of the "Know-Nothings," which is just sweeping over the States with the rapidity of the whirlwind, but which, for this very reason, cannot last long in this particular form, is mainly directed against the influence of Romanism.

If, however, the great question of the relation of church and state be not by any means fully solved even in the United Staes, still the two powers are there at all events much more distant than in any other country.

The natural result of this arrangement is a general prevalence of freedom of conscience and religious faith, and of the voluntary principle, as it is called: that is, the promotion of every religious work by the free-will offerings of the people. The state, except in the few cases mentioned above, does nothing towards building churches, supporting ministers, founding theological seminaries, or aiding indigent students in preparation for the ministry. No taxes are laid for these objects; no one is compelled to contribute a farthing to them. What is done for them is far, indeed, from being always done from the purest motives — love to God and to religion — often from a certain sense of honor, and for all sorts of selfish by-ends; yet always from free impulses, without any outward coercion.

This duly considered, it is truly wonderful, what a multitude of churches, ministers, colleges, theological seminaries, and benevolent institutions are there founded and maintained entirely by free-will offerings. In Berlin there are hardly forty churches for a population of four hundred and fifty thousand, of whom, in spite of all the union of church and state, only some thirty thousand attend public worship. In New York, to a population of six hundred thousand, there are over two hundred and fifty well-attended churches, some of them quite costly and splendid, especially in Broadway and Fifth Avenue.* In the city of Brooklyn, across the East River, the number of churches is still larger in proportion to the population, and in the country towns and villages, especially in New England, the houses of worship average one to every thousand, or frequently even five hundred, souls. If these are not Gothic cathedrals, they are yet mostly decent, comfortable buildings, answering all the purposes

---

* In 1854 there were in New York city, forty-eight Episcopal churches, forty-eight Presbyterian, thirty-five Methodist, nineteen Reformed Dutch, twenty-nine Baptist, eight Congregational, five Lutheran, and twenty-four Roman Catholic; besides the church edifices of several smaller denominations and sects, which must swell the number now to nearly 300.

of the congregation often even far better than the most imposing works of architecture. In every new city district, in every new settlement, one of the first things thought of is the building of a temple to the Lord, where the neighboring population may be regularly fed with the bread of life and encouraged to labor, order, obedience, and every good work. Suppose the state, in Germany, should suddenly withdraw its support from church and university, how many preachers and professors would be breadless, and how many auditories closed!

The voluntary system unquestionably has its great blemishes. It is connected with all sorts of petty drudgery, vexations, and troubles, unknown in well endowed Established Churches. Ministers and teachers, especially among the recent German emigrants in America, who have been accustomed to State provision for religion and education, have very much to suffer from the free system. They very often have to make begging tours for the erection of a church, and submit to innumerable other inconveniences for the good cause, till a congregation is brought into a proper course, and its members become practised in free giving.

But, on the other hand, the voluntary system calls forth a mass of individual activity and interest among the laity in ecclesiastical affairs, in the founding of new churches and congregations, colleges and seminaries, in home and foreign missions, and in the promotion of all forms of Christian philanthropy. We may here apply in a good sense our Lord's word: "Where the treasure is, there the heart will be also." The man, who, without coercion, brings his regular offering for the maintenance of the church and the minister, has commonly much more interest in both, and in their prosperity he sees with pleasure the fruit of his own labor. The same is true of seminaries. All the congregations and synods are interested in the theological teacher, whom they support, and who trains ministers of the Word for them; while in

Europe the people give themselves little or no trouble about the theological faculties.

It is commonly thought that this state of things necessarily involves an unworthy dependence of the minister on his congregation. But this is not usually the case. The Americans expect a minister to do his duty, and they most esteem that one who fearlessly and impartially declares the whole counsel of God, and presents the depravity of man and the threatenings of the Divine Word as faithfully as he does the comforting promises. Cases of ministers employed for a certain time, as hired servants, occur indeed occasionally in independent German rationalistic congregations, and perhaps among the Universalists, but not in a regular synod. A pious congregation well knows that by such a degradation of the holy office, which preaches reconciliation, and binds and looses in the name of Christ, it would degrade itself; and a minister, in any respectable church connection, would not be allowed to accept a call on such terms, even were he willing.

Favored by the general freedom of faith, all Christian denominations and sects, except the Oriental, have settled in the United States, on equal footing in the eye of the law; here attracting each other, there repelling; rivalling in both the good and the bad sense; and mutually contending through innumerable religious publications. They thus present a motley sampler of all church history, and the results it has thus far attained. A detailed description of these at present is forbidden, both by want of time and by the proportion of the discourse. Suffice it to say, in general, that the whole present distracted condition of the church in America, pleasing and promising as it may be, in one view, must yet be regarded on the whole as unsatisfactory, and as only a state of transition to something higher and better.

America seems destined to be the Phenix grave not only

* This is given in the second lecture.

of all European nationalities, as we have said above, but also of all European churches and sects, of Protestantism and Romanism. I cannot think, that any one of the present confessions and sects, the Roman, or the Episcopal, or the Congregational, or the Presbyterian, or the Lutheran, or the German or Dutch Reformed, or the Methodist, or the Baptist communion, will ever become exclusively dominant there; but rather, that out of the mutual conflict of all something wholly new will gradually arise.

At all events, whatever may become of the American denominations and sects of the present day, the kingdom of Jesus Christ must at last triumph in the New World, as elsewhere, over all foes, old and new. Of this we have the pledge in the mass of individual Christianity in America; but above all, in the promise of the Lord, who is with his people always to the end of the world, and who has founded his church upon a rock, against which the gates of hell shall never prevail. And his words are yea and amen.

With this prospect we finish this outline miniature of life in the United States. You see from it, that all the powers of Europe, good and bad, are there fermenting together under new and peculiar conditions. All is yet in a chaotic transition state; but organizing energies are already present, and the spirit of God broods over them, to speak in time the almighty word: "Let there be light!" and to call forth from the chaos a beautiful creation.

Perhaps, in the view of many of my respected hearers, I have drawn too favorable a picture. But I beg to remind them, first, that the dark side, which, indeed, I have not concealed, has been only too often presented in disproportion and caricature by European tourists or distant observers; and, secondly, that it would be very ungrateful and dishonorable for me to disparage my new fatherland behind its back, to uncover its nakedness with unsparing hand, and neglect its virtues and its glorious prospects.

81

In general, however, notwithstanding all differences on particular points, few intelligent and unprejudiced Germans certainly will think me wrong in designating America as a world of the future. I do so, not in disparagement of old and venerable Europe. She, indeed, unquestionably trembled to her foundations in 1848, and seemed on the verge of a fearful anarchy and barbarism; but she has since already shown, that in Christianity and civilization she has the power and the pledge of regeneration. I do not believe, that Europe, which we Americans revere and love as our bodily and spiritual mother, must become a second Asia, in order that America may become a higher Europe. In fact, this critical moment itself gives promise of regeneration of the East and of the venerable birth-place of Christianity. This we may hope, in the providence of God, will be the final result of the present contest between Russia and the Western Powers for Constantinople and the key of the holy sepulchre. The partition walls between nations and countries are gradually being removed by the facilities of communication, which must serve in a higher hand as instruments for spiritual and eternal ends. Europe, Asia, Africa, America, and Australia, all belong to the Lord, who died for them all. They come nearer together every year, and must at last, without distinction of old and new, whether called into the vineyard early or late, exchange the hand of brotherhood, submit in free obedience to the common Lord, glorify his name, and fulfill the promise of one fold under one shepherd.

PART II

The Churches and Sects

THE CHURCHES AND SECTS

"Westward the star of empire takes its way." This verse of a celebrated English philosopher is a characteristic watchword of the American's restless reachings into the future. It flatters his vanity, it spurs his ambition, it rouses his energy, it constantly excites and strengthens in him the impression that his nation is one day to be the greatest of the earth, to attain the perfection of church as well as state, and then to react with regenerating power on Europe, and from California to convert China and Japan. These are, to be sure, extravagant notions, favored no less by ignorance of the state of Europe than by American vanity.

Yet this verse has truth. It expresses the general law of the geographical march of history both secular and sacred. Thus far civilization and Christianity have followed in the main the course of the sun from East to West. The East, the land of the morning, is not only the cradle of mankind and of civilization, but also the birthplace of the church. Around the venerable countries of Palestine, Syria, Asia Minor, now desolate, and groaning under the yoke of the false prophet, cluster the earliest and holiest associations of Christendom. Hence Christendom now, at this critical moment, looks out upon them from Europe and America with the intensest interest, and in hope of an approaching regeneration of the Eastern churches. From Asia Christianity spread to Greece and to Rome; and thence flowed the conversion and civilization of the Romanic and Germanic tribes. But as early as the close of the Middle Age Paris — still further West — became a model of higher culture, and a chief seat of the scholastic and mystic theology, and of reformatory efforts in the church, which gradually and steadily spread, and struck deepest root in Germanic soil.

In the sixteenth century, Germany and Switzerland, became the starting-place of another grand movement of history, in which we now have our place, and whose end cannot yet be seen. Germany, lying geographically in the centre of Europe, was commissioned in the age of the Reformation to furnish the heart's blood for the modern history of the world and the church, to bring out from the inexhaustible mines of the word and the spirit principles and ideas, which should embody themselves as institutions and become flesh and blood in other lands.

From Germany and Switzerland the great Reformation passed to the west of Europe, visiting especially that remarkable Anglo-Saxon island, which has since risen to the dominion of the sea and of commerce, and at the same time to the vast duty of spreading Christianity and European culture in all its colonies. From England and Scotland the northern half of the western hemisphere has been, and in our own day the still newer world of Australia is being, colonized and prepared for political and religious independence. The history of England and North America for the last three centuries is utterly unintelligible without the Reformation. It is at bottom a continuation of the movement, which, starting from Wittenberg, Zurich, and Geneva, spread into the Germanic countries North and West, and has given the Anglo-Saxon race especially the most powerful impulse towards the fulfillment of its mission for the world.

In North America all sections and interests of European Protestantism are now more or less fully represented. There they all find a free asylum and room for unrestrained development. There the Roman Church also finds the same freedom. There all confessions and sects come into contact, and into a conflict, the result of which must greatly affect the future fortunes of all Christendom. America will also in time take a very active part in the Christianizing of China and Japan, and a lively interest in all great missionary operations. However unfavorable our judgment, therefore, of its present ecclesiastical condition — and I confess my own dissatisfaction with it — we have every year less room to deny or, save from sheer prejudice, to overlook its great prospective importance.

From this point I will now endeavor to present, first, a general ecclesiastical view of North America, and then a sketch of each of the most prominent confessions and sects.

I. GENERAL ECCLESIASTICAL CONDITION OF THE UNITED STATES

As the present can be duly understood only in its connection with the past, allow me to premise a few historical remarks.

North America, as already observed, follows strictly in the train of the ecclesiastical revolution of the sixteenth century, and is in its prevailing religious character primarily a continuation of European Protestantism. The American historian, Bancroft, throughout his extensive work, proceeds on the presumption, that even the entire civil constitution and social life of North America, is a product of the English Puritanism, which is itself a modification of the Genevan Calvinism. This is an exaggerated view. Bancroft, in his "History of the United States," writes in general as a propagandist of Republicanism — and of Republicanism, too, as conceived by the Democratic party — and hence sees some things in an entirely false light. Yet his view has somewhat of truth. It certainly cannot be denied, that the American system of general political freedom and equality (which, however, has a restriction and counterpart in the slavery of the Southern States), with its kindred doctrine — not by any means fully applied, yet aiming to be — of the rights and duties of self government and active coöperation of the people in all the affairs of the Commonwealth, is, in some sense, a transferring to the civil sphere the idea of the universal priesthood of Christians, which was first clearly and emphatically brought forward by the Reformers. With the universal priesthood comes also a corresponding universal kingship; though, of course, this no more excludes a special kingship, or a rank of rulers, than the other, a particular ministry. This universal kingship is what the American Republic aims at. Whether it will ever realize it is a very different question. Certainly not by the unfolding of any powers of mere nature. The Bible idea of a general priesthood and kingship can be realized only by supernatural grace, and will not appear in its full reality before the consummation of all things at the glorious coming of Christ.

The Germanic and Protestant character of the United States reveals itself particularly in their uncommon mobility and restless activity, contrasting with the mournful stagnation of the Romanic and Roman Catholic countries of Central and South America. The people are truly a nation of progress, both in the good sense and in the bad; of the boldest, often foolhardy, enterprise; a restless people, finding no satisfaction, save in constant striving, running, and chasing after a boundless future. I state here an actual fact, palpable to every one, who sets foot in the New World, and observes, for instance, the bustle and headway of such a city as New York. This spirit of enterprise is shared also by the religious bodies, even by the Roman Church, which promises itself a glorious future in America.

The connecting link between European and American church history is England, — poorer in ideas, than Germany, but exhibiting Protestantism more as an institution, and in far greater political and social importance, than any country of the continent; as, in fact, she is to this day the mightiest bulwark of Protestantism against Rome. The six Northeastern States, collectively called New England, have thus far exerted the leading religious influence in the Union. Through these especially the ecclesiastical life of North America strikes its deepest roots in those mighty religious and civil contests, which shook England in the seventeenth century; in that Puritanic movement, which may be called a second Reformation, a more consistent, though an extreme, carrying out of the Protestant principle against the semi-Catholicism of the Episcopal Establishment.

Apart from what was merely preparatory, the church history of the United States properly begins with the emigration of the Puritan "Pilgrim Fathers." These pious, bible-reading, earnest, and energetic Puritans, persecuted in England for their faith, and sacrificing to religious conviction their father-land, and all associated with that sweet word, first sought refuge in Holland in the year 1611; thence in 1620 crossed the Atlantic; landed, after a long, stormy voyage, on the lonely rock of Plymouth, and here first of all kneeled in tears, to thank their Lord and God for their happy deliverance from the perils of death and from all bondage of conscience. Soon reinforced by larger emigrations of their brethren in faith, especially in 1630, they founded in Massachusetts, according to the principles of the strictest Calvinism, a theocratic state, and became the fathers of a republic, of whose power and importance they did not dream; — a striking proof, that the greatest results may flow from small beginnings.

True, the settlement of Virginia, with the planting of the English Episcopal Church there, was of earlier date (1607); but this proceeded mainly from commercial interests, and has accordingly had no such influence in forming the religious character of the Americans. The same may be said of the founding of the New Netherland colony by the Hollanders, who established a trading port on Manhattan island as early as 1614, thus laying the foundation for the town of New Amsterdam, as New York was originally called, and some years afterwards transplanted the Reformed Dutch Church with the Heidelberg Cathechism, and the Decrees of Dort to the banks of the Hudson and the Delaware.

Pennsylvania, on the contrary, had a decidedly religious origin. The renowned William Penn, designed it (1680) primarily as an asylum for his persecuted brethren in faith, and stamped it from the first with the main features of the Quaker sect, which may be plainly discerned to this day, especially in Philadelphia, the "city of brotherly-love." At the same date Maryland (so called after Henrietta Maria, daughter of Henry IV., and wife of Charles I.) became a refuge of persecuted Catholics under Lord Baltimore. After the infamous revocation of the Edict of Nantes by the grandson of Henry the Fourth, many Huguenots betook themselves to North and South Carolina, New York, and New Jersey, and there gradually merged themselves in the Presbyterian and Episcopal churches. In the beginning of the last century began the emigration of the German Lutherans and Reformed from the provinces on the Rhine. This emigration passed chiefly to Pennsylvania, and was occasioned in part by the devastation of the Palatinate, and the oppression of the Protestants by the army of Louis the Fourteenth. Somewhat later the Salzburgers sought and found in Georgia a home of peace, and freedom for their Lutheran faith. About the middle of the eighteenth century Zinzendorf and Spangenburg planted in the same State, but more especially in Pennsylvania (at Bethlehem and Nazareth), several communities of Moravian Brethren; while Mühlenberg, as commissioner of the Halle Orphan House, organized the Lutheran Church, and the Swiss Schlatter the German Reformed, in Pennsylvania. In the same period John Wesley and Whitefield several times appeared on the soil of the New World, as mighty evangelists and revival preachers; and the great movement of Methodism, in connection with the awakening influence from New England, mainly from

90

the metaphysical divine and powerful preacher, Jonathan Edwards, stirred and fructified the whole land.

Thus was North America from the first, like Geneva in the time of the Reformation, only on a much larger scale, an asylum for all the persecuted of the Old World. And so it has remained to this day; though the later emigration has rather lost the religious character, and is mostly ruled by secular interests. It is an incalculable advantage for that land, that its first settlements sprang in great part from earnest religious movements. Modern infidelity and indifferentism, which are likewise imported, cannot do it near so much harm, as if they had laid the foundation of its institutions.

From this history of the rise of the United States, we can understand, in the first place, how the principle of religious toleration should be so deeply rooted in the people. They must give up their own tradition and their holiest associations, before they can ever bow to ecclesiastical despotism and exclusiveness. The persecuted man has always been an advocate of toleration for his own interest, and, to be consistent, must also sympathize with all the persecuted. In America universal freedom of faith and conscience came by necessity, and with this a separation of Church and State, even in those colonies where they were originally united.

But this is only one side of the matter. From the above allusions to American church history it is at the same time clear, that the principle of religious freedom rests there on a *religious* basis, as the result of many sufferings and persecutions for the sake of faith and conscience; and thus differs very materially from some modern theories of toleration, which run out into sheer religious indifference and unbelief. The American is as intolerant as he is tolerant; and, to appreciate his character, we must keep this paradoxical fact always in view. In many things he is even decidedly fanatical. Think only of the Puritanic origin of New England, and of the enormous influence which the strict Calvinism still exerts on the whole land. In the same Geneva, which so hospitably received all hunted Protestants from France, Italy, Spain, England, and Scotland, there reigned at the same time a rigoristic church discipline, and Servetus was burned as a blasphemer. The American leaves every man at liberty to belong to any church, confession, or sect, or to none, according to his own free conviction. But within the particular confessions the lines are far more sharply and strictly drawn than in Europe. There every church member is required to adhere closely to the doctrines and usages of the particular body, to which he belongs.

Hence in America a preacher or theological professor far more easily than here incurs suspicion of neology and heresy, and, though not indeed imprisoned nor banished, much less burned, as in Papal times, is yet forthwith deposed, and, if necessary, formally excommunicated, if after due investigation it appear, that he teaches and acts contrary to his church, which called him and bound him to a certain confession of faith. A rationalist, like Paulus, Wegscheider, Röhr, Bretschneider, Uhlich, Wislicenus, could not find a place in the pulpit or professorial chair of any respectable communion, not even the Unitarian; while in Germany even the majority of the theological chairs and superintendencies have for twenty years, in spite of all obligation to symbols, been filled by men of this or some similar school. That even at this day a man like Dr. Baur, who denies the genuineness of all the New Testament books, except four epistles of Paul and the Apocalypse, and treats the Gospel history almost like a heathen mythology, should still hold the first theological chair of the evangelical church of Würtemberg, is absolutely incomprehensible to a Presbyterian, a Puritan, or an Episcopalian. A man, who does not believe in the divinity of Christ, the inspiration and authority of the Bible, the necessity of conversion and regeneration, and who does not at the same time live a strictly moral life, must in America enter any other calling sooner than the ministry. In the pulpit he will appear to the people, who have a very sound discernment in the matter, as a hypocrite, or as an objective lie, in bold contradiction with the nature and spirit of his calling.

From the decidedly Protestant character of the country, however, one can also, much more easily than in Germany, incur the opposite charge of hyper-orthodoxy, of Puseyism, and of Romanizing tendencies; as, for example, by objecting to the Puritanic views of Catholicism and of church history, by insisting on the import of the church, its unity, and historical continuity, or on a mystical view of the sacraments, in opposition to the prevailing symbolical theory. I might, if it were proper, give some striking instances of this from my own experience. In this respect the German churches of America are more tolerant, by reason of their connection with the German theology; whereas the English and Anglo-American theology has adhered far more to the lines of the old Protestant, especially the Puritanic, extremely anti-Catholic orthodoxy of the seventeenth century, and has been more directly under the control of the ecclesiastical authorities.

This supervision of theology by the church is a valuable remnant of discipline, and ought, I think, to be preferred to too broad and latitudinarian a freedom of doctrine; though I grant, and that from bitter personal experience, that it is very often associated with shallowness, bigotry, and the spirit of persecution; and thus in many ways hinders the free development of theology.

The religious character of North America, viewed as a whole, is predominantly of the Reformed or Calvinistic stamp, which modifies there even the Lutheran Church, to its gain, indeed, in some respects, but to its loss in others. To obtain a clear view of the enormous influence which Calvin's personality, moral earnestness, and legislative genius, have exerted on history, you must go to Scotland and to the United States. The Reformed Church, where it develops itself freely from its own inward spirit and life, lays special stress on thorough moral reform, individual, personal Christianity, freedom and independence of congregational life, and strict church discipline. It draws a clear line between God and the world, Church and State, regenerate and unregenerate. It is essentially practical, outwardly directed, entering into the relations of the world, organizing itself in every variety of form; aggressive and missionary. It has also a vein of legalism, and here, though from an opposite direction, falls in with the Roman Church, from which in every other respect it departs much further than Lutheranism. It places the Bible above every thing else, and would have its church life ever a fresh, immediate emanation from this, without troubling itself much about tradition and intermediate history. Absolute supremacy of the Holy Scriptures, absolute sovereignty of Divine grace, and radical moral reform on the basis of both, these are the three most important and fundamental features of the Reformed type of Protestantism.

In the ecclesiastical condition of America, with all the differences among particular branches, these general characteristics are all clearly defined. The religious life of that country is uncommonly practical, energetic, and enterprising. Congregations, synods, and conventions display an unusual amount of oratorical power, and of talent for organization and government; and it is amazing, what a mass of churches, seminaries, benevolent institutions, religious unions and societies, are there founded and supported by mere voluntary contribution. In all these respects, Germany and the whole continent of Europe, where the spirit of church building and general religious progress does not keep pace at all with the rapid increase of population in large cities, could learn very much from America.

With these virtues, however, American Christianity, of course, has also corresponding faults and infirmities. It is more Petrine than Johannean; more like busy Martha than like the pensive Mary, sitting at the feet of Jesus. It expands more in breadth than in depth. It is often carried on like a secular business, and in a mechanical or utilitarian spirit. It lacks the beautiful enamel of deep fervor and heartiness, the true mysticism, an appreciation of history and the church; it wants the substratum of a profound and spiritual theology; and under the mask of orthodoxy it not unfrequently conceals, without intending or knowing it, the tendency to abstract intellectualism and superficial rationalism. This is especially evident in the doctrine of the church and the Sacraments, and in the meagreness of the worship, which lacks not only all such symbols as the cross, the baptismal font, the gown, but even every liturgical element (except in the Episcopal and most of the German churches), so that nothing is left, but preaching, free prayer, and singing, and even the last is very often left merely to the choir, instead of being the united act of the congregation.

Here now is the work of the German church for America; not only of the Lutheran, but also of the German Reformed, which in fact was never strictly Calvinistic, but has always been rather Melanchthonian, moderate, mediating between Lutheranism and Calvinism, between the Germanic and the Romanic Protestantism, and has accordingly in recent times almost everywhere, especially in Prussia, fallen in with the Evangelical Union. The German church, with its hearty enjoyment of Christianity, and direct intercourse with a personal Saviour, its contemplative turn, its depth of inward view, its regard for history, and its spirited theology, might and should enter as a wholesome supplemental element into the development of American Protestantism; and this it has, in fact, within a few years begun in a small way to do, assisted by the increasing number of translation of the standard works of German theology. It is still more plainly the mission duty of the Episcopal church in that country to restrain the unchurchly and centrifugal forces of ultra-Protestantism. By her excellent Prayer Book she supplies to a much greater extent than the German denominations the defects of a purely subjective and jejune worship, and she would recommend herself still more if she would allow greater freedom and variety in the liturgical service. Her theological mission too is to mediate between the extremes of Romanism and Puritanism; but her native American literature so far does not correspond with her great material resources and social standing, and has not exerted much influence yet to shape the theological thinking of the country; partly on account of her pedantry and exclusiveness.

As to the good and the evil effects of the voluntary principle, which follows unavoidably from the separation of church and state, and underlies the whole American church system, I have already expressed myself in the first lecture, and will not here repeat my remarks.

I must here, however, speak more fully of the Sect system, which I then only briefly touched upon. America is the classic land of sects, where in perfect freedom from civil disqualification, they can develop themselves without restraint. This fact is connected indeed with the above-mentioned predominance of the Reformed type of religion. For in the Reformed church the Protestant features, and with them the subjective, individualizing principle, are most prominent. But in the term *sect-system* we refer at the same time to the whole ecclesiastical condition of the country. For there the distinction of church and sect properly disappears; at least the distinction of established church and dissenting bodies, as it is commonly understood in England and Germany. In America, there is, in fact, no national or established church; therefore no dissenter. There all religious associations, which do not outrage the general Christian sentiment and the public morality (as the Mormons, who, for their conduct, were driven from Ohio and Illinois), enjoy the same protection and the same rights. The distinction between confessions or denominations (as the word is there) and sects is therefore likewise entirely arbitrary, unless perhaps the acknowledgment or rejection of the ecumenical or old Catholic symbols be made the test; though this would not strictly apply even in Germany.

Favored by the general freedom of conscience, the representatives of all the forms of Christianity in the Old World, except the Greek — for we here leave out of view the isolated Russian colony in the Northwest of America — have gradually planted themselves in the vast field of the United States by emigration from all European countries, and are receiving reinforcements every year. There is the Roman with his Tridentinum and pompous mass; the Episcopal Anglican with his Thirty-nine Articles and Book of Common Prayer; the Scotch Presbyterian with his Westminster Confession, and his presbyteries and synods; the Congregationalist, or Puritan in the stricter sense, also with the Westminster Confession, but with his congregational independence; the Baptist, with his immersion and anti-paedobaptism; the Quaker, with his inward light; the Methodist, with his call to repentance and conversion, and his artificial machinery; the Lutheran, now with all his symbols, from the Augustana to the Form of Concord, now with the first only, and now with none of them; the German Reformed and Reformed Dutch, with the Heidelberg Cathechism and the Presbyterian Synodal church polity; the Unionist, either with the consensus of both confessions, or indifferently rejecting all symbols; the Moravian community, with its silent educational and missionary operations; and a multitude of smaller sects besides, mostly of European origin, but some of American. In short, all the English and Scotch churches and sects, and all branches of German and Netherland Protestantism, are there represented. Each one alone is, of course, weaker than its mother church in Europe, except the Puritanic, which has attained its chief historical importance only in New England. But they are all there, not rarely half a dozen in a single country town, each with its own church or chapel; and, where they have any real vitality at all, they grow there proportionally much faster than in Europe. Some, as the Presbyterian, the Methodist, the German Protestant, and the Roman Catholic, have even almost doubled their numbers within the last ten or twenty years.

This confusion of denominations and sects makes very different impressions on the observer from different theological and religious points of view. If he makes all of individual Christianity, and regards the conversion of men as the whole work of the church, he will readily receive a very favorable impression of the religious state of things in America. It is not to be denied, that by the great number of churches and sects this work is promoted; since they multiply the agencies, spur each other on, vie with each other, striving to outdo one another in zeal and success. We might refer to the separation of Paul and Barnabas, by which one stream of apostolic missionary labor was divided into two, and fructified a greater number of fields with its living waters. There are in America probably more awakened souls, and more individual effort and self-sacrifice for religious purposes, proportionally, than in any other country in the world, Scotland alone perhaps excepted. This is attributable, at least in part, to the unrestricted freedom with which all Christian energies may there put themselves forth; and to the fact, that no sect can rely on the favor of the State, but that each is thrown upon its own resources, and has therefore to apply all its energies to keep pace with its neighbors and prevent itself from being swallowed up.

The charge that the sect system necessarily plays into the hands of infidelity on one side and of Romanism on the other has hitherto at least not proved true, though such a result is very naturally suggested. There is in America far less open unbelief and skepticism, than in Europe; and Romanism is extremely unpopular. Whether things will continue so is a very different question.

But on closer inspection the sect system is seen to have also its weaknesses and its shady side. It brings all sorts of impure motives into play, and encourages the use of unfair, or at least questionable means for the promotion of its ends. It nourishes party spirit and passion, envy, selfishness, and bigotry. It changes the peaceful kingdom of God into a battle-field, where brother fights brother, not, of course, with sword and bayonet, yet with loveless harshness and all manner of detraction, and too often subordinates the interests of the church universal to those of his own party. It tears to pieces the beautiful body of Jesus Christ, and continually throws in among its members the fire-brands of jealousy and discord, instead of making them work together harmoniously for the same high and holy end. It should not be forgotten, that Christianity aims not merely to save individual souls, and then leave them to themselves, but to unite them with God and therefore also with one another. It is essentially love, and tends towards association; and the church is and ought to become more and more the one body of Jesus Christ, the fullness of Him who filleth all in all. If, therefore, the observer start with the conception of the church as an organic communion of saints, making unity and universality its indispensable marks, and duly weighing the many exhortations of Holy Scripture to keep the unity of the Spirit in the bond of peace; he cannot possibly be satisfied with the sect system, but must ever come out against it with the warnings of Paul against the divisions and parties in the Corinthian church. A friend very near to me, and a thoughtful, deeply earnest theologian, has keenly assailed and exposed the sect system as the proper

99

American Antichrist. The noblest and most pious minds in America most deeply disapprove and deplore at least the sect *spirit*; and fortunately too, this spirit recedes in proportion as the genuine spirit of Christianity, the uniting and co-operative spirit of brotherly love and peace, makes itself felt. In the American Bible and Tract Societies and Sunday School Union, the various evangelical denominations work hand in hand and get along right well together, although their Catholicity is more of a negative character, not reconciling, but concealing the confessional differences, and although their charity is at an end as soon as the Romish church is mentioned, as if she was simply an enemy of Christ. Several of the most prominent churches maintain a friendly inter-delegation; and even in those which do not, or which make it a mere form, all the true children of God, when they see one another face to face, exchange the hand of fellowship in spite of all the jealousy and controversy between their respective communions.

Sectarianism, moreover — and this I might especially commend to the attention of German divines — is by no means a specifically American malady, as often represented; it is deeply seated in Protestantism itself, and is so far a matter of general Protestant interest. Suppose that in Prussia church and state should be suddenly severed; the same state of things would at once arise here. The parties now in conflict within the Established Church, would embody themselves in as many independent churches and sects, and you would have an Old Lutheran Church, a New Lutheran Church, a Reformed Church, a United Church — and that again divided into a union positively resting on the symbols, and a union acknowledging only the Scriptures — perhaps, also, a Schleiermacherian Church, and who knows how many spiritualistic and rationalistic sects and independent single congregations besides. America in fact draws all its life originally from Europe. It is not a land of *new* sects; for those which have originated there, as the Mormons, are the most insignificant, and have done nothing at all to determine the religious character of the people. It is only the rendez-vous of all European churches and sects, which existed long before, either as establishments or as dissenting bodies. England and Scotland have almost as many different religious bodies as the United States, with the single difference that in the former countries one (the Episcopal in England, the Presbyterian in Scotland) enjoys the privilege of state patronage, while in America all stand on the same footing.

In forming our judgment of the American sect system, therefore, we are led back to the general question, whether Protestantism constitutionally involves a tendency towards denominationalism and sectarianism, wherever it is not hindered by the secular power. This we cannot so very easily deny. Protestantism is Christianity in the form of free subjectivity; of course not an unregenerate subjectivity, resting on natural reason — for this is the essence of rationalism — but a regenerate subjectivity, based on and submitting to the Word of God. It is thus distinguished from Catholicism, which takes Christianity in an entirely objective sense, as a new law, and as absolute authority, and does not therefore allow national and individual peculiarities at all their full right and free development. In the first, the centrifugal force predominates; in the second, the centripetal — there freedom, here authority. And to harmonize perfectly these two opposite yet correlative principles, is the highest, but also the most difficult, problem of history.

Accordingly it is the great work and the divine mission of Protestantism, to place each individual soul in immediate union with Christ and his Word; to complete in each one the work of redemption, to build in each one a temple of God, a spiritual church; and to unfold and sanctify all the energies of the individual. But, through the sinfulness of human nature, the principle of subjectivity and freedom may

101

run out into selfish isolation, endless division, confusion, and licentiousness; just as the principle of objectivity, disproportionately applied, leads to stagnation and petrifaction; the principle of authority, to despotism in the rulers and slavery in the ruled. In North America, the most radically Protestant land, the constitutional infirmities of Protestantism, in religious and political life, are most fully developed, together with its energy and restless activity; just as the natural diseases of Catholicism appear most distinctly in the exclusively Roman countries of southern Europe.

Now in this unrestrained development and splitting up of Christian interests, most palpable in America, the Roman Catholic sees symptoms of an approaching dissolution of Protestantism and the negative preparation for its return into the bosom of the only saving church. But such a relapse to a position already transcended in church history, such an annulling of the whole history of the last three centuries, is, according to all historical analogy, impossible. How inconceivable, that in this age of the general circulation of literature, the Book of all books can again be taken away from the people, and all the liberties, hard won by the Reformation, obliterated! Catholicism can, indeed, draw over to itself as it has lately done in Germany, England, and America, individuals, tired of the Protestant confusion and uncertainty, having no patience with the present, and no faith in the future, longing for a comfortable pillow of absolute, tangible authority. But Protestantism in the mass can never be swallowed up by it; or if it should be, it would soon break out again with increased violence, and shake the Roman structure still more deeply than it did in the sixteenth century.

We believe, indeed, by all means, that the present divided condition of Protestantism, is only a temporary transition state, but that it will produce something far more grand and glorious, than Catholicism ever presented in its best days. Protestantism after all still contains the most vigorous energies and the greatest activity of the church. It represents the progressive principle of history. It is Christianity in motion. Hence more may be expected from it than from the comparative stagnation of the Roman or Greek Catholicism. Converted regenerate individuals, these subjective Protestant heart-churches, are the living stones for the true Evangelical Catholic Church, which is to combine and perfect in itself all that is true and good and beautiful in the past. But this requires the previous fulfillment of the mission of Protestantism, the transforming of each individual man into a temple of God. Out of the most confused chaos God will bring the most beautiful order; out of the deepest discords, the noblest harmony; out of the most thoroughly developed Protestantism, the most harmonious and at the same time the freest Catholicism. What wild controversy has already raged, what violent passion has been kindled among theologians, about the doctrine of the Eucharist! And yet this sacrament is the feast of the holiest and deepest love, the symbol of the closest fellowship of Christ and the church. The one, holy, universal, apostolic church is an article not only of faith, but also of hope, to be fully accomplished only with the glorious return of Christ.

In America are found, in some degree, as a preparation, for this great end, all the data for the problem of the most comprehensive union. For there, not only the Lutheran and Reformed confessions, but also the English and all the European sections and forms of the church are found in mutual attrition and in ferment. But, of course, Europe likewise, especially Germany and England, must have its part in the work; nay, must make the beginning. For Europe still stands at the head of Christian civilization, and is ever producing from her prolific womb new ideas and movements, which, through the growing facility, and frequency of inter-communication, the swelling emigration, and the exportation of elements of literature and culture of every kind, at once make themselves felt in America, perpetuate themselves there in modified forms, and come into immediate contact and conflict, so as to bury themselves in each other, and rise again as the powers of a new age in the history of the world and the church. Therefore have I called America, even in respect to religion and the church, the Phenix-grave of Europe.

II. THE SEVERAL CHURCHES AND SECTS

I proceed now to consider the several confessions; — "denominations" they are called in America, because the difference is in fact often merely nominal, and relates not so much to the doctrinal confession, as to government, worship, and outward usage. In this sketch I will confine myself to the most important and influential denominations which represent the proper ecclesiastical life of the United States. Besides these there is, to be sure, a legion of smaller sects, some of English origin, some of German, and some of American; the Shakers, the Tunkers, the River Brethren, the Seventh-day Baptists, Schwenkfeldians, Weinbrennerians, Swedenborgians, Universalists, &c. But it were unfair and ridiculous to judge American Christianity by these. They have not, in fact, made near so much noise, nor exerted near so much influence on the American church, as even the German Catholics and the rationalistic "free societies" upon the German. Most of these smaller sects, too, soon run their course and become mere petrifactions.*

---

* I must warn my German readers against the ridiculous caricatures of American Christianity which abound in European works. Such an one has appeared quite recently in the last volume of the learned Roman Catholic Encyclopaedia of Wetzer and Welte (vol. xi., Freiburg, 1854, p. 49 sq.). There, in a long article on America, we read of a number of sects, of which we never heard in our life, and whose existence must be confined to the private opinions of some eccentric and deranged heads, and such may be found anywhere in the Romish Church as well as the Protestant. It was

In America, as elsewhere, the leading and most comprehensive division in the church is that of Protestantism and Romanism. The former embraces the great mass of the population; many thousands, however, holding only a very loose and outward connection with it, and not being formal members of any particular church, though they regularly attend public worship. The nominal Protestants, many of them not even baptized, correspond to the numberless nominal Christians in European state churches, who, though they have been baptized and have professed their Catholic, or Lutheran, or Reformed faith, care no more about the church, than if they were heathens or Mohammedans.

In Protestantism we may again distinguish the English and the German groups of confessions. To the English belong the Congregationalists, the Presbyterians, the Episcopalians, the Quakers, the Methodists, and the Baptists; the last two having also German branches. The Reformed Dutch are, it is true, of Low Dutch origin, but they have become in language entirely English, and are closely related to the Presbyterians. The Huguenots, who emigrated after the revocation of the edict of Nantes, have nearly all fallen in with the Presbyterian and Episcopal churches, and the French language is rarely used in public service in the United States, excepting for the numerous Roman Catholic Frenchmen in some of the Southern States, especially Louisiana. The German group embraces the Lutheran, Reformed, and United Churches, and the Moravian Brethren.

All these may be reckoned to orthodox and evangelical Protestantism, since they adhere in their symbols to the

---

not without a smile that we saw there "Bethlehemites," "Sionites," "Bryonites" (who are reported to pluck out their right eye in literal understanding of Matth. 5, 29!), "Ranters of the right arm," "Latitudinarians," "Six Article and Ten Article Baptists," "Tabernaculists," "Bible-Christians" (who live on water and vegetable food!) and "Atheists," figuring along side of Presbyterians, Episcopalians, Puritans and Methodists, as if they were of equal importance.

fundamental doctrines of the Scriptures and the Reformation, and manifest a corresponding Christian life. The Baptists and Quakers stand on the extreme limit of orthodox Protestantism, and accordingly come nearest to being sects in the strict sense; though the Baptists are very numerous. The Episcopalians, on the other hand, form the extreme right wing of Protestantism and are the nearest akin to Catholicism, especially in the high-church or Puseyite section. The German churches, we may say, generally hold middle ground between the Episcopal and the Presbyterian.

There are other religious parties, which stand in radical opposition to both the Evangelical Protestant and Roman Catholic Churches, and thus form a group by themselves — as the Universalists and the Mormons. The latter have recently attracted so much notice, though undeservedly, even in Europe, that I must pay them also some attention here.

We will first consider the Protestant communions, partly in the order of their importance for America, partly in the order of their age; then contrast with them the Roman Church; and lastly describe Mormonism, the irreconcilable foe of both; only remarking further, that for want of the necessary helps I cannot enter into detailed statistics; though these at any rate change every year. All I wish to do is, briefly and clearly to exhibit the reigning life and spirit and the distinguishing features of the various denominations.

(a) THE CONGREGATIONALISTS

The Congregationalists, or Independents, or Puritans in the strict sense,* sprang up in the later years of Queen Elizabeth; but their roots run back to the Calvinistic reformation in Geneva. As early as the reign of Edward VI., in

---

* In the wider sense the Presbyterian theology also, and still more the Baptist, may be called Puritanic, i. e., radically Protestant; for they push the opposition to Catholicism in doctrine as far as the Congregationalists.

fact to some extent under Henry VIII, two tendencies may be observed in the English Church; the semi-Catholic, which, with all its opposition to the Roman Papacy, would still preserve as far as possible the mediaeval character, especially in government and worship; and the radically Protestant, which broke all connection with the Catholic tradition, considering it a development of the Antichrist, and with deep moral earnestness, but also with intolerant and stormy zeal, insisted on transforming the whole church life directly from the Bible on the model of Geneva and Zürich. The former party triumphed under the gifted and masculine Elizabeth, who hated Puritanism even more than the Papacy, and, on political grounds, preferred the Episcopal order as forming a surer support for monarchy ("no bishop, no king," being the motto of her successor, James I.), and a more splendid court and state attire. True, Puritanism afterwards gained the ascendency under Cromwell after a bloody civil war of religion; but the restoration of the Stuarts soon re-established the Episcopal Church; yet with unmistakable evidence of the mighty influence of Calvinism and Puritanism, which it to this day cannot deny.

But in New England Puritanism found a safe refuge and an unmolested home. There it has revealed, since the landing of the "Pilgrim Fathers" in 1620, its proper importance for the history of the world. It is the ruling sect of the six Northeastern States, and has exerted, and still exerts, a powerful influence upon the religious, social and political life of the whole nation.

Congregationalism is, in general, an extreme Calvinism, modified by the English character and peculiar views of church government. It forms the extreme left wing of orthodox Protestantism, maintaining the keenest and most unyielding hostility to Romanism; though allied to it on the other hand by a certain Judaizing spirit and rigid legalism. Calvin, with all his religious horror of the Papacy, had confessedly a strong churchly vein; and, with all his logical acuteness, a turn for mystic depth. This is especially discernible in the beginning of the fourth book of his Institutes, and his doctrine of the Holy Supper, which is in reality more akin to the Lutheran, than to the jejune, or to use his own exaggerated and unjust term, the "profane" theory of Zuingle. These churchly and mystic elements passed on, indeed, into the German Reformed and the Anglican Churches, but were gradually thrown aside by the Presbyterian and Puritanic communions. It is a remarkable fact, that where Calvin's rigid doctrine of predestination has prevailed, his view of the Eucharist, though undeniably contained in all the leading symbols of the Reformed Church of the sixteenth and seventeenth century, even in the Westminster Confession, has almost entirely given place to the more meagre and the clearer common sense view of Zuingle; and *vice versa*. In their doctrine of the church and the sacraments, as well as in their views of history and tradition, the Congregationalists approach the German Rationalism, or at least that last form of Supernaturalism, which, through the intermediate steps of the Rational Supernaturalism and Supernatural Rationalism, finally passed into formal Rationalism. In all other respects, however, they are strictly orthodox, still holding to the Westminster Confession and Catechisms, drawn up by an assembly of Calvinistic divines in London in 1642. On many points, particularly the inspiration, authenticity, and authority of the Scriptures, they still maintain the Protestant orthodoxy of the seventeenth century, and charge most modern German theologians, often not unjustly, with a dangerous looseness. New England has produced a series of able divines, such as Jonathan Edwards (a man of rare piety, deep metaphysical talent and powerful eloquence, the friend and co-laborer of Whitefield in the extensive revival of the last century), Bellamy, Hopkins, Emmons, Dwight, Wood, &c., who are hardly known by name in Germany, but who fill an important chapter in the development of Calvinistic theology, and may claim a place in our manuals of doctrine history. This "New England theology," however, is upon the whole rather dry and jejune, also too local in its character, and not sufficiently connected with the general history of theology. At present it is in an unsatisfactory transition state. The old-fashioned Puritanism of the seventeenth century does not satisfy the scientific wants and present taste; while a great deal of New School Congregationalism has deviated from the path of Catholic truth, and resolves the process of conversion and regeneration into a scheme of Pelagian Utilitarianism. Of late, German philosophy and theology is receiving greatly increased attention in New England, and the professors in Andover, the most important Congregational seminary, Drs. Park, Stowe, and Shedd, are well acquainted with it; Moses Stuart, author of several Biblical commentaries, having broken the way. This study of the German literature will undoubtedly greatly stimulate, enliven, and invigorate the New England mind, which is naturally strong, clear, and active; but it may also play into the hands of rationalistic and transcendental tendencies. All depends upon the character of the German works, and upon the natural turn of mind and heart.

But the leading peculiarity of Congregationalism, which essentially distinguishes it even from the Genevan Calvinism and the Scottish Presbyterianism, lies in its theory of church government, which exalts and develops the independence of single congregations. In this it goes a step beyond the Reformation of the sixteenth century, and forms a new stage in the unfolding, or at least in the application, of the Protestant principle of religious subjectivity. It proceeds on the ground, that each congregation (hence the name Congregationalism) is a complete church of Christ, and as such independent of all earthly supervision (hence the name Independency); directly united to Christ, and responsible only to him; therefore entitled and bound to choose and maintain its own officers, and conduct all its own affairs, internal and external, as prescribed by the divine word itself. Here, accordingly, the idea of the church coalesces entirely with the idea of a local congregation, and in place of an organism embracing all believers, we have a loose conglomerate of independent religious societies, at best only invisibly united. It is, however, a very good feature of this system, that a congregation has only one pastor at a time, and is never allowed to be so large as to put any individual member beyond the reach of a conscientious pastoral supervision. For this reason there are forming among the Congregationalists, and in America in general, immigration entirely out of view, many more daughter churches with their own houses of worship and their own pastors, than in Europe. In Berlin there are many congregations, each of which, on the American plan, would easily make a dozen. Then there is an important distinction made in each congregation between the church, in the strict sense of the term, or the number of communicants, who constitute a spiritual association, and manage all the spiritual concerns of the charge; and between the parish or ecclesiastical society, which is a civil corporation consisting of all those who attend public worship and contribute to the support of the pastor, and have the control of the secular matters. The transition from the latter to the former is marked by a solemn covenant and act of reception, which in fact, though not in form, corresponds to our confirmation, but which is left, of course, in America to the free will of each individual.

This idea of the independence of single congregations was expressed, as is well known, even by Luther in his correspondence with the Bohemian Brethren, whom he advised in their isolated condition to manage their own affairs without regard to ecclesiastical authority; and still more clearly by the fugitive Franciscan, Lambert of Avignon, at the Homburg Synod in 1526. But it could never be practically carried out in Germany for want of the material for such independent congregations. In England it was first brought forward by one Brown, a preacher, towards the end of Elizabeth's reign; and hence the Congregationalists were at first called Brownists. But, as he afterwards from impure motives returned to the Episcopal Church, they would have nothing more to do with him, and rejected the name. With better reason may the worthy minister, John Robinson, be regarded as the proper father of the American Puritans. He, with his congregation, fled before an unrighteous persecution, in 1611, from the north of England, first to Holland; thence, in 1620, he sent his people, with solemn prayer and fasting, and the most earnest exhortations to be steadfast in the faith and grow in the knowledge of the holy word and law of God, to America, intending to follow them with the next party of emigrants; but he soon after died, without seeing with his bodily eyes the beloved land of his hopes. On the inhospitable shores and in the unbroken wilds of Massachusetts, which have since been transformed by Puritan industry into a garden, his followers and friends increased under the severest privations and self-denials, and became the stock of a great nation.

The Congregationalist principle, however, is not fully carried out even in New England. Its operation has been modified by the theocratic institutions of the early settlers and the principle of Catholic churchly unity, without which the principle of independency must run out into complete atomism. The Pilgrim Fathers were soon followed by a great number of other Puritans, particularly in 1630 by the founders of Boston, Salem, Hartford, New Haven, &c.; and these, like most of their English brethren in faith, were not properly Independents at all, but either held the Presbyterian principles of church government or were willing to retain even the Episcopal system, with essential modifications.

Cotton and Wilson of Boston, Hooker and Stone of Hartford, Davenport and Hooke of New Haven, and the other ministers who accompanied these trains of emigrants, were mostly educated in Oxford and Cambridge, and regularly ordained ministers of the Church of England, only suffering for nonconformity, but never having established a separate church organization. The Rev. Mr. Higginson, of Leicester, on taking the last view of the coast of England, in May, 1629, for Massachusetts, addressed the large company of his spiritual children and fellow-passengers in these words: "We will not say as the Separatists (Brownists) are wont to say, at their leaving England: — Farewell, Babylon — Farewell, Rome; but we will say, Farewell, dear England — Farewell, the Church of God in England, and all the Christian friends there. We do not go to New England as Separatists from the Church of England, though we cannot but separate from corruptions in it; but we go to practise the positice part of church reformation, and to propagate the Gospel in America." He concluded "with a fervent prayer for the king, the Church and State in England, and for the blessing of God in their present undertaking for New England."

From the co-operation of these two classes of Puritans, there arose in New England, in the course of the seventeenth century, a theocratic state church, with a common Calvinistic confession of faith, and a rigid discipline; thus limiting the independence of the several congregations by their connection with the whole. The "Saybrook Platform" of 1708 is evidently a compromise between the Presbyterian and the Congregational principle. And even now that the union between church and state is dissolved, the Congregationalists have their annual and semi-annual associations and consociations, for the settlement of difficulties and cases of discipline, the examination and ordination of candidates of the ministry, and the furtherance of the general interests of the church. These, indeed, are not permitted to trespass on the jealously guarded rights of the single congregations, and have not legislative, but only advisory, power; yet they have such a moral influence, that ministers or congregations obnoxious to their discipline cannot well maintain themselves in public opinion. In general ecclesiastical operations, as home and foreign missions, educational schemes, the establishment and support of theological and scientific institutions, they work together without difficulty, and display very great activity. Thus the Congregational theory in New England is always associated, more or less, with Presbyterian practice.

From this state of things, therefore, one should by no means judge that independent system, to which so many of the late German emigrants incline, on account of their hatred of all church authority in matters of faith. For these, no form of church government is more miserable than the independent; and no congregations are in a worse condition than those cut off from all synodal supervision. Every one would rule and govern, yet no one understands even the A B C of church government. Nay, would that they were Puritans, in the good sense of the word! Would that we had multitudes of living independent congregations, which the truth had made truly free, and able to govern and discipline themselves according to the word of God! This were a real advance, to be desired even for Germany; nay, most especially for Germany. Here — at least in the northern and eastern parts — Protestantism, to its shame, has in three whole centuries produced no proper congregational life at all; and Luther's lamentation over the want of material for an efficient congregational government growing out of the congregation itself, must still prevail. But those independent German churches in America are infinitely different from the Bible-reading, earnest, rigid Puritans. They are, in fact, nothing but licentious rationalistic communities, which employ a preacher as a hired servant, exclude him from the church council, and thus trample on the dignity of the sacred office, and rather hinder than favor the kingdom of God; whereas, among the Anglo-American Congregationalists the ministers always preside *ex-officio* in the church councils, take the lead in all ecclesiastical matters, and are in general very honorably treated by the congregations, and held in greater respect than any other class.

The congregational principle, however, even in its best form, and in union with living faith and a pure confession, is after all one-sided, and must be balanced by the idea of the universal church. We need unquestionably independent congregations, in which the general priesthood shall be no empty name, but a living reality — and this is the sinew of truth in Anglo-American Congregationalism; but these congregations ought, at the same time, to feel themselves living members of the church universal, the one undivided body of Christ, and to help one another with the hand of brotherly love in every good work. In this respect the Episcopal and Presbyterian principles of church government have the advantage; since they hold fast the idea of the organic unity and authority of the universal church, which must never be given up. True independence and freedom is not, in fact, inconsistent with rational authority, but can rightly thrive only in union with it. Most of the Congregationalists, too, who move from New England to the middle, southern, and western states, commonly attach themselves to the Presbyterians of the New School, whose synods have legislative power. Of late, however, there is a tendency in New York and the western states to form strictly Congregational churches, and it is not impossible that the New School Presbyterian body may split yet on this question, and on the rock of slavery.

Finally, as to the form of worship, Puritanism stands at the extreme of simplicity and meagreness. In this, also, it goes beyond Calvin. Even those symbolical forms and ancient church usages, which he either approved or at least tolerated as innocent, it rejects on account of their real or supposed connection with the abominated Catholicism; such as the cross, the altar, the clerical costume, all liturgical forms of prayer, and the church festivals, even Christmas, Easter, and Whitsuntide. In the war against these things the Puritans displayed, in the days of Cromwell, the same pedantry and fanatism, nay, we may say the same formalism — only reversed, negative — as the Papists and Episcopalians in their zeal for them; and gave proof, that an extreme spiritualism, which overlooks the true import of the divinely created body, very easily passes unawares into its own opposite. Of late, however, they have considerably softened and changed in this respect. The former aversion to church steeples, bells, organs, and choirs has almost disappeared; and even the Gothic architecture, which really grew out of the Catholic idea of worship, is now frequently employed in Puritanic New England. In general, as taste and artistic talent are cultivated, prejudice against any union of religion with art will disappear, and Christianity will be seen to be a thoroughly penetrating and transforming leaven for architecture, painting, sculpture, music, and poetry, as well as for everything else. Nay, there is even danger that this progress of taste in America may lead to an unwholesome predilection for outward pomp, splendor, and mere form in church matters, and extinguish the old Puritanic earnestness.

For it is not to be denied, that this Puritanic worship, with all its nationalistic nakedness and its barrenness for the imagination and the heart, has yet its excellences. If, from fear of mechanical formality, the use of liturgies is unjustly rejected, so that even the prayer of all prayers, which the Lord himself taught the disciples, and expressly enjoined upon them, is hardly ever heard from the Puritanic and Presbyterian pulpits of America — though the case is somewhat different in England and Scotland — the gift of free prayer, on the contrary, is most cultivated in these communions. This free prayer, however, in the pulpit itself, commonly assumes involuntarily a stereotyped form, employing from Sabbath to Sabbath nearly the same phrases, yet making it difficult for the hearer to join, since he has first to appropriate what he hears, before he can form it into his own prayer. Just in proportion as the altar service and the sacramental element of worship is lost sight of, the sermon receives increased attention. It is in general decidedly evangelical, urging on the hearers repentance, conversion, and sanctification; but it is often too didactic, at least for the German taste, and resembles rather a theological essay; while, conversely theological lectures in America are less scientific and more practical than in Germany. Finally; although the Puritans and Presbyterians likewise go too far in rejecting all the church festivals and the whole idea of the church year, as matters of merely human tradition and liable to frequent abuse; yet it must be granted, that they observe Sunday — or as they very characteristically prefer to call it the Sabbath — much more earnestly and worthily, than any other section of Christendom. That this day, appointed by God, and no more abolished by Christ than any other precept of the decalogue, but only spiritualized by association with the resurrection, should be profaned and degraded to a day of worldly amusement and dissipation, as it is on the European continent, especially in such a city as Paris, is to any American, but particularly to the Puritanic New Englander, a real abomination and one of the chief sources of infidelity and moral corruption. If this regard for the Sabbath often runs into Pharisaic legalism and scrupulousness, this extreme is still far less injurious to the public morals, especially in a country where church and state are separate, than the opposite extreme of Sadducean and heathen licentiousness.

Puritanism, from its proper home in the six New England states, has directly and indirectly exerted a greater and in general more beneficial influence on the whole religious life of America, than any other denomination. I make this concession the more readily, since I myself am no Puritan, and, according to my theological education, never can be one. Puritanism has been the main source of the energetic spirit of enterprise, the moral earnestness, the practical organizing talent, the wholesome principle of the multiplication of congregations, each with only one pastor, the zeal for the Bible and Tract Societies, for missions, for general education, for higher institutions of learning, the liberality towards religious and benevolent causes, the strict observance of the Sabbath, the temperance movement, the opposition to slavery, and most of the social reforms of that country.

But it has also nourished unchurchly tendencies and all forms of fanaticism and radicalism. In the midst of the Puritan churches there has quite imperceptibly arisen since the end of the last century Unitarianism, a semi-rationalistic sect in doctrine, but highly respectable as regards scientific and esthetic culture and natural morality, especially benevolence. It embraces many of the most worthy and cultivated families of Boston, the American Athens; almost the whole faculty of the University at Cambridge, Mass., and many of the first authors, poets, and statesmen of America, as Channing (who was certainly not far from the kingdom of heaven), Prescott, Bancroft, (who, however, quite recently professed something like Trinitarian opinions), Ticknor, Longfellow, John Quincy Adams, Everett, Fillmore, etc. From New England principally, although not exclusively, originates Universalism, which goes much further and undermines the foundations of the Gospel. New England is the chief scene of the extravagances of Garrisonian abolitionism and female emancipation, in connection with dangerous leanings to a skepticism and pantheism, which have been promulgated in writings, public assemblies, and sometimes even from the pulpit, by such men as

117

Theodore Parker and Ralph Emerson, to the great sorrow not only of the orthodox Puritans, but even of all earnest and sober-minded Unitarians.

But we confidently believe, there is yet salt enough in New England to counteract these workings of decay. The days of the stiff, gloomy, old-fashioned Puritanism, however, are over. Its virtues will abide; but its defects must give place to a more free, living and spiritual conception of Christianity and the church.

(b) THE PRESBYTERIANS

The Presbyterian church of America came chiefly from Scotland and North Ireland; but it has received also a great deal of material from the anglicized descendants of the Dutch, French, German Reformed and Lutheran emigrants. Its first presbytery, consisting of seven ministers was organized in Philadelphia in 1705. The first General Assembly met in 1789, when the number of ministers amounted to 188 with 419 congregations. It now extends over all the States of the Union except New England, where Puritanism takes its place. It is without question one of the most numerous, respectable, worthy, intelligent, and influential denominations, and has a particularly strong hold on the solid middle class.

My sketch of this church may be brief, as the Presbyterians essentially agree in doctrine and worship with the orthodox Congregationalists just described, and have also the same confession of faith, viz., the Westminster Confession and Catechism.

Presbyterianism really differs from Puritanism only in its form of government, from which it takes its name; showing what importance it attaches to this matter in opposition to Independency on the one hand, and Episcopacy on the other. It holds to the idea of a common church government and of binding authority of synods, to which single congregations are subject; but it rejects all hierarchical orders and teaches on the contrary the official parity of all the clergy. The organization is essentially the same as that of the Scotch Reformed church — a consistent application of the synodical and presbyterial principle on the basis of strictly Calvinistic theology and discipline. At the head of each congregation stands the consistory or congregational council, called in the old Scotch phrase the *kirk-session.* This consists of the pastor, who is president *ex-officio,* and of elders chosen for life from the congregation; it is entrusted with the administration of all local affairs of a spiritual nature. A certain number of ministers, not less than three, with as many lay elders form a Presbytery, which holds generally semi-annual meetings; and three or more Presbyteries form a synod, which convenes annually and superintends the affairs of its district. Over all the synods stands the General Assembly, which meets every spring, and is composed of an equal number of clerical and lay delegates from all the Presbyteries. It is the highest tribunal in all matters of doctrine and discipline, and has not only advisory power, like the Associations of the Congregationalists, but legislative functions, so that a minister or congregation, which obstinately resists its decrees, is liable to a formal excommunication.

In 1837 the Presbyterian church split into two parts, nearly equal in size and influence, the Old School and the New School branches, as they are called, which are very jealous of one another, and hold no formal intercourse. The separation, which with more patience and love perhaps might and should have been avoided, was occasioned as much by personal collisions and local interests as by any real differences in doctrine. It has contributed, however, to the numerical increase of the churches, ministers, colleges, seminaries, and benevolent contributions; for the Old School alone is now as large as the whole Presbyterian church was at the time of the division. The Old School is in general the more strictly orthodox, conservative, and centralized in its operations. The New, indeed, likewise acknowledges the Westminister Confession as its symbol, and reckons among its members many as decided Calvinists as there are in the other branch; but it reserves to itself, as a body, greater freedom and a wider range in the theological development of its standards, especially as regards the doctrines of original sin and predestination; and as to church polity it holds in some respects middle ground between the old Scotch Presbyterianism and Congregationalism. There is a like difference among the Congregationalists in New England; but, in the absence of a general church organization, it has taken no such organized form. The New School also is composed of quite heterogeneous material, and by the perpetual agitation of the slavery question and other points of difference is threatened almost every year with a new division, which it can hardly long escape; while some of its members have already returned into the bosom of the Old School.

Both branches of the Presbyterian church have recently, like the Puritans, felt the influence of German theology, which in spite of very strong and sometimes certainly not unfounded prejudices, will exert an increasing influence for good and for evil. The professors at Princeton, the leading seminary of the Old School, Drs. Hodge, Add, Alexander, and Green, and the professors, Drs. Robinson and Smith, in the Union Theological Seminary at New York, the most important institution of the New School, have made themselves acquainted with German theology, some of them by a residence in Germany for the purpose, and pay constant regard to it in their writings.

Besides these two sections of the Presbyterian family, there are in America other smaller Presbyterian communions, differing from the former only in some very unessential usages, and originating in the older secessions from the Scottish Establishment; as, the Seceders, the Associate Reformed, and Reformed Presbyterian bodies. The Cumberland Presbyterians are, on the contrary, of American growth, and were excommunicated by the Presbyterian General Assembly in the beginning of this century (1810) for leaning to Arminianism and Methodistic measures.

(c) THE REFORMED DUTCH

Next in order we may mention the Protestant Reformed Dutch Church, not on account of its numerical strength and importance, which is very limited, but on account of its age and its close affinity with the communion just described and its medium position, as it were, between Old School Presbyterianism and Episcopacy, to which we shall presently come. It is properly the oldest Protestant denomination in the United States, with the exception of the Episcopal church, which dates from the colonization of Virginia in 1607. For as early as 1614 the Hollanders, in whose service the English commander, Henry Hudson, had discovered the river called by his name a few year before, began to settle on its beautiful banks and laid the foundation of New Amsterdam, which subsequently changed its name to that of New York and became the commercial metropolis of the New World. The Dutch Reformed church was even the established church in the New Netherlands, though it freely tolerated the others till the surrender of the colony to England in 1664. Thus it is closely interwoven with the history of the "Empire State." It formed, for more than a century, only a branch of the mother church in Europe, and stood under the immediate jurisdiction of the Classis of Amsterdam, which to this day has the charge of the churches in the Dutch colonies. But this dependence, at first natural and beneficial, became gradually troublesome on account of the intervening distance, and interfered with the growth of the daughter. Finally, after a good deal of violent controversy between the old Dutch and the young Dutch parties, which led even to a formal, though but temporary, schism, is assumed an independent organization with the consent of the Classis of Amsterdam and the Synod of North Holland in 1771, under the conciliatory influence mainly of the venerable Dr. Livingston, the first theological professor of its own Seminary.

From that time nearly all connection with the mother church ceased, and even the Dutch language rapidly passed away from the pulpit and the school, where for a long time it had been exclusively employed. The young generation grew up altogether English, and received no new increase from Holland, which preferred sending its surplus population to its own colonies in the East and West Indies. The neological movements, which have agitated the Reformed church of Holland, especially the Universities of Groningen and Leyden, since the end of the last century, and nearly set aside there the authority of the articles of Dort, have not affected the American Dutch church in the least. But it is equally true that the modern Evangelical movements, and the influences of the better German theology, which are now increasingly felt in the mother country, as they were from the time of Ursinus and Olevianus to that of Lampe, and which are now doing a good commensurate with the evil wrought by the German rationalism of the preceding period, have left it entirely untouched. A pretty large party in this denomination, consisting mostly, I suppose, of ministers who originally came from the Congregationalists and Presbyterians, has even seriously agitated the question, recently, of the propriety of giving up the name *Dutch* altogether, which has a rather bad sound in some of the States, being improperly used as a term of contempt for *German.* But others feel justly proud of the land of their forefathers, which occupies such a distinguished position in the history of modern civilization, political liberty, and Protestant Christianity, and of the honorable connection of their church with the history of New York. They also fear, not without reason, that the repudiation of the distinctive name would prepare the way for the final absorption of their congregations by the more influential and progressive Episcopal and Presbyterian churches, to which in fact a great many of their members have already gone over. To this must be added legal difficulties in reference to the title to church property; so that, for the present at least, this unimportant, though characteristic project of a change of the denominational name may be considered as abandoned.

The Dutch Reformed church is confined to the States of New York, and New Jersey, and the city of Philadelphia. But it has there very wealthy and respectable congregations, especially the Collegiate churches in the city of New York, which, in consequence of the enormous increase of the value of certain donations in land, became the richest ecclesiastical corporation in America, with the exception of the Episcopal Trinity church in the same city. It has also at New Brunswick, N. J., a theological Seminary and College (Rutger's College), which are among the best endowed literary institutions in the land, although their number of students is small and almost entirely confined to this particular denomination. In the absence of an original field of home missionary labor — for the recent emigration from Holland to the Western States is confined to a small number of separatists and isolated individuals — it has lately made an effort to enlarge its territory and influence by establishing congregations out of foreign German and German Reformed material, and published a new German hymn-book.

In doctrine this denomination holds to the Heidelberg Catechism, but more especially to the Decrees of the Synod of Dort. The former is practically very little used now amongst the Dutch. They neglect the regular catechetical training of youth in the old style; reject the rite of confirmation; observe none of the leading festivals, and have no sympathy whatever with the churchly elements of primitive Protestantism, in which they can see only relics of Popery. In their current views of the sacraments and kindred subjects they have, it seems, fallen in entirely with the reigning spirit of modern American Puritanism and Presbyterianism, which adopt, with few exceptions, the low Zuinglian theory in spite of the Calvinistic teaching of all the Reformed confessions. The 76th Question of the Heidelberg catechism must appear to them, accordingly, as obsolete mysticism and superstition. They are hardly able, in their present condition, properly to understand, and to appreciate the German origin and genius, the Melanchthonian, conciliatory, and catholic spirit of this admirable production. But in regard to the mystery of predestination they are said to be more rigidly Calvinistic than even the Old School Presbyterians, and determine here the sense of the cautious and moderate Catechism by the express teaching of the anti-Arminian Synod of Dort, held more than fifty years later. They are generally considered, with the above qualification, as the stiffest and most immovable of all the most respectable Protestant churches in America, and would fain be regarded as the very Gibraltar of old-fashioned Protestantism, in the happy dream that the venerable Synod of Dort settled all theological questions in 1618, and left us nothing to do but to renew from time to time a sweeping commonplace protest against Arminianism, and more especially against Popery, as the veritable Antichrist and enemy of all civil and religious freedom. It would be more important to make this claim good by positive achievements in theological science. But the ruling party in the Dutch Synod seems to be singularly averse to every movement which threatens to disturb in the least the comfortable pillow of an easy traditional orthodoxy, and to lead to more liberal views.*

---

* We ought, perhaps, to make an honorable exception in favor of the "New Brunswick Review," which was designed to parade the learning and

This aversion to anything new, in connection with some disappointments of a personal and sectarian nature (not to mention less honorable motives), was the principal cause of its recent conduct towards the German Reformed sister church, which, however, we must in justice add, is sincerely regretted by many of the most worthy Dutch ministers and laymen as meddlesome and presumptuous, uncharitable and unwise. Since the American Dutch Church has no prospect of enlarging its territory without interfering, more or less, with the home missionary field of other denominations, the emigration from Holland having almost entirely ceased, it is the more desirable that it should yield to a freer motion within, and justify its separate denominational existence and increase its usefulness by such contributions to the theology of the age, as might be expected from its historical origin, its own resources, and its social standing in American Christendom.

Apart from this theological stagnation, which characterizes a considerable portion of the Dutch ministry, it is said to be inferior to none in America as regards general culture and ability, and takes an active part in the benevolent operations of the day, especially the foreign missionary, Bible, and tract causes, and the American and Foreign Christian Union.

The government and discipline of the Dutch church is almost entirely the same with the Presbyterian, except that

---

orthodoxy of a *part* of the Dutch body before the theological and literary world. But it has been already suspended after one year's existence (1854–55). We sincerely hope it may not sleep as long as the famous Low-Dutchman, Rip Van Winkle, and that it may find more noble and profitable work to do hereafter, than to publish ill-natured and ill-mannered abuses and absurd caricatures of the so-called Mercersburg Theology, else the editor might bring upon himself another such withering castigation as his searching neighbor of New Brunswick felt it his duty to inflict upon him, in the service of truth and justice, through the columns of the "N. Y. Observer," for June 15, 1854, unless he should be regarded by such an one with the silence of contempt, according to the proverb: Le jeu ne vaut pas la chandelle. We wish him neither the one nor the other.

in it, as in the German Reformed body, the elders and deacons are chosen not for life, but for a term of years. This seems to us rather an advantage, since it brings more of the lay force of the church into official activity for the common good.

In worship, the Dutch Reformed denomination has not given itself up to the exclusive dominion of extemporaneous prayer, which rules in the Puritan and Presbyterian bodies of America, but still holds fast to a part, at least, of the old Palatinate liturgy, though it is now engaged in revising and modernizing it.

(d) THE PROTESTANT EPISCOPAL CHURCH

This is the oldest Protestant church in the United States, and although less numerous, popular, and energetic than the Puritans, Presbyterians, Methodists, and Baptists, has easier access to the higher circles of society, especially in the large cities, and the best prospects of a steady and substantial growth. It was transplanted as early as 1607, with the new colony of Virginia, and enjoyed there the privileges of an established church. It obtained the same advantage afterwards under the protection and influence of the English government in the colony of Maryland, and also in New York, since 1693. Nevertheless, it was only a weak plant before the Revolution, and was merely an appendage to the diocese of the bishop of London. Its clergymen could be ordained only in England, and were mostly sent to it, and in part supported, by the "Society for the Propagation of the Gospel in Foreign Parts," founded in 1701. Different attempts were made, indeed, to choose a proper colonial bishop — without which a district so far from the jurisdiction of the London prelate could not possibly thrive — but they always failed. At last, the separation of the colonies from the mother country made an independent organization indispensable, and after many difficulties, an act of parliament was finally passed, after the conclusion of the war of independence, empowering the Archbishop of Canterbury and the Bishop of London to consecrate three bishops for the dioceses of Pennsylvania, New York, and Virginia (1787). Another bishop, Seabury, had been already ordained a few years before, in 1784, in the independent Episcopal Church in Scotland for the diocese of Connecticut. From these descends the American Episcopal succession, which, on account of difficulties arising in England, but soon removed, Bishop White, of Philadelphia, has already been searching for, in the Lutheran Church of Denmark, where the succession was confessedly broken in the sixteenth century.

Since that time the Anglican church has formally established itself in the United States, under the name of the Protestant Episcopal Church, and has made, not very rapid, but quiet and steady progress.

It does not properly correspond so well as the Puritan and Presbyterian churches to republican institutions; and on account of the English sympathies, which a large number of its clergy cherished for very obvious reasons, during the Revolutionary war, it incurred suspicion of a want of patriotism, and was, therefore, for a long time unpopular. Yet, it has in its favor stanch old English traditions, an important theological and practical religious literature, and a name of renown even in the history of America — for Washington, for instance, and most of the great statesmen of Virginia, belonged to it — and by its compact, imposing, and personally responsible form of government, and its liturgical worship, without any special missionary efforts, it has a strong attraction for the higher classes and the polite, yet would-be religious world. It may be called, in a certain sense, the aristocratic and fashionable church of the United States, which, however, involves at the same time a serious defect, since in the church of Christ all distinctions of society ought to disappear in the feeling of common guilt and common salvation, and before the awful realities of the eternal world. From its clergy the President chooses most of the chaplains for the army and navy. In the country, in the lower orders of society, and in the west, it has very feeble hold; but in the great cities of the east it is wealthy and strong. In New York, for example, it possesses, not by any means the most intelligence and piety — in these it must yield to the Presbyterian — but the greatest outward splendor, the most imposing and costly churches, and the fattest livings. With a mass of high-flying men of the world, who attend its worship merely for fashion's sake, and perhaps also for the music, but never think of such a thing as thorough conversion, it numbers among its members many truly pious persons, whose religious life is more evenly and harmoniously formed, than that of most Puritans. The large accession which the Episcopal Church continually receives from other denominations, is, by no means, to be referred entirely to outward considerations, but, in many cases, to deeper inward grounds. Many laymen, and even Puritanically or Methodistically educated clergymen, pass over to it, because they see in it the true mean between the extremes of Puritanism and Romanism, and because they think, that it alone equally meets both the evangelical Protestant and the Catholic interests. Yet many such Episcopal clergymen, who have come from other Protestant denominations, have been driven by the same desire for a fixed objective ecclesiasticism and a liturgical altarservice, beyond this *via media* into the Roman camp.

I will now briefly present the leading features of this denomination and its differences from the mother church.

The Protestant Episcopal Church is primarily the natural continuation of the English established or national Church, which broke off from Rome under Henry VIII, and was afterwards under Edward VI, and especially under Queen

Elizabeth, fixed in its present form.* Its peculiarity, it is well known, consists in this: that in the work of reformation it took not only the Bible, but also church antiquity for its rule, and hence did not push its changes so far as the Protestant churches on the continent and in Scotland, but took a middle position between the two great opposites. It is, so to speak, the result of a treaty or compromise between the Catholic and Evangelical Protestant principles, outwardly secured by the Erastian principle, or the supremacy of the crown. On the one hand, in the Thirty-nine Articles it is Protestant, and indeed moderately Calvinistic, therefore Reformed; in many points, as the observance of the Sabbath and aversion to pictures, the cross and altar, it shows even the influence of Puritanism. On the other hand it is essentially Catholic in its episcopal hierarchy (though deprived, to be sure, of the papal head, to make room for a royal papacy) and in its liturgy, which with only the omission of some specifically Roman elements, is an altogether faithful compilation and an uncommonly successful translation of the old Catholic church prayers and formularies. Thus it stretches out one hand to Geneva, the other to Rome. It does not bring the two principles into vital, organic union, but merely into juxta-position. It is not a work of one design and moulding, but, as it were, an unfinished pile of heterogeneous materials, and yet the mightiest and most influential national church which Protestantism can show, and the one which can most nearly rival Rome. It is not the beating heart and the thinking head, but the right arm and the political and social bulwark of Protestantism.

Hence, there have always been in this church two parties, which have as little real communion with one another as two separate confessions; and which both have equal ground

* The designation "High-church," as still frequently used in German works for the Church of England, is altogether wrong. "High-church," in English, is not a noun at all, but an adjective, denoting only a particular party in the Anglican church, opposed to the Low-church party.

in the symbols and history of the church, and are on the
other hand equally inconsistent. The High-church party,
which for the last twenty years has been most earnestly and
worthily represented by Puseyism, takes its stand on the
episcopal constitution and the theory of apostolic succession,
and more than all on the Book of Common Prayer. In spite
of all its defects, we regard this book as a truly national
English work, and — excepting perhaps the German church
poetry — the greatest production of Protestantism in the
sphere of worship. It is known and venerated as far as the
English tongue extends, even by non-episcopalians, for its
admirable language, if for nothing else, in regard to which
it stands related to English literature as Luther's translation
of the Bible to German. If now this party should pursue only
the churchly, priestly, and sacramental element, it must run
into Romanism; and many Puseyites, following their former
learned leader, Dr. Newman, have in fact gone over to the
Roman Church. But there are also fortunate and morally
estimable inconsistencies; and in matters of religious conviction one ought not to follow merely the laws of logic — otherwise the most rational were always the most true — but to
regard other far deeper considerations. The Low-church
party stands with equal right on that thoroughly Protestant
symbol, the Thirty-nine Articles of the Anglican church, and
can appeal to its reformers and many of its greatest bishops
and divines, who were not only Calvinistic in the doctrine of
election, but even in part at least Zuinglian in the doctrine of
the sacraments. In logical consistency this party ought to be
Presbyterian or Puritanical in its fanatical hatred of everything Catholic, and in many respects it actually is so in
principle; but at the same time it still cleaves with honest
love to the episcopal constitution and to that "venerable
daughter of the Bible," the Book of Common Prayer.

Thus there are unreconciled antagonisms in the Anglican
Church. It contains, in some sense, the material for a Protes-

tant Catholicism or Catholic Protestantism; but it lacks that unity of principle and idea, which inwardly reconciles the antagonism, and brings the Catholic and Evangelical elements together into an organic whole. I know some young, talented, and amiable Episcopal clergymen in America, some of them educated in German theology and philosophy, who feel this want, and see more or less clearly, that above the abstract antagonism of the stiff objectivity of the high church party and the arbitrary subjectivity of the low church, a third party must form itself, which shall combine the elements of truth on both sides, give their due weight to the interests of both objective and subjective, Catholic and Protestant Christianity, and thus reconcile the two. These gentlemen sympathize most with Hare, Trench, Maurice, Kingsley, Alford, Conybeare, Howson, and such English divines, who cannot be numbered with either of the extreme parties, and have therefore been called the Broad-Church School.

This general character the American Episcopal Church shares throughout with her mother in England. The whole Puseyite controversy, one of the most remarkable and important phenomena in the history of Protestantism, somewhat analogous to that of the more recent strictly confessional Lutheranism in Germany, was long ago transplanted to American soil, whither indeed the vibrations of all European movements at once extend. Almost half the Episcopal ministers there are more or less Puseyistic, and several among them, even a bishop (Dr. Ives of North Carolina, a well-meaning, but weak man), disgusted with Protestantism, which they have never fully understood, have, like many of kindred mind in England, deserted to the Roman camp; while most content themselves with the idea of an Anglo-Catholicism, in hope of a future closer union with the Eastern churches and the Roman bishop as patriarch of the West. The antagonism and party spirit of the high-church and low-church sections, reveal themselves in America even in all the elections of bishops and in all the diocesan and general conventions; yet a formal rupture has thus far been avoided. They have had much to do, also, with the late scandalous processes, to which some high-church bishops, the now justly deposed Onderdonk of New York and the still acting Doane of New Jersey, who holds his office on a sort of confession of his guilt in squandering other people's money for his educational establishment at Burlington, have been subjected by their colleagues, primarily for moral offences. These trials have seriously injured the Puseyite party in public opinion; yet they show at the same time, that this church still exercises a discipline, which even a prelate, in high official station, cannot escape. It must also be as readily conceded, that Puseyism has infinitely more worthy representatives, than either of the above-named prelates, who have acquired a celebrity, anything but enviable, more by their outward position, than in any other way.

But with this general resemblance to the English Church, the American Episcopal Church has certain peculiarities growing out of her condition there, which give her even an advantage over her still far larger and more powerful mother in England. We refer not to the inconsiderable omissions in the liturgy (the Athanasian Creed, the prayers for the royal family, the services which relate to the death of Charles I, the restitution of the Stuarts in 1660, and the gunpowder treason under James I), most of which her altered political condition has required; but to modifications in the whole organization and government.

In the first place, by its separation from the state it is entirely relieved of the inconsistency of a royal lay episcopacy, or the ecclesiastical supremacy of the crown, as it is called, which in England, to add to the absurdity, resides at present, as formerly in the days of the maiden Elizabeth, in a woman; and the relative passages in the Thirty-nine Articles, the Liturgy and the Canons have been stricken out, or essentially modified. The Protestant Episcopal Church in the United States has full freedom, and the invaluable right of self-government. This was wrested from the Anglican church by Henry VIII, when he cut off from the hierarchy the Roman head and set his own tyrant head on the bleeding stump. True the convocation or legislative synods continued; but they stood altogether under the authority of Parliament and the crown. Since 1717 they have sunk to a mere shadow and solemn farce; and the earnest endeavors of some of the Puseyite party under bishop Wilberforce of Oxford to revive them, have, at least thus far, been frustrated by the obstinate opposition of the Erastians or emperor-papists.

Then, again, the American Episcopal Church has full lay representation — a Presbyterian element — which we must likewise regard as a decided advantage.

Its organization is this: It is divided into dioceses according to the political divisions of the country, the names of the dioceses corresponding to the number and names of the States; while the Roman Catholics name their sees after the larger cities. Only the great State of New York, has two dioceses — an eastern and a western. At the head of each diocese stands a bishop, who is usually at the same time rector of one of the more important congregations, and is in part supported by it, or draws his salary from the interest of a special fund, or, if there is no such fund, or if it is not sufficient, from the annual collections made by his Presbyters. Every spring he assembles all the Presbyters of his district, with as many lay delegates as there are parishes, in a diocesan convention. He, as president, opens the convention with *a charge*, consisting of a statistical report of his official labors during the past year, with appropriate exhortations, and sometimes theological expositions. Here all the affairs of the diocese are attended to. To this body belongs also the power of electing the bishop of the diocese, of choosing a standing committee as his council, and of presenting him for trial.

Every three years the General Convention, as it is called, assembles in one of the larger cities of the Union, for the most part in New York and Philadelphia alternately. Agreeably to the arrangement of the old English convocations and of the British Parliament and the American Congress, this convention consists of two houses, an upper, or the house of Bishops (now numbering thirty-one or two), which sits with closed doors, and is presided over by the oldest or senior bishop — for there are no archbishops as in England — and a lower, or the house of clerical and lay deputies, which is composed of an equal number of Presbyters and lay delegates from all the dioceses, none being allowed to send more than four of each order, and which holds its deliberations in open church. This triennial General Convention is the supreme judicatory of the Episcopal Church in all matters of doctrine, worship and discipline. The concurrence of both houses is necessary to the enactment of a law. The vote is counted by dioceses. The house of bishops has a veto upon the acts of the lower house. This power may prevent many useful reforms but also many useless changes or dangerous innovations, especially in an age and country, which has a morbid passion for law-making.

All this now looks very well on paper. But in reality one has to observe with regret, that at these conventions, as is true indeed also of Presbyterian synods, and as must be said perhaps still more of the ancient ecumenical councils, to say nothing at all of the Council of Trent — too must party spirit and passion appear, too much of the notorious *odium theologicum*, all sorts of intrigue and worldly policy, and an unhealthy tendency to empty declamation and immature and unprofitable legislation; so that the idea has already been suggested of having these conventions only once in ten years. Yet the free synodal constitution, with all its evils, which flow from sinful flesh, and are in fact incident to every other form of government, we far prefer to a slavish dependence of the church on the temporal power and the changing humors of individuals; and we believe, that its advantages and its happy influence in awakening and promoting the general life of the church infinitely outweigh its defects.

Though the party impulses in this church, its exclusiveness, its pedantry, its high pretensions, especially with its obvious deficiency in original contributions to theological science, are much to be lamented; yet it has also many excellences and advantages, occupies a very important conservative position in American Christianity, and has, perhaps, of all Protestant denominations the best prospects of ultimate success in the United States. There is at present a movement on foot, headed by several worthy and even high-church Presbyters, but not favored, as it seems, by the bishops, of increasing the efficiency and popularity of this church, by allowing greater liberty in the use of the Prayer Book, with the privilege of preferring even free prayers in certain cases; by providing a greater variety of forms for many occasions; by relaxing somewhat the rigor of the Episcopal succession theory, and entering into a more liberal and friendly relation to other evangelical churches. In this way, it is thought, the Episcopal Church, which was heretofore almost exclusively confined to the higher classes of society, and has rather discouraged the poor man from joining it, would be able to reach the masses, and accomplish a much greater amount of good among the American people.

(e) THE METHODISTS

In the bosom of the Church just described has arisen, since 1729, Methodism, the third great movement of religious reform in England. It forms almost as important an epoch in the development and application of the Protestant principle, as the Puritanic revolution in the seventeenth century; while now on the other hand Puseyism represents the counter movement of Anglicanism towards Catholicism, and is therefore mainly, though by no means wholly, retrograde. Methodism, however, may almost as well be called an American product, as an English. Its founders, John Wesley and George Whitefield, themselves labored a long time as clergymen of the Episcopal Church in Georgia; and the latter, who died in New England (1770), went through all the colonies repeatedly, as a genuine evangelist and a powerful revival preacher; ever testifying against natural depravity with awful earnestness, as in the immediate presence of heaven and hell, and warning men to turn from the gaping abyss; everywhere, as lightning, striking the conscience, and kindling new divine life — an incalculable blessing to his whole age. In fact Methodism established itself independently in America, even before it did in England, although the first Methodist congregation was not founded before 1766 in New York. Confessedly it originally contemplated no separation from the Evangelical establishment, but only a revival of that church. It aimed not to make itself a distinct sect, but, at most, like the German Pietism, an *ecclesiola in ecclesia*, and especially to introduce practical religion among the dreadfully neglected lower classes of the people. But when the American colonies declared themselves independent, and thus all connection was dissolved between the Episcopal Church and England, an emergency presented itself which John Wesley, then already eighty years old, who had openly disapproved the war for liberty, and thus drawn upon himself the sarcastic censure of that well-known yet unknown political writer, Junius, thought could be met only by a departure from the usual church order; and he, though only a Presbyter of the Anglican church, on his own responsibility, in 1784, ordained one of his friends and fellow Presbyters, Dr. Coke, bishop or superintendent of his American Methodist Societies, and by this act gave them the character of an independent religious body, which has since borne the name of the Methodist Episcopal Church. At the same time he made an abridgment of the Common Prayer Book and the Thirty-nine Articles, as a directory for the worship and doctrine of this new organization.

However we may think of this bold step, which was, in any case, an ecclesiastical irregularity, like Luther's ordination of Nicolas of Amsdorf, as bishop of Naumburg, and the ordination of Teasel by Œcolampadius; it is obvious, that Methodism has, since then, grown with uncommon rapidity, and is one of the most important facts in the modern history of Protestant christendom. It has not been entirely without influence, even on the Anglican mother church. The active zeal of the evangelical or low-church party for practical Christianity and missions is, at least in part, an effect of the Methodistic movement. In America, this has had, perhaps, of all sections of the church, next to Puritanism, the greatest influence on the general religious life, and especially, as we shall hereafter see, on the German churches. It must be regarded as the chief author and promoter of *revivals*. These, in this particular form, are peculiar to that country, and date from the time of Whitefield and Jonathan Edwards. They commonly appear in "camp-meetings," and "protracted meetings," and sometimes spread, as by contagion, over whole districts. The Methodist is, at all events, one of the most numerous denominations in America, perhaps the most numerous, and in the State of Indiana it even controls the political elections. It has uncommon energy and activity; and enjoys an organization eminently fitted for great general enterprises and systematic, successful cooperation. Its preachers have, in general, little or no scientific culture, but, on an average, a decided aptness for popular discourse and exhortation, and they often compensate by fidelity and self-denial for their want of deeper knowledge. They are particularly fitted for breaking the way in new regions, for aggressive missionary pioneer service, and for laboring among the lower classes of the people. Their zeal, however, is very frequently vitiated by impure motives of proselytism, and indulges in the boldest aggressions on other churches, thinking that it alone can really convert. Amongst the negroes, too, both free and slave, Methodism has most influence, and seems, with its emotional excitements, well adapted to their sanguine, excitable temperament. Formerly, appealing to the apostles and evangelists of the primitive church, it used to condemn learning and theology from principle, as dangerous to practical piety; and to boast, that its preachers had "never rubbed their backs against the walls of a college," and yet knew the better how to catch fish in the net of the kingdom of God. But in this respect, a considerable change has been, for some years, going on. The Methodists are now beginning to establish colleges and seminaries, to publish scientific periodicals, and to follow the steps of the culture of the age. But it is a question whether they will not thus lose more in their peculiar character and influence with the masses, than they will gain in the more cultivated circles.

The Methodist Episcopal Church in the United States has been divided since 1847 into two almost equal parts, a northern and a southern. These have broken off all intercommunion, and have recently had a vexatious lawsuit about the division of the common property. The sole cause of the separation was slavery. The Methodists of the northern and western States are mostly abolitionists, and would not suffer that their brethren in the south should hold, buy, and sell immortal men as property.

In its character, Methodism holds the same relation, both in light and shade, to English Christianity, as the Pietism of Spener and Francke to the German; and it stands towards the Episcopal Church just as this Pietism does towards the Lutheran, except that it is organized as a distinct sect, while Pietism still forms only a party within the Lutheran and

German Reformed churches. Hence it takes most with the Würtemberg emigrants, among whom there are so many Pietists. Wesley himself had been in Germany. He was acquainted with the German church hymns, many of which he reproduced in English (as he afterwards did Bengel's Gnomon in his Commentary on the New Testament), and was at first in very close intercourse with Zinzendorf and the Moravian Brethren, to whom he owed much, though he afterwards separated from them. Whitefield particularly admired the Francke Orphan House, and endeavored to found one like it in Georgia.

Methodism and Pietism have in common an earnest interest for subjective experimental religion, repentance, conversion, regeneration; and this in a particular way or method (whence the name Methodism). The reigning spirit of the system demands for a full "getting through," violent birth-throes, a powerful struggle of repentance, a definite sum of experiences of sin and grace, and commonly also a distinct recollection of the time and place of regeneration or conversion; — for with the Methodists these two are the same. They entirely reject the doctrine of election, and frequently preach from the pulpit against Calvinism. They are Arminian, and teach, often even to the extreme of Pelagianism, the freedom and accountability of the human will, the possibility of resisting and losing the divine grace, and the possibility and relative necessity of repeated regenerations. This, it is well known, was the main reason of Wesley's final separation from Whitefield; the latter decidedly holding the doctrine of predestination, though in his sermons he never made imprudent use of it. In other respects the confession of Methodism is a simplification of the Thirty-nine Articles; and the Wesleyans, in England at least, have retained much even of the Book of Common Prayer, while their brethren in America are in this matter also more free and radical, and are almost entirely addicted to extemporaneous prayer.

139

Yet, after all, there is a very considerable difference between Methodism and Pietism, founded in the difference between the English and German national character.

Methodism lacks throughout the German depth, and inwardness, the contemplative turn for the mystical, and a vigorous, fruitful, and profound theology; while on the other hand, it far surpasses Pietism in energetic outward activity, going forth to conquest. They are related in this respect like Martha and Mary, Peter and John.

While Pietism contents itself with working as salt within the church, and in the use of the ordinary means of grace, Methodism has a complete, separate, and indeed in its way admirable organization. John Wesley was not only a pungent preacher, but also a legislative genius, an exceedingly shrewd, skillful business man; while his brother Charles, the sweet writer of spiritual songs, was of a more inward, reflective turn, and in this respect supplied the defect of the other. Had John lived in the Middle Age, or in the Roman church, he would have been, without doubt, like Dominicus, Francis of Assisi, and Ignatius of Loyola, the founder of a great monastic order; and had the Anglican church rightly understood and appreciated him, and possessed the tact which the Roman shows in such cases, it would not only not have persecuted Methodism, but would have formally sanctioned and patronized it as a society for home and foreign missions, and thus prevented a secession.*

The constitution, drawn up by John Wesley, but afterwards in many respects modified and developed, is in principle entirely hierarchical, and is so far in remarkable contrast with the political republicanism of the United States.

* Says Macaulay in his brilliant article on Ranke's History of the Popes: "At Rome the Countess of Huntingdon would have a place in the Calendar as St. Selinda, and Mrs. Fry would be foundress and first Superior of the Blessed Order of the Tails. Place Ignatius Loyola at Oxford. He is certain to become the head of a formidable secession. Place John Wesley at Rome. He is certain to be the first General of a new society devoted to the interests and honor of the Church."

It has often been remarked, that Methodism is a full Protestant counterpart to the order of Jesuits in the Roman Church.
The legislative power resides in the general conference,
which consists of a certain number of delegates from the
annual conferences of the various districts; the executive,
in bishops and presiding elders. The Anglican theory of
apostolic succession, however, of course falls away; for the
first Methodist bishop was never Episcopally ordained. It
is thus not an Episcopacy exclusively of principle, but of
order and expediency, as with the Moravian Brethren. The
congregations are entirely passive, and have not even a voice
in the choice of their minister. The clergymen themselves
are in their turn wholly dependent on the presiding elders
and bishops, and must have their stations changed by them
every two years; so that a continual rotation is established,
and no room given for a really close union, a patriarchal
relation, between pastor and people. Hence, also, the clergymen are not supported exclusively by their congregations,
but partly from the common Conference funds, for which,
however, collections in the congregations are required, and
from the proceeds of their large Book Concern in New York.
They receive a moderate but respectable and fixed salary for
themselves, their wives, and each of their children; the income rising with the growth of the family. Then the super-
numerary and superannuated clergymen, and missionaries,
and the widows and orphans of deceased ministers, are well
provided for by a large and well-managed sustentation fund
for the purpose. In addition to this ministry, Methodism has
the faculty of employing the gifted and experienced laity in
a sort of clerical activity, using them very successfully as
local preachers and class-leaders — a work, which then commonly forms, for the more talented, the stepping stone to the
proper clerical office, and a practical preparation for it.

The hierarchical character of the Methodist Church constitution is, on the one hand, its strength and one main cause

141

of its success and compactness. But, on the other hand, it is ever provoking reactions in the suppressed lay element, and has already produced several secessions in England and America. The largest sect which has gone out from it in (1830), and has exchanged the Episcopal constitution for a tolerably independent one, is the Protestant Methodist Church, commonly called Radical Methodists. A still more dangerous and probably incurable schism has appeared within the last few years among the Wesleyans in England, and has thrown them into the greatest excitement.

In worship, Methodism is not satisfied with the usual divinely ordained means of grace. It really little understands the use of the Sacraments, though it adheres traditionally to infant baptism, and four times a year celebrates the Lord's Supper, as a simple commemoration. It has far more confidence in subjective means and exciting impressions, than in the more quiet and unobserved but surer work of the old church system of educational religion. The main point with it is always effect on the sinner by special efforts of the preacher; and with this view it has invented and perfected, especially in America, a machinery for the purpose, altogether foreign to Pietism — the system of what is called *new measures*. This includes not only prayer-meetings — an institution as old, by the way, as Christianity, and only invested by Methodism with a particular meaning and importance; but also and especially camp-meetings, commonly held in forests or under tents, often for weeks together in a good season of the year; protracted meetings, which may be held also in the church and in the winter season, and are designed to compensate for the regularly returning church festivals rejected by the Methodists, as by the Puritans; class-meetings, anxious or inquiry meetings on appointed week days for the interchange of religious experience, and a special personal conversation with anxious sinners (a kind of substitute for the Roman Catholic confessional); and, finally, the anxious-bench, a genuine modern American invention, *i. e.*, a seat before the pulpit, to which after sermon the penitent hearers are invited, and where they are pressed with special exhortations, and wrought up to the most intense nervous excitement, till the new life "breaks through," and then the sense of forgiving grace often vents itself in a jubilee of ecstacy, as boisterous as the violent lamentations, groans, and not rarely convulsions, in which the sense of sin had just before found utterance.

One can conceive how many of these "new measures," some of which are, however, only modifications of old ones, may, under wise direction, be very powerful means of awakening and promoting religious life. I well remember what favorable representations I had made to myself of a Methodist camp-meeting before my removal to America. The idea of a great assembly in the forest by moonlight, and under heaven's blue, starry dome of peace, devoutly listening to the solemn warnings and precious promises of the divine word, wrestling with the Lord in fervent prayer, like Jacob at Jabbok, till break of day, and filling the vast silence of nature, that living temple of God, with the praises of the crucified and risen Friend of sinners — is sublime and captivating. And preaching in the open street and the markets, in the large cities, where churches are wanting, may be a real duty, which the societies for Inner Missions in Germany ought particularly to consider. Nor have I a moment's doubt, that in those exciting Methodist meetings, and even on the anxious-bench, many thorough conversions, and still more superficial but real awakenings, needing further care, have taken place. But unfortunately in reality very much that is human and impure, mingles itself in, and these new measures have led to the most injurious outbreaks of religious fanaticism; above all they have nourished a most dangerous distrust of the ordinary means of grace, the calm preaching of the Word, the sacraments, and catechetical instruction. The

143

Methodists reject not only confirmation, as a useless or hypo-critical form, but also the idea of objective baptismal grace; and they often dreadfully neglect all religious training of children, in the vain, presumptuous expectation that some exciting revival-sermon in a camp-meeting or a few hours on the anxious-bench, will answer the purpose of the tedious process of parental discipline and care, and regular pastoral instruction. No wonder that, under such influences, the young generation grows up rude and immoral, and that in many districts where the quick straw fire of Methodistic revivals has burned brightly, it has left a complete desola-tion, with frivolous mockery of all religion.

The new measures have passed from Methodism into other churches, the German among the rest, and are there very frequently still more wantonly abused. The Lutheran and Reformed have, however, within the last twelve years, at least in the eastern States, almost entirely come back from these wild extravagances, feeling that they do not correspond to the genius of their church; and they have returned to the good old measures, which in the end prove better, than the most artistic stimulants of human invention. The flourishing period of new measures is now, in general, pretty much past, and even among the Methodists the swollen stream of reli-gious excitement seems to be again seeking its natural, fixed channels, especially in the more cultivated city congrega-tions, which have never really approved those unwholesome excesses.

(f) THE GERMAN CHURCHES *

It is commonly estimated, that the Germans in the United States, including their English-speaking descendants, num-

* In the original volume, which was designed for Germany, this section stands as a distinct third part, of almost equal compass with the present second part. It is here abridged, to give the work its due proportion for the general American reader. — TRANSLATOR.

ber now, at least, four millions; thus forming almost one-sixth of the whole population.

But the strength of the German churches ought not to be estimated accordingly. These Germans are scattered over all the Union, especially the middle and western States, and divided into a multitude of sects. They have not naturally the practical talent for organization, and, under the State-church system of their fatherland, did not learn how to take care of themselves. They emigrated, with few exceptions, not from religious, but from secular motives. Perhaps more than half the later emigrants are almost entire strangers to Christianity. And finally, the German emigrants have been ecclesiastically left almost entirely to themselves by the mother churches. These things fully explain why the German churches of America are yet in their childhood, compared with the Presbyterian, the Congregational, or the Protestant Episcopal, at least in general culture, social influence, and church activity.

Nevertheless, I am firmly convinced, on account of the number of pious and educated Germans and Anglo-Germans, which is now considerable, and is rapidly growing; on account of the late great increase of life and activity among them; on account of the decrease of transition to the English churches, and the growing sense of their peculiar calling; that the German church and theology in America have a highly important work, which they alone can properly fulfill.

The great body of German Christianity in the trans-Atlantic world belongs to Protestantism, and to the Protestant Germans we shall accordingly confine ourselves. Perhaps one-fourth, at most one-third, of the emigrants, particularly from Bavaria, Würtemberg, Baden, the Rhenish provinces, and Austria, may be Roman Catholics. The German Protestants, however, are, like Protestantism itself, much divided, and represent almost all branches of the church in the

145

mother country. The great mass belong to the Lutheran and Reformed confessions. Besides these there are the United Church, the Moravian Brethren, and the older sects, as the Mennonites, Tunkers, and Schwenkfeldians; with several others of American and mostly Methodistic origin, the Albright Brethren, the United Brethren, the German missions of the Methodist Episcopal Church, and a few Baptist congregations.

The German emigration to America began in the time of Penn, about 1680, and directed itself particularly to the colony of Pennsylvania, which is accordingly, to this day, the principal theatre of the German-American churches. The ecclesiastical organization did not begin till towards the middle of the last century. It was mainly the work of Count Zinzendorf, the Lutheran pastor Mühlenberg, a missionary of the Halle Orphan House, and the Reformed pastor, Schlatter, of St. Gallen, who was sent about the same time, by the Dutch Reformed Church, as a missionary to the Germans in Pennsylvania. These three worthy men may be regarded as the patriarchs of American German Protestantism. Various causes — the rise of Rationalism in Germany, and wars in Europe and America, the cessation of emigration, and of the interest of the mother church for her distant children, want of educational institutions and embarrassing ignorance of the English language — brought the German church in America to a stand, and occasioned the transition of many of its children, especially of the richer and more influential families, to the Presbyterian, Episcopal, or Methodist bodies; though, on the other hand, its separation from Germany saved it from Rationalism, and left it firm in the pious traditions of the fathers. About 1820, it was awakened from its lethargy, first by the influence of the Anglo-American churches, then by the fresh stream of renewed emigration, which, with much bad, brought also much good from the newly-awakened Christian life of Germany. Under the influence of Puritanic Presbyterianism and Methodism, favored by the irresistible spread of the English language even into purely German settlements, this newly-aroused life at first bore, and still, in some measure bears, a predominantly English character, partly Puritanic, partly Methodistic, and was for a while in danger of losing its peculiarity, especially the churchly elements of German Protestantism, its liturgy, festivals, catechetical training, confirmation, mystical view of the Lord's Supper, &c. But of late, since about 1840, the German church has vigorously awakened to a sense of her origin, history, and mission, and has revealed what we may term a decided evangelical-catholic and Anglo-Germanic tendency, occupying itself with some of the weightiest religious problems of the age, establishing theological and literary institutions, and beginning to exert an influence even on the Anglo-American communions. Emigration also has very rapidly increased since the close of the Napoleonic wars, and has of late so swelled as to attract the attention of the German governments and American statesmen, and to involve one of the most important social questions of the age. The number of German emigrants to the United States at present averages at least 150,000 a year, and surpasses now that of every other nation, even the Irish.

These emigrants by no means at once exchange their language for the English; and the conflict of the two tongues is a peculiar phenomenon and a great practical difficulty in the history of the American German church. That the German language, unless constantly reinforced by emigration, must gradually become extinct as a medium of popular intercourse in the United States, is inevitable; not on account of any outward prohibition of its use; but through the irresistible silent influence of the English tongue, which seems destined and better fitted than any other, to become the universal language for the Western Hemisphere; and through the working of that mysterious energy, by which

147

all the nationalities of the Old World are fusing into a peculiar American national character. In very many Lutheran and German Reformed congregations of Pennsylvania, New York, Maryland, Virginia, Ohio, and even further out, the English language is now either mostly or exclusively used in worship; and it is due to truth to say, that these congregations are often among the most active and zealous of their confessions. In most cases the transition to the English language and customs is at the same time an advance in cultivation and piety. In the older counties of Pennsylvania there has existed for perhaps a century, a dialect formed by a singular cross between the Palatinate German and the English, which, though it has passed from Pennsylvania into other States, may be termed, from its origin, Pennsylvania German. The foreign elements consist of unchanged English words, Germanized forms of English words and expressions, and literally translated English idioms and phrases. Characteristic of the two nationalities is this yielding of the German language to the English; while in the midst of German settlements, the English has appropriated only two German expressions: souerkrout and smierkäs! Such corruption of the German tongue is commonly in America the bridge to its extinction.

But the extinction of the German even as a popular language, must be put at least a hundred years in the future, on account of the vast and still increasing emigration. And then again, this language is, like the Greek and Latin, probably destined to even a distinct perpetuity as a learned language and a means of higher intellectual culture, on account of its exceedingly copious and valuable literature in all branches of science and poesy.

This contact of the two languages is a source of great difficulty and constant collisions in the German churches, often involving even the passionate and bitter opposition of narrow Native-Americanism and bigoted Europeanism. The

148

native Germans are often strenuous for even the exclusive use of the German in worship; the native Americans are as strenuous for the English. The only true position here is what we may call the Anglo-Germanic, allowing both languages their due, and working towards a higher religious union of both the nationalities, which Providence has thrown together in America undoubtedly to be thus united.

Of the several branches of German-American Protestantism, we place first.

(1) THE LUTHERAN CHURCH. — This is the most numerous and, in its origin and history, the most German of all. Its organized existence in America dates from the middle of the previous century, when Dr. Mühlenberg, a missionary of the Halle Orphan House, collected the long present but neglected material into congregations, and (A. D. 1748) laid the foundation of what was called the United Ministry, and of the still existing Pennsylvania Synod of the Evangelical Lutheran church. It drew its material from almost all the German countries, first from the Palatinate, afterwards mainly from Wütemberg, Baden, Alsace, Bavaria, Hannover, the Saxon provinces, and from Sweden and Norway. Though a multitude of nominal Lutherans in America, as the older emigrants from Sweden and Norway, have gone over to other communions, as the Episcopal and Methodist, yet this church has, within the last ten or twenty years, grown with great rapidity; and if its internal condition and its influence had corresponded with its numbers, it must have already been counted among the leading denominations in America. It stretches over all the Middle and Western States, and some of the Southern. According to its latest statistical reports, it numbers near nine hundred ministers, and perhaps thrice as many congregations. It has eight theological seminaries, five colleges, or at least beginnings of colleges, and nine periodicals, four in English and five in German. Its home missionary field is larger than that of any other Ameri-

can denomination, and its missionary spirit and liberality is growing every year.

The multifarious differences of opinion and schools in this body, representing almost all those of the mother church, besides specifically American tendencies, make it no easy matter to describe the character and internal condition of the Lutheran confession. Leaving out of view unimportant and local fractions, we may distinguish in general three divisions, which we may briefly style the New Lutheran, the Old Lutheran, and the Moderate Lutheran or Melancthonian.

The New Lutheran party is an amalgamation of Lutheranism with American Puritanic and Methodistic elements. It consists chiefly of native Americans of German descent, and hence prides itself on being emphatically the American Lutheran Church. It is perhaps the most numerous, at any rate the most active, practical, and progressive, and indeed almost entirely English, not only in its language, but in all its sympathies and antipathies. It makes little of thorough theological education, and much of oratorical talent, practical activity, and business tact. To it properly belong the literary institutions at Gettysburg, Pa., Springfield, O., Springfield, Ill.; and it has thus far spoken the great word in the General Synod.

The Old Lutheran section consists of a portion of the more recent emigrants from Saxony, Prussia, Bavaria, and other countries. They are still entirely German, having not yet amalgamated at all with the English and American body; though they outwardly prosper very well, if we are to judge from the rapid increase of their ministers and congregations. Their pastors are mostly well instructed, faithful, conscientious, and self-denying, though, except in cases of happy inconsistency, very exclusive, and narrow-minded, and unable or unwilling to appreciate properly other churches and nationalities than their own. Luther is their highest human authority; and indeed, not the free, bold, world-shaking reformer, but the reactionary, scrupulous, intolerant Luther, who at Marburg refused Zuingle's hand of brotherhood offered with tears. In their congregations they maintain a certain discipline and order, and are zealous for the parochial school. Over the experimenting New Lutherans they have the advantage of a fixed principle, a well-formed doctrinal basis, and general logical consistency. They are, however, not harmonious. The office question, which has thrown even the strictly symbolical Lutherans of Germany into discord, in spite of all their boasted doctrinal compactness and unity, has arrayed them against each other in two parties, the Synod of Missouri and the Synod of Buffalo, which wage a newspaper war with a bitterness little creditable to Lutheranism and Christianity, and not at all fitted to inspire the Anglo-American, if ever he hears of it, with respect for this section of German Christendom. I refer to the controversy between the two views of the clerical office — one, the common Protestant view, which makes the clerical office only the organ of the general priesthood; the other, the Romanizing doctrine of a separate clerical office, resting on ordination, and specifically different from the general priesthood of the baptized.

The Moderate Lutheran tendency strikes a middle course between these two extremes, which are bound together only by the accident of name. It has the oldest American Lutheran tradition on its side; for the first missionaries came mostly from the Halle Orphan House and the Pietistic school of Spener and Francke, which is well known to have been never strictly symbolical, but somewhat latitudinarian in doctrine. It is represented by the oldest and largest Synod — the Pennsylvania — and to some extent also by the United Synod of Ohio. A considerable number of ministers in these and kindred synods, especially of the older men, have indeed very indefinite views, are uneducated and mentally indolent, and care more for their farms than for theology and the Church, and for the most part blindly follow some leading minds. But within a few years past a higher intellectual life and church activity has sprung up in the Pennsylvania Synod, which now includes some venerable old and promising young theologians, partly educated in America, others transferred from Europe. The true problem of this synod is to mediate, not only between the old churchly and the Puritanic Lutheranism, but at the same time between European-German, and American interests; and thus to facilitate a consolidation of the Lutheran Church in America. This it has only just rightly begun to do, by the recent passage of two important measures, viz.: acts of union with Gettysburg (by establishing a German professorship there), and with the General Synod, from both of which it had hitherto held off through strong, and in some cases not unfounded prejudices against the un-Lutheran and un-German spirit reigning in them.

The difference between these three grand divisions of American Lutheranism is more or less manifest in all departments of church life.

In the first place, in doctrine, and in the posture of the parties towards the symbolical books. The Old Lutheran Synods of Missouri and Buffalo, of course, like the strict Lutherans in Germany, hold the whole Book of Concord, laying special stress on the Formula Concordiæ, as the consistent logical continuation of the unaltered Augustana, and as precisely defining the pure Lutheran doctrine, both against the Reformed and the Roman Catholic churches. The Pennsylvania Synod contents itself with only the Augsburg confession and the smaller catechism of Luther. With these the Melancthonian tendency is safe; whereas, by the Form of Concord it is repudiated as crypto and semi-Calvinistic.

The New Lutherans, on the contrary, have, in reality,

entirely given up all the points which distinguished the Lutheran theology from the Reformed, substituting for the Calvinistic doctrine of predestination, however, the still un-Lutheran, Arminian theory of free will; while they not only retain the Lutheran opposition to Romanism, but run it to a Puritanic excess. True, the General Synod and the Gettysburg Seminary go upon a certain acknowledgement of the Augustana, but only as to substance of doctrine, therefore with a restricting *quatenus*, which of course leaves it to be twisted by every one according to his own notions. The zealous theological leader of this American Lutheranism has more particularly defined his own doctrinal position and that of his numerous disciples and brethren, stating as its main features: (1) Rejection of the binding authority of all Lutheran symbols except the Augsburg Confession; (2) Acknowledgement of the latter only as an expression, "in a manner substantially correct," of the cardinal doctrines of the Bible, which is the only infallible rule of faith and practice. He then rejects as unscriptural the following Lutheran doctrines and practices: exorcism; the doctrine of original sin and guilt; private or auricular confession, as taught in Luther's smaller catechism; the lax view of the Augustana respecting the Christian Sabbath; the Lutheran doctrine of baptism in its relation to regeneration and the Lord's Supper.

This last point of difference is the most important. For it was from this, in fact, that the separation of the two evangelical confessions began; and it was on this, that Luther, during the conference at Marburg, and on every other occasion, showed himself most unyielding. How completely is the case now reversed! When the Reformed Dr. Nevin, in 1846, vindicated the Calvinistic doctrine of a real spiritual presence, and a real participation by faith of the body and blood of Christ, that is, the life-power of his humanity, the editor of the "Lutheran Observer" attacked and ridiculed this view as Romanizing, superstitious, and senseless. Dr. Schmucker adopts the Puritanic, essentially Zuinglian theory prevalent in America, and in a special article on this subject, rejects not only the substantial, but even the dynamic or virtual presence of the human nature of the Redeemer, declaring, that "there is no real or actual presence of the glorified human nature of the Saviour, either substantial or influential, nor anything mysterious or supernatural in the Eucharist." Anywhere in Germany this would not even be called Zuinglianism, much less Lutheranism, but the purest Rationalism of common sense. Even Bretschneider and Wegscheider leave as much as this of that holy mystery of faith, that centre of the Christian worship. But in America the lowest and coldest views of the sacraments and the church are not seldom joined with orthodoxy on other points and much practical Christian zeal. The same is true also, to some extent, of the English Dissenters, nay, even of the Scotch Presbyterians and the Low-church Episcopalians; so also the leader of the Low-church American Lutheranism, though he has translated Storr's Dogmatic into an English abridgment, and has studied the Supranaturalistic literature of Germany, is, in his theology, properly altogether Anglo-American, partly after the Puritanic Presbyterian stamp, partly after the Methodistic, which appears in his Pelagianizing views of the freedom of the will, and his theory of conversion and regeneration; but he would feel highly insulted to be classed with the German Rationalists, since he holds the divinity of Christ, as well as the Divine inspiration and authority of the Holy Scriptures, as fundamental articles of faith. He has also endeavored to show that almost all the leading men of the Lutheran church of America, had no higher views of the sacraments than himself, and that even in the old Pennsylvania Synod very few rose above the Zuinglian theory; which may certainly, till within a few years, have been the case.

Since about the year 1848, however, a remarkable reaction has arisen in the bosom of this Anglo-American New Lutheranism, in consequence partly of the growing study of German theology, partly of occurrences in a sister church. Many of the best minds and the most influential disciples and friends of Gettysburg have forsaken their former views. In the first zeal of opposition to a pseudo-Lutheranism, they even inclined to the extreme of the exclusive Lutheranism of the Form of Concord. But it soon appeared that this could never rightly take root among Christians of the English tongue, and in such a country as America. It is, indeed, the Reformed confession in its various branches, especially the Calvinistic, which there forms the central stream of the Christian life; and in the face of this perfectly palpable fact, a theory which really lops off this confession from the tree of the kingdom of God, and treats it as a complication of heresis, seems a most glaring injustice, if not an absurdity, and destroys itself without giving any one the trouble of refuting it. Accordingly, on the pages of the Quarterly Evangelical Review — established in 1849, as the organ of this new orthodox churchly party of the Anglo-Lutherans — we see, for example, a vindication of the symbolical books in the spirit of Sartorius and Rudelbach, followed by a demonstration of their unscriptural errors, and of the entire impropriety of such clogs on Christian progress. This Quarterly is thus a faithful mirror of the unreconciled doctrinal antagonisms and the theological agitation, which have for the last six or eight years disturbed the English, and therefore most active and zealous, section of the American Lutheran Church. These controversies will, it is to be hoped, lead in time to fixed results, and, much as disputes among brethren are in themselves to be regretted, will certainly on the whole prove to be for the best.

In respect to church government, the Lutheran denomination presents as little unity as in doctrine. It is a con-

glomerate of Synods, not united, and in some cases overlapping, thus occasioning an almost hopeless confusion.
Thus, for example, within the territory of the Pennsylvania
Synod there are an East Pennsylvania Synod and a West
Pennsylvania, divided on the subject of new measures. There
are distant ministers in the State of New York belonging
not to the New York Synod, but to the Pennsylvania; and
ministers in Pennsylvania belonging to one of the two likewise overlapping synods of Ohio and Missouri; and the
reverse. This confusion results in part from doctrinal differences, in part from the unpractical, helpless character
of the Germans, who have never accomplished much anywhere in the matter of church government, being in fact
accustomed to regard it as of very little importance. In my
opinion, the different Lutheran Synods ought to be entirely
reorganized, their territories clearly separated and defined,
and a union of them established for common objects. This,
however, can never be done, till greater doctrinal unity
can be secured.

Such a union was attempted in the triennial General
Synod, instituted in 1820. This is now, especially since the
annexation of the most numerous Synod — the Old Pennsylvania — more worthy of the name than formerly; though
perhaps half the Lutheran Synods will still have nothing to
do with it, partly from opposition to the New Lutheran or
properly un-Lutheran tendency which formerly prevailed
in it, but has now already given way. The Old Lutheran
Synod of Missouri will, of course, never fall in, unless this
General Synod should make all the symbols, from the Augsburg Confession to the Form of Concord, the binding doctrinal basis, which it will never do. The General Synod,
however, assumes no legislative power, but only advisory.
It does not enter into doctrinal differences as such; though
these involuntarily intrude themselves even into purely

business discussions. It only aims at coöperation and greater efficiency in the causes of education and missions.

The constitution of the Lutheran church in America is in some sense a mean between synodal Presbyterianism and independent Congregationalism; a position which some regard as a great excellence, others, as half-way and undecided. The German consistorial system, resting on the basis of a royal episcopacy and supremacy, of course falls to the ground in a country where church and state are separated; and no one there seems to lament it much; for though large revenues cease with it, yet the freedom of the church, the freedom of all freedoms, is an estate so precious, that for the sake of it great disadvantages are gladly borne. A return to the Episcopal constitution is out of the question, in spite of the contact with a flourishing Episcopal church; for there are only very few and isolated sympathies in this direction, perhaps among the Scandinavian emigrants and some Old Lutherans. Even the system of superintendencies, to which these latter lean, would not rightly thrive there; and besides, this is only a defective substitute for the Episcopal supervision, which comes recommended by so old historical tradition. Thus there remains only the Reformed synodal and Presbyterial constitution, which certainly best answers the idea of an independent Protestant community, and has been also introduced into the Lutheran churches of the Rhine and Westphalia.

But the three leading features of Presbyterianism — the regular introduction of the laity into church government, the legislative authority of synods, and strict discipline — are still very imperfectly formed in the American Lutheran church. Besides the synod there is nothing but a ministerium, as it is called, consisting entirely of clergymen; the synods have only advisory power; the congregations are in many cases wholly independent and under no fixed system, and

157

in exclusively German churches all children are baptized and confirmed without any strict regard to religious qualifications, either in themselves or in their parents. Thus there is much room here also for further development in American Lutheranism.

Finally, as to worship and Christian life. In the first place, the Old Lutherans have a more or less complete liturgical altar-service, even with the crucifixes and candles burning in day-time; and in all such matters they cleave to historical tradition; while the New Lutherans incline to the Puritanic system of free prayer, the strict observance of Sunday, neglect of the church festivals, and of all symbolical rites and ceremonies; or they allow at most only a restricted use of liturgies, of which they have several, as well as a number of German and English hymn-books.

Then they disagree still more in reference to the means of awakening and promoting religious life in congregations, particularly in reference to the so-called "new measures," which we have already described in speaking of their native confession, Methodism. The New-Lutherans used these, especially the anxious bench, from about the year 1830, to the greatest extent, and not rarely with the wildest hyper-Methodistic excess; while not only the strictly symbolical Lutherans, but also the ministers and congregations of the Pennsylvania Synod, set themselves against them with the greatest decision. One might make a book on the anxious-bench controversy in the German church of America (for the Reformed church also was deeply agitated by it); though the task would hardly be a very profitable or interesting one. Very often, it is true, the opposition arose from religious indifferentism and lifeless formalism, and went again all living piety along with the Methodistic excesses. The healthy tendency here took a middle course, and insisted on the revival and maintenance of a solid churchly religious life, resting on sound knowledge, wrought through the old yet ever new and effective measures of the Word and the sacraments — in short, the means of grace not invented by men, but appointed by God himself, and accompanied by his blessing. This tendency is now constantly gaining the upperhand. The system of new measures has already outlived itself, and is almost confined to the Western States. The wild straw-fire has burned out; and what good there was in this Methodistic thunder-storm and whirlwind, has remained, and been taken up into a sound churchly life.

The Lutheran Church has an important calling in the new world. This it cannot fulfill by being unfaithful to its genius and history, and casting away its doctrinal and practical peculiarities; nor by thrusting them forward in rough opposition to the Reformed and English communions, and thus depriving itself of all influence on them; but by faithfully preserving its gifts, and at the same time proceeding in wise and cordial accommodation to the circumstances of a new country and people, and so making itself available and profitable both for the emigrants from its old home, and for the whole development of Anglo-American Christianity. Confused and unsatisfactory as its condition may appear in general and in detail to an outside observer, yet its rapid progress in latter years, and its great number of excellent, laborious, and self-denying clergymen, and plain, virtuous, and substantial laymen, give promise of a fair future before it.

(2) THE GERMAN REFORMED CHURCH. — If we take the word *Reformed* in its original sense in church-history, as including all the non-Lutheran Evangelical Protestants, the Reformed Church is the prevailing one in America. It exists there, however, not as one organization, but in various mutually independent bodies, which take their names either from their national origin (German Reformed, Dutch Reformed), or from their forms of government (Episcopal,

Presbyterian, Congregational). The German branch of this tree, which has struck deeper roots in Switzerland, France, Holland, England and Scotland, than in Germany, was transplanted to America, and organized there at the same time with Lutheranism; first in Pennsylvania. In language, manners, and customs, as well as in their general course of development, the two confessions are so closely allied, that the people and even many of the clergy in many places have lost almost all sense of difference. When Pennsylvania farmers are asked about it, they commonly answer: the Lutherans pray, "Vater Unser," the Reformed, "Unser Vater." The Reformed, as in the case also in Germany, are not near so numerous as the Lutherans, though in influence and efficiency they are not a whit behind them, and in some cases even in advance. The proper home of the German Reformed Church of America is the Palatinate, from which the first emigrants proceeded about the time of Penn. It receives accessions from the Rhenish provinces, from the different cantons of German Switzerland, and from Lippe, whither many worthy and earnest men emigrated some years ago, from attachment to the Heidelberg catechism and aversion to a rationalistic church administration. Many of the Unionists also attach themselves to this church; the majority, however, to Lutheran congregations or the Church Union of the West. Its main strength lies still in Pennsylvania, and next to this in Ohio, where it has made considerable progress within a few years. In Maryland, also, and Virginia, it numbers several good congregations; but lower south and far west it is as yet a weak plant, while in the states of New Jersey and New York it has permitted its material to be almost entirely absorbed by the Dutch and other denominations.

It is divided into two closely connected synods, an Eastern and a Western, separated by the Alleghany Mountains; and each synod is subdivided, into a number of classes or district synods. Its constitution is the Presbyterian, which answers its purpose very well; but does not so stiffly oppose itself to other forms of government as the Scottish *jure divino* Presbyterianism. It has now over three hundred ministers, and perhaps a hundred thousand communicants; three theological seminaries, and as many colleges; two German and four English popular and scientific periodicals. Of late years it has been zealously working its way up, has vigorously increased in the midst of perpetual conflicts and agitations from without and within, and has taken a peculiar theological position before the American public.

As to doctrine, the German Reformed Church still holds, and for some years past with increased veneration and love, the Heidelberg catechism, the most genial, profound, and spiritual symbol which the history of the Reformed Church has to show. It dates, indeed, as is well known, from the Pentecostal age of Protestantism, but from the later, maturer days of that age, when the leading phases of the Reformation could already be seen and compared, and its results systematically put together. Accordingly it combines warm religious enthusiasm for evangelical truth with calmness, clearness, and command of material; and, as the joint product of a disciple and intimate friend of Melanchthon (Zacharias Ursinus) and an earnest practical follower of Calvin (Caspar Olevianus), it presents the theological and ecclesiastical position of the German Reformed Church in its whole relation, both as to agreement and difference, to Rome, Whittenberg, and Geneva. This position is decidedly evangelical, and intermediate between the German and the non-German, the Lutheran and the rigid Calvinistic Protestantism. In language, nationality, warmth, and depth, nearly allied to Lutheranism, especially in its milder, conciliatory, Melanchthonian shade, and always inclining even towards union with it, the Reformed Church varies from it, and approaches Calvinism in its conception of the sacraments, its predilection for the synodal and Presbyterian constitution, for a more complete independent congregational life, stricter church discipline, and greater simplicity in worship; though without being in the narrower sense Calvinistic. For the harsh doctrine of a *double* predestination is, by the entire silence of the Heidelberg Catechism respecting a *decretum reprobationis,* thrown out of the province of public authoritative teaching into that of private opinion and theological speculation; and the Puritanic severity of radical disruption from history have always found but very few advocates among the Reformed of the German tongue.

From this middle, or, if we may so speak, central position between Wittenberg and Geneva, between the German nationality on the one hand, and the Romanic, English, and Scotch on the other, the denomination of which we are speaking can the more readily exert a theological and religious influence in both directions; recommending to Lutheranism, to which it is in America, as everywhere else, bound by a thousand cords, the peculiar excellences of the strictly reformed churches, and to the latter the good gifts and treasures of the Lutheran confession. And for this work it has in the United States the best opportunity; for there all these theological and national antagonistic forces are brought into immediate daily contact with each other, and there the German Reformed branch of the kingdom of God has the freest room for the execution of its special mission.

This its mission, too, it has come clearly to apprehend. After having shown for a long time too strong a leaning to Anglo-American Presbyterianism and Puritanism, and come into danger of losing its German character, and with this of course its influence on the German emigration, it has now become aware of its historical and theological peculiarity, and attached itself wholly to the development of the modern Evangelical United Theology of Germany, which, being the joint product of both confessions, no longer allows so rigid a separation of their respective doctrinal ideas.

162

Indeed, the opposition of the Old Lutherans to the Union arises from the presence of the Reformed elements in it. This following of the German theology is plainly the most natural course for a German Church, and is found even in Switzerland, many of whose sons study in Berlin, Halle, Bonn, and Tübingen, and whose professors are in part from Prussia and Würtemberg. Almost all the Reformed divines of Germany and Switzerland, as Ebrard, Hundeshagen, Heppe, Lange, Hagenbach, Herzog, Schenkel, &c., are quite identified with the development of the United Evangelical theology.

But in the United States German philosophy and theology come into living contact with the whole Anglo-American form of Christianity, and thus become essentially modified. While they act upon the latter, they undergo themselves a process of transformation. From the collision, the mutual attraction and repulsion, of these two elements there has arisen, since Dr. Rauch and Dr. Nevin, the first presidents of the literary institutions of Mercersburg, a theological movement, which, on account of the practical character of the American ecclesiastical system, under favor of the free synodal life, and in consequence of much bitter and unjust opposition from other denominations, has kept the whole German Reformed communion, laity as well as clergy, for the last ten or twelve years, in an almost constant agitation, the end of which cannot yet possibly be seen. The whole movement is not the result of any design or calculation, but evidently providential, and hence will ultimately result in good. It has, under God, even already been beneficial, by consolidating the church, and exciting a considerable amount of serious theological investigation and practical activity. As to the landmarks of this denomination, they have not been removed in the least, as is erroneously supposed by some; on the contrary, the Heidelberg Catechism is now more faithfully adhered to and more generally used by its

163

ministers, than ever before. They look, it is true, upon the present distracted and confused state of Protestantism as unsatisfactory and transitory; but they expect no help from a retrograde movement to Romanism; they hope and pray rather for a new reformation, which should save all the positive elements of truth and piety in Protestantism, and unite them with the excellences of Catholicism. They look not backward to the fleshpots and chains of Egypt, but forward to the unity and freedom of the land of promise, to which God will surely lead all his people from the wilderness in his own good time.

(3) THE GERMAN EVANGELICAL ASSOCIATION OF THE WEST. — This Union is to be regarded as the prolongation of the Evangelical United Church of Prussia, and those German States which follow its example in this respect. It operates in America as in Germany; instead of fusing the Lutheran and Reformed confessions into one body, as it was designed to do, it has thus far become a third church besides the first two; it contains, indeed, the germs of a future reconciliation, but its proper work is still far from being accomplished. We do not say this in censure; for the greater and more important a work is the more of time and labor is required to effect it. Previous feeble attempts at union have failed, though the two denominations there come into so close contact; and now a renewed vigor of church life has re-aroused the confessional opposition, and retarded the present effort. Yet favorable conditions exist in the two confessions — some outward ones peculiar to America, which encourage the hope of a final accomplishment of the object; and this, too, on a far grander scale than the Prussian, Baden, and Würtemberg Union at first could have contemplated.

In America, where almost all branches of the Protestant church, and, indeed, almost all forms of Christianity, are represented and thrown into contact, the idea of union necessarily expands. In fact, the true idea of union, in the real spirit of the modern German evangelical theology, covers the whole field of evangelical Protestantism, and looks even to the final reconciliation of the all-comprehending antagonism of Protestantism and Catholicism — a work, for which the present Church-Union of Prussia and other German States may, perhaps, in the hands of Providence, prepare the way, but which it will require a great many other agencies, and even a new reformation, for its completion, and may never fully appear before the second coming of Christ. And to the *idea* of union in this comprehensive sense, every theologian, who has an intelligent and warm interest in the body of Christ, must be devoted, whatever objections may be raised to the present actual operation of the movement in some of the German churches.

The Evangelical Association here before us, though of course at present confined to a much smaller and more modest sphere, still meets an actual want. It provides a home for numbers of late emigrants, who have been born, baptized and confirmed in the United Evangelical Church of Germany; especially in regions where there are no Lutheran or German Reformed congregations. It was instituted on the 4th of May, 1841, at St. Louis, Mo., by seven clergymen of the United Church of Germany, under the style: "The German Evangelical Church Union of the West (Der deutsch-evangelische Kirchenverein des Westens);" and now numbers some thirty ministers. According to the first paragraph of its revised statutes, "the object of the Association is, to work for the establishment and spread of the Evangelical Church in particular, as well as for the furtherance of all institutions for the extension of the Kingdom of God. By the Evangelical Church we understand that communion which takes the Holy Scriptures of the Old and New Testaments as the Word of God and our only infallible rule of faith and practice, and commits itself to that exposition of the Scriptures laid down in the symbolical books of the Lutheran and Reformed Churches, chiefly the Augsburg Confession, Luther's Catechism, and the Heidelberg Catechism, so far as these agree; and where they differ, we hold alone to the relevant passages of Scripture, and avail ourselves of that freedom of conscience which prevails on such points in the Evangelical Church."

With many difficulties to encounter, and perhaps many modifications to undergo, this institution still has, in the character of its members, in the matter of its documents, and in attainments already made, the pledge of continuance and the warrant of the best hopes for its future. It was primarily intended only for the more Western States. Yet there is in Ohio a like association in connection with this; and in the large Atlantic cities there would be German material enough for Evangelical congregations. Should it succeed even there in keeping pace with the times, it must place itself the more as a connecting link between the Lutheran and German Reformed Churches, reach towards both the hand of love and peace, and thus draw them gradually nearer together, and by contributing its share to their final reconciliation in spirit and in truth, accomplish the proper object of the Union.

(4) SMALLER GERMAN DENOMINATIONS AND SECTS. — Among these, very honorable mention is due to the Moravian "Brethren," a society of whom was founded in America as early as the Lutheran and German Reformed Churches, by the distinguished Count Zinzendorf and Spangenberg themselves. The Herrnhuters are still a very small community, with little or no prospect of growth; yet they exert a wholesome influence in their way, like the silence of the country, against the prevailing busy devotion to the practical and material; especially through their well-known male and

female schools at Bethlehem, Nazareth, and Lititz in Pennsylvania, and Salem, N. C., which are sought by some from a considerable distance. They have kept the German language and customs more pure than any other class of emigrants, and are distinguished in America, as elsewhere, for a contemplative turn, missionary zeal, freedom from bigotry and exclusiveness, warm-hearted quietness, fine manners, love of music, order, cleanliness, and chaste ornament. After having been sunk for some time into a pretty stagnant condition, they seem to have latterly awakened somewhat to new life, and it is much to be desired that this most amiable, harmless, and peaceful of all Protestant sects should, with the warmth of its first love, still make itself long felt in America.

Other older sects, transplanted from Europe in the first half of the last century, the Mennonites, Tunkers, and Schwenkfeldians, are particularly numerous in Lancaster Co., Pa. They consist chiefly of farmers, of good name as industrious, quiet, harmless citizens. But as communions they have no influence, being either distracted by subdivision, or petrified.

The influence of Methodism on the Lutheran and German Reformed Church at the close of the last and beginning of the present century, produced several new sects, in doctrine, discipline, government, and worship entirely conformed to the Methodist Episcopal model. Such are the United Brethren in Christ, founded about 1800, by William Otterbein, a pious Reformed Minister from Germany; the Evangelical Communion (Evangelische Gemeinschaft), commonly called the Albrecht Brethren, founded somewhat later by Jacob Albrecht, a Lutheran layman of Pennsylvania; the German Methodists, regularly connected with the northern section of the Methodist Episcopal Church, and forming its most promising home missionary field; and the Weinbrennerians, or as they ridiculously presume to style themselves, the

167

"Church of God," founded in October, 1830, in the town of Harrisburg, Pa., by John Weinbrenner, an excommunicated German Reformed Minister. They combine the new measures and revivalism of the Methodists with the peculiarities of the Baptists, and practise feet washing as a sacrament on the ground of John xiii. Besides these there are some few Baptist congregations unconnected with the older Mennonites and Tunkers, and chiefly of American origin.

All these sects are a reproach and humiliation to the Lutheran, Reformed, and United churches; but should at the same time stimulate them to persevering self-purification, to greater activity, and more faithful discharge of duty, and thus become a blessing to them, as the dissenters to the Anglican church, as Protestantism to Catholicism. The more life and zeal there are in the church, the less warrant is there for sects, and the less progress can they make. But so long as the church neglects its duty, sects are necessary and beneficial, as taskmasters and troublers.

(g) THE BAPTISTS

It is often asserted, that the Baptists are the most numerous sect in the United States. But in this case the term must at any rate be taken in its widest sense, as including all parties which agree in rejecting infant baptism, though they have no other connection with each other. There would then come in the Calvinistic and Arminian Baptists, who are of English and Anglo-American origin; the free communion and close communion Baptists; the Mennonites and Tunkers, who emigrated from Germany and settled mostly in Pennsylvania; the River Brethren, a section of the Tunkers; the Seventh Day Baptists, English and German, who follow the letter of the Old Testament, and keep holy the seventh day of the week instead of the first, and have on this account lately, but unsuccessfully, petitioned the legislature of Pennsylvania for a modification of the Sabbath laws in their favor; the Disciples of Christ, commonly called Campbellites (from their still living founder, Alexander Campbell, originally a Scotch Presbyterian), who identify baptism, that is immersion, with regeneration itself, reject all creeds and sectarian names, although they added to the catalogue of sects a new one, and have within a short time greatly increased; the "Christians," who boast of having no founder, and having sprung up as by magic, about 1803, in three different localities at once, New England, Ohio, and Kentucky, in opposition to the bondage of creeds and sectarian distinctions, reject the doctrines of the Holy Trinity and the divinity of Christ, as unscriptural, and baptize only adults, by immersion. There is even a Baptist party in the Southern States, called the Hard-Shell Baptists, because, I think, they oppose missionary, tract, and temperance societies, and similar movements, as unscriptural inventions.

Of course I cannot here go into an account of all these subdivisions of the Baptists; but will confine myself to the most commanding body of them, to which the term Baptist is in America generally meant to apply. I mean the Regular, or Calvinistic Baptists, as they are commonly styled, to distinguish them from the Free-will Baptists, who hold Arminian or Pelagian views on the relation of the human will to the divine in conversion and sanctification, and date in America from 1780, when the first congregation was formed in New Hampshire.

The Calvinistic Baptists have not the slightest historical connection with those fanatics of the days of the Reformation, whose excesses in the Peasant War and the transactions at Munster are so notorious. They originated in the times of those violent Puritanic commotions, which, in the seventeenth century, disturbed the whole ecclesiastical and religious life of England. They are really not distinguished from the Independents, except by their theory of baptism. In

169

America they arose simultaneously from the Puritanic colonies, the first Baptist church having been founded in Providence, Rhode Island, by Roger Williams in 1639; they were first much persecuted, fined, whipped, and imprisoned, especially in Massachusetts and Virginia; but grew with great rapidity after the Revolutionary War, and are now more numerous in America than in England. In their history shine such names as those of Bunyan, the author of the world-renowned "Pilgrim's Progress," one of the best books of edification ever produced; Roger Williams, an exile from the colony of Massachusetts, founder of the State of Rhode Island, and one of the first advocates of the principle of universal religious toleration; and more recently, Robert Hall, one of the greatest pulpit orators of England. They are perhaps most largely and worthily represented in New England and the State of New York, and have latterly made great exertions for the spread of the Bible, and in the work of heathen missions. They have also lately established several colleges and seminaries, and taken a commendable interest in the cause of liberal education. Many of their most prominent divines, as Sears, Hackett, Conant, are acquainted with German literature; and one of their literary institutions, the university of Rochester, in the State of New York, some years ago purchased the whole library of the late Dr. Neander, whom the Baptists particularly venerate and love for his latitudinarian views on infant baptism.

In regard to doctrine, government, and worship, the Calvinistic Baptists really agree in all essential points with the orthodox Congregationalists; and what we have already said of these, both in praise and in censure, is true of the denomination now before us. We need only mention, therefore, the points of distinction which make them Baptists in the specific sense.

The first relates to the proper subjects of baptism, and consists in the rejection of infant baptism. This they consider an innovation which crept into the church in the third century, which is contrary to the teaching and practice of the apostles, and which should have been discarded by the Reformers of the sixteenth century, with all other papal traditions. Baptism, in their view, necessarily presumes the preaching of the Gospel to the subject, and repentance and faith within him. But both these are impossible in unconscious infancy; hence baptism is here unmeaning, nay a very profanation, and a violation both of the rights of God, who calls every man when he will, and of the rights of man, who ought to move of his own free will towards God. They certainly have against them the typical relation of circumcision to baptism; the passages of the Acts of the Apostles, which record the baptism of whole families; the practice of the ancient church; and many theological and philosophical arguments drawn from the organic unity of the Christian family, the constitutional adaptation of Christ to be the Redeemer of all ages and conditions, the extent of his covenant of grace, the susceptibility of the child to the regenerating influence of the Holy Ghost, &c.

But in the first place, the Baptists have a strong hold on the lamentable fact, that infant baptism is so very often profaned, and particularly in state churches, is administered even where the parents and sponsors are either downright infidels, or at best altogether spiritually dead and indifferent, and where consequently there is no foundation of religious family life, and no guarantee of a parental discipline answering to the baptismal vow, and fitted to unfold and mature the covenant grace. No wonder, then, that there are innumerable baptized persons who are worse than unbaptised heathens, and in whom the blessing of the sacrament has turned into a curse. The practice of the Baptists, however, by no means secures them against such profanation. For they are no more infallible than other Christian communions; they must baptize many hypocrites and unworthy persons;

and their effort to attain absolute actual purity in the church on earth, and fully separate the tares from the wheat before the judgment — an effort in itself entirely praiseworthy — must prove as unsuccessful as that of the Donatists and other sects of ancient and modern times.

Then again the Baptists in America have the advantage over most modern Puritanic and Presbyterian divines at least on the score of logical consistency. For the latter either directly deny the idea of objective baptismal grace, or at least so weaken it, that in the absence of subjective faith, on which they make the whole efficacy of the sacrament depend, infant baptism becomes pretty much an empty ceremony, being at most a solemn assumption of the obligation of Christian training on the part of the parents. If infant baptism be not at the same time the beginning of the gracious operation of the Spirit of God in the child, and the positive seal of a covenant of grace, it were better to drop it entirely. Meantime, it must not be thought that the Baptists have any higher conception of baptism, and of the sacraments in general, than the Puritans. The common idea with them is, that baptism is only the authentic legitimation, the seal of regeneration and conversion, and therefore really imparts nothing new, but only confirms what is already present. The idea of a proper objective baptismal grace and of a real regenerative efficacy of this sacrament, they reject as mysticism or popery. Their theology generally is, if possible, still more unchurchly and anti-catholic, than that of the Puritans.

The second peculiarity, which distinguishes the Baptists from the other Protestant churches, as well as from the Roman Catholic, regards the form of baptism; which they make immersion, in opposition to sprinkling. This rite they administer, winter and summer, either in baptisteries constructed for the purpose, or in streams and lakes. On this point they have a far greater advantage from exegesis and

172

church antiquity, than in the rejection of infant baptism, which must at all events have been very generally introduced as early as the latter part of the second century, as appears from Tertullian's isolated opposition against it, and from the somewhat later testimony of Cyprian and Origen in its favor. For immersion, the Baptists appeal to the original and almost uniform meaning of the Greek word βαπτίζειν; to all those passages of the New Testament, where total or partial immersion is unquestionably implied in the act of baptism; to the general practice of the ancient church, which has continued to this day in the Eastern churches; and to the symbolical appropriateness of this mode of baptism, — this alone answering the idea of burial with Christ and resurrection with him, and an entire washing from guilt; while sprinkling effaces this idea.

The Baptists, however, are not content with only giving the preference to immersion, and regarding sprinkling also as a valid though less expressive form. They would make the latter entirely unscriptural and void, and accordingly require converts from other denominations to be re-baptized; as if the operation of the Holy Ghost depended on the quantity of water and the outward form. A part of the Baptists have for some years been prosecuting with great energy and considerable expense, a revision of the English version of the Bible; in which, among many other improvements, the words *baptize* and *baptism* (which, by the way, are formed from the Greek original itself, and properly mean submerge), are to be exchanged for the unequivocal *immerse* and *immersion*.

It is no more than consistent with this narrow, exclusive view of the mode of baptism and of infant baptism, that the close-communion Baptists, as they are called, debar Christians of other denominations from their celebration of the Lord's Supper; as lacking the necessary pre-requisite for a place at the Lord's table, viz., baptism, in the above sense of immersion. Besides these, however, there is a more liberal party, which regards the doctrine of infant baptism and the admission of the right of sprinkling as no obstacle to real communion in faith and in the Supper. Hence these are called open-communion Baptists. The most distinguished Baptists of England, both of former and later times, Bunyan, Robert Hall, Forster, and Baptist Noel, advocate open communion; while in America, so far as I know, the stricter and logically more consistent theory prevails, at least among the ministers.

(h) THE QUAKERS

The Society of Friends, as they call themselves, or the Quakers, as they are commonly called by others, likewise dates from that most remarkable period of deep religious motions in England, the first half and the middle of the seventeenth century. It was founded by George Fox, who, from a shoemaker and a shepherd, rose by inward experiences and visions to a reformer and a prophet, and plays a similar part in the history of religious sects with the well-known Gorlitz shoemaker and *theosophus Teutonicus* in the history of philosophy. One of his first and most distinguished followers was William Penn. He was born, indeed, in England, and educated in Oxford, and also ended his life in his native land, in 1717; but he belongs as much, if not more, to the history of America, and became there the father of a great and powerful state, which justly bears his name. He purchased from the English crown, which owed his father a considerable sum, the land on the Delaware river, and founded, in 1680, under English jurisdiction, the colony of Pennsylvania, and the city of "brotherly love," Philadelphia, which has since attained a population of half a million. He designed this colony originally as an asylum for his brethren in faith, who were at that time still bitterly persecuted in England, till by James II, in 1686, they were allowed the rights of dissenters. But from the beginning he granted all other Christian confessions free access and equal rights, and made treaties of peace also with the wild Indians, who always received the most humane treatment in this Quaker colony.

The religious peculiarity of the Quakers, you are aware, is a sort of mysticism; the only one which has proceeded from the bosom of English Protestantism — a mysticism, which derives all Christianity and moral life from the principle of the "inward light," as a divine communication to every man, and repudiates all outward forms. The Quakers carry their spiritualism even to the rejection of the ministerial office and of the sacraments; so that an attempt to define their relation to the visible Church of Christ, in the proper and strict sense, brings us into a strait; for, on the one hand, the Word and sacraments are essential marks of the church (especially according to the definition of the Augsburg confession), and on the other, it cannot be denied, that the Quakers bring forth the moral fruits of Christianity, and are at all events enlightened and warmed by Christian ideas. They reject the sacraments, indeed, only as outward acts and rites, and would hold fast, and indeed lay all the more stress on the idea of a baptism of the spirit, and of a purely inward communion with Christ. But this leaves no sacrament at all; for the essence of a sacrament consists in the mystical union of invisible grace with a visible sign. They keep, indeed, the written word of God; but they in reality put the inward light above it. They have no separate clerical office. They exalt to the place of this the universal spiritual priesthood and prophetic gift, disregarding even the difference of sex. I myself once attended a great yearly festival of the Quakers in London, where eight women and only one man were moved by the Spirit of God, and addressed prayers to God and exhortations to the assembly in that peculiarly tremulous prophetic tone, from which they are supposed to have received the name of Quakers, or tremblers.

Often, however, after sitting together for two hours, they separate without a sound having been uttered. For no one is to preach or pray, unless inspired at the moment by the Spirit. This one-sided spiritualism of the Quakers remarkably avenges itself, we may add, by passing into a pedantic formalism, which adheres most scrupulously to the most trivial forms, such as a particular color and cut of the coat, hat, and bonnet. Their fairest traits are their simplicity, general philanthropy, and sympathy for all the persecuted and oppressed. That this is not simply a natural feeling with them, but the effect of divine grace, a spark of the infinite love of the Saviour, and their peculiar mission in the household of Christendom, no one can deny who has carefully read the life of Elizabeth Fry (who, if she had been a Roman Catholic, would have been canonized as the foundress of the "Blessed Order of Sisters of the Tails"), and the memoirs of her brother, Joseph John Gurney, recently published by Braithwaite.

This original sect has never become very numerous either in America or in England. It has no spirit of proselytism; and the fanaticism which characterized the first stage of its history, it long ago abandoned. But through the thoroughly democratic character of its constitution, its spirit of toleration, and its rigid separation of religion from politics, it has exerted a greater influence on American affairs, than many a larger denomination; though Bancroft exaggerates its effect by his idealizing rhetorical exhibition of its principles. It is still a respectable religious party, especially in Philadelphia and the immediate vicinity, where is has its largest meetinghouses. There the Quakers may often be seen on the street, in their peculiar, but uncommonly clean and neat dress, with fresh, fair countenances, and the evident marks of inward content and outward prosperity. They are mostly merchants, or farmers, or men of fortune and leisure. They take an active part in the philanthropic movements, and have done real service in the reform of prison discipline. The so-called Pennsylvania system of solitary confinement to favor earnest reflection, and so promote the improvement of the prisoners, is to be traced chicfly to the influence of the Quakers. They still oppose the oath and war — though there was during the American Revolution a patriotic party, called the "Fighting Quakers" — and seek to spread the principles of peace by special societies and publications. They are likewise decided enemies of slavery, and are generally ultra-abolitionists.

Their views are altogether in favor of universal freedom and equality of religious toleration. But this sect has an unfavorable influence in spreading amongst the people the dangerous opinion, that the ministry and the sacraments are really altogether unessential, and that a man may be a good Christian, without attaching himself to any particular branch of the visible Church. In the self-sufficiency of the inward light, they think they may dispense with science and theology, as an unprofitable work of man. Their education is merely of a general kind. The only theologian they can show is Barclay, and he was a theologian before he joined them. They live pretty much by themselves, and they may perhaps be the chief cause of the comparative unsociableness of Philadelphia.

Beyond Eastern Pennsylvania they have few congregations. In New England they were even from the first, about the middle of the seventeenth century, bitterly persecuted and banished from the land, on account of the fanatical and indecent excesses of some Quaker women; and since then they have not been able to gain much foothold there. They will undoubtedly still long maintain themselves, and fill their place in the great family of Christendom; but they will always be limited to a very small sphere. Their youth of the richer and higher families desert largely either to the Episcopal Church or to the indifferent world.

Among the American Quakers there are two schools: the old or orthodox, who firmly hold to the Bible and their traditional customs, and the Hicksites (from their founder, Elias Hicks), commonly called "Hickory Quakers," who hold Unitarian and rationalistic opinions on the trinity and the divinity of Christ, and identify the inward light with natural reason. These liberal Quakers are among the loudest advocates of the wildest extravagances of Garrisonian abolitionism, and female emancipation. I have myself heard a Quakeress, Lucretia Mott, of Philadelphia, in company with Garrison, and regardless of all true female delicacy, deliver before a mixed assembly of whites and blacks, in the Baptist Church of Norristown, in 1848, a perfectly fanatical discourse against the American Constitution, and in favor of the full equalization, not only of all races, but also of both sexes. The moment religious life is extinguished, Quakerism sinks into the lowest rationalism and skepticism, or wanders into the wildest excesses of ultra democracy; the overstrained spiritualism ends in the flesh.

(i) THE ROMAN CHURCH

The doctrine, constitution, and worship of this church I need not describe. They are the same in the New World as in the Old. In fact, this church is wont, you know, to boast of this unity and unchangeableness as one of its greatest virtues. We confine ourselves, therefore, to a view of its actual condition and its prospects in America.

If we look to America at large, the Roman Catholic Church is older there than Protestantism itself, the first discoveries of Columbus, John and Sebastian Cabot, Amerigo Vespucci, all Roman Catholics, and natives of Italy (with the exception of the younger Cabot, who was born in England), having preceded the Reformation of the sixteenth century. We heartily rejoice, as Christians, that the idea of our holy

178

religion entered largely into the bold enterprise of the noble Genoese, whose monument is a whole continent in fact, though not in name, and of his royal patroness, Isabella the Catholic. When he first presented to the Queen of Castile and Aragon the temptation of extending her dominions, and pictured the dazzling wealth of the Indies, it made no impression upon her. But when he spoke of the poor heathen on the distant islands, made after God's image, with souls to be saved, he touched her inmost heart, and the pious queen poured her jewels into the cap of the enthusiast, who, a few months afterwards, planted the cross on the island of San Salvador, and took possession of a New World in the name of Christ our Saviour, and the Crown of Spain. Soon after his return he wrote from Lisbon to Sanchez, the treasurer of Spain: "Let processions be made, festivals be celebrated, temples be adorned with branches and flowers: for Christ rejoices on earth and in heaven in view of the future redemption of immortal souls. Let us rejoice also over the temporal advantage, which will grow out of the discovery to Spain not only, but to all Christendom." Ferdinand and Isabella, after hearing the report of the discoverer, fell on their knees and joined in the *Te Deum* of the choir of the royal chapel in celebration of the glorious conquest to the church as well as to the State. They immediately ordered the Indians, whom Columbus had brought with him, to be educated as missionaries, and sent as early as 1498, twelve priests in addition, to the western hemisphere.

Our joy in this beautiful prelude of American history would be still greater and purer, if the first emigrants from Spain had not dishonored their Christian profession by barbarous cruelty against the native heathens, and by the worst vices of civilization, which force even from a Roman Catholic historian the honest confession: "In vain almost was the building of Christian churches and the founding of episcopal sees under such circumstances; for the Indians had such a just aversion against the religion of their oppressors, that the Cazike Hatney said, the money was the God of the Christians, and he did not wish even to go to heaven, if Spaniards should ever get there." *

If the Pope of Rome were infallible in the exercise of his power, the whole of the American continent together with the islands would now be the sole property of the Roman Church and the Crown of Spain. For in the consciousness of the mediæval papacy, that the successor of Peter and the vicar of Christ had a right to dispose of all the kingdoms of the world, and in grateful consideration of the merits of the Spanish monarchs in suppressing Mohammedanism in their territory, Alexander VI, of infamous memory, himself a Spaniard by birth, gave the whole western hemisphere to the Crown of Spain as an inheritance.† But in this, as well as in regard to the geographical situation of the new discovery,‡ both Rome and Spain were greatly mistaken, and doomed to disappointment. God in his providence had destined the northern half of the New World as a hospitable asylum for all nations and churches of Europe, and more especially for the Anglo-Saxon race and for Protestantism, which so soon followed the discovery of America, as if this had prepared a new home for it. In Central and South

---

* Hefele, Der Cardinal Ximenes und die Kirchlichen Zustände Spaniens am Ende des 15, und Anfang des 16 Jahrhunderts (1844), p. 513.

† In two bulls of the 3d and 4th of May, 1493, Pope Alexander VI. assigned to Spain, "omnes insulas et terras ferinas inventas et inveniendas, detestas et detegendas versus occidentem et meridiem, fabricando et constituendo unam lineam a Polo Arctico, scilicet septentrione, ad Polum Antarcticum, scilicet meridiem (sic!)."

‡ It is well known that Columbus and Amerigo Vespucci died in the firm conviction that they had only touched parts of Eastern Asia. Columbus made even his men swear to their belief, that there was a *land* route from Cuba to Spain ("que esta tierra de Cuba fuese la tierra firme al comienzo de las Indias y fin á quien en estas partes quisiere venir de España por tierra"). Whosoever ventured to deny it, should be punished with a hundred strokes and the loss of his tongue. See Alex. v. Humboldt's Kosmos, ii. 277 and 462 (German edition) and his Examen crit., etc. t. iv. p. 233, 250, 261, and t. v. p. 182–185.

America, Romanism and the Romanic race are still in undisturbed possession of power, it is true, but they present the gloomy picture of an almost hopeless stagnation; * while the United States, with their predominantly Germanic and Protestant population, are the very embodiment of life and progress.

On the free Republican and Puritanic soil of North America the Roman Catholic Church with its mediæval traditions, centralized priestly government, and extreme conservatism, seems to be almost an anomaly, but is perhaps just on this account necessary and useful as a check and corrective for the extremes of Protestantism and religious radicalism. Her first appearance on the territory now belonging to the Union, was in Florida, which was discovered by the Spaniards, under Juan Ponce de Leon, in 1512, but not annexed to the United States till 1820. After several unsuccessful attempts the Spaniards, more than twenty-five hundred strong with five hundred negro slaves, took possession of Florida on the 28th of August, 1565, the day of St. Augustin, founded the town called by that name, which is thus forty years older than any other town in the Union, and butchered about nine hundred Huguenot settlers a little further north, with their wives and children, without any provocation, "not as Frenchmen, but as Calvinists." The French government of Charles IX cared nothing for this outrage upon its Protestant subjects, who were murdered at home in the terrible St. Bartholomew's night of 1572. But the Huguenots effected a

---

* This is admitted even by Roman Catholic writers. See e. g. "Brownson's Review" for July, 1855, p. 820. "A traveller through Mexico is struck with what appears to be monuments of the piety of the Spanish government. Large and magnificent churches were built, and richly endowed, wherever needed, and in no country was more ample provision made for the material support of religion; and yet in no country was the religious and secular instruction of the people more shamefully neglected. . . . Spain wanted loyal subjects, not free and enlightened citizens. The state of religion in Cuba, the queen of the Antilles, is most deplorable, and would gain immensely by the annexation of the island to the American Union."

private expedition for bloody revenge in 1563, and after having killed some Spaniards, "not as Spaniards and sailors, but as traitors, robbers, and murderers," they returned to France, not being strong enough for a permanent occupation. May this bloody prelude of North American church history never be repeated on American soil.

In broad and most honorable contrast with this Spanish bigotry and cruelty, working of the palmy days of the Inquisition, stands the conduct of the two hundred people, mostly English Catholic gentlemen with their servants, who under Leonard Calvert, brother of George Calvert, better known as Lord Baltimore, landed near the mouth of the Potomac in 1634, and laid the foundation of the colony of Maryland. It is certainly a very remarkable fact, that this Roman Catholic colony, one hundred and forty years before the War of Independence, about contemporaneously with the persecuted Baptist Roger Williams, but more fully than he, and nearly fifty years before the settlement of Pennsylvania through the equally tolerant Quaker William Penn, proclaimed the principle of the fullest religious liberty, and acted upon it, until the Protestants temporarily overthrew it.

As the power of tradition is nowhere greater than in the Roman church, we believe that this example of Lord Baltimore and his friends will always have a very decided influence in filling the minds of the most enlightened American members of that communion, with aversion to all penal laws in matters of conscience, and with a strong attachment to the principle of religious liberty.

But although the Roman church is thus closely and honorably identified with the history of one of the oldest of the original States of the North American confederation, it remained very small and unimportant till a comparatively recent period. Of all the signers of the Declaration of Independence, only one was a catholic.

At the beginning of the Revolutionary War, there was hardly a place in the colonies except Philadelphia, where the laws of the land permitted a Catholic priest to celebrate mass; and even the Constitution of Rhode Island, which from the days of Roger Williams allowed freedom of conscience, had a brief disqualifying clause against the Roman Catholics, which was not removed till 1784. The first Episcopal see was founded at Baltimore, in 1790, by the election of the Rev. John Carroll, a Jesuit, and cousin to Charles Carroll of Carollton, the last though not least of the signers of the Declaration of Independence.

Only within perhaps the last twenty years, has this church begun to make its influence felt in the public life of the United States. This has been the natural result, partly of the acquisition of Louisiana (1803), Florida (1820), and Texas (1844), but especially of a perfectly massive emigration from Catholic Ireland, which was for several years greater than that from all other European countries put together, and has done as much to depopulate and un-Romanize Ireland, as to people and Romanize America and Australia. The emigrants from the southern parts of Ireland have, indeed, many good traits, among which are prominent, generosity, chastity, and a love for the religion of their fathers undestroyed by years of oppression and misery; but they are in general terribly neglected, ignorant, addicted to drunkenness and profanity, quarrelling and fighting, not seldom in the open street; and they form on the whole the roughest class of the American population. Hence, too, they are by no means fitted to inspire the American, who, like the mass of men generally, judges from appearances and single concrete cases, with much respect for the Roman church; for they do not seem to be morally improved by any number of masses and confessions, which they scrupulously attend. The Irish and their descendants form the majority of most of the Catholic congregations, especially in the large cities, and

183

they furnish also most of the priests and bishops. Archbishop Hughes of New York, for example, and Archbishop Kenrick of Baltimore, the former the shrewdest, the latter the meekest and most learned of the Roman prelates of America, as also the latter's brother, the Archbishop of St. Louis, and Archbishop Purcell of Cincinnati, are all natives of Ireland.

Then the Roman Church draws a constant accession from Germany, especially from Bavaria, Würtemberg, Baden, and the Rhenish provinces; also from France, and to some extent from Spain and Italy. Of the German emigrants perhaps one third are Roman Catholic. They do not however agree very well with the Irish. They have their own religious journals, perhaps half a dozen, and sometimes, with commendable zeal, build themselves churches of their own, of which St. Peter's in New York, and St. Alphonsus' in Baltimore (both founded by the Redemptorists), are among the largest and finest in all America. The French have settled principally in the State of Louisiana, and have hitherto formed in New Orleans the majority of the population; but they are now obliged gradually to adopt the English language. These likewise furnish many priests, bishops, and sisters of charity.

On the proper body of the American nation, the substantial middle class, if such we may speak of in a republic (and such one must find after all), the Roman Church has very slight hold. As in England and Scotland, so in America, it meets only the extremes of society, especially the lowest, poorest, and most uncultivated class of emigrants, who form, so to speak, its flesh and blood; embracing also, almost everywhere, a larger or smaller number of influential families of the higher and educated order, including many converts from the different Protestant denominations, especially the Episcopal.

The Roman Church may now number near two millions of members, not quite one twelfth of the population of the

Union. She is, there as everywhere, very well organized, and in all more important enterprises operates as a compact unit; while Protestantism is full of discord. She already has a diocese in almost every State of the Union; including six archepiscopal sees, of which Baltimore (the metropolitan), New York, and Cincinnati are the most important and influential. Her higher clergy are wisely chosen, and among them are many very able, earnest, self-denying, and worthy men. The jealous watching of thousands of Protestant eyes has a good effect on their morality and zeal; and places them in these respects far in advance of the dead and corrupt priesthood of purely Catholic countries, like Mexico, or Portugal, or Sicily. In the larger cities she is building costly and imposing cathedrals, for which she is receiving constant aid from Europe, especially from France. At the same time she is everywhere establishing schools (very frequently attended by Protestant youth), infirmaries, and orphan asylums under the direction of the Jesuits, Redemptorists, and Sisters of Charity; nay, even monasteries and nunneries, in striking contrast with the driving secular activity of the country. She knows how to use the lever of the public press for her purposes, and endeavors to keep pace with the enormous journalizing zeal of America. Besides many weeklies and monthlies, she brings out reprints and translations of the most important Catholic works of ancient and modern times, and many original productions. She is beginning also to mix in politics and control the elections. But this very effort for power and political influence may prove extremely dangerous to her, if not fatal. Quite lately, at the instance of the National Council of Baltimore, she has made systematic attacks, in the States of New York, Pennsylvania, Maryland, Ohio, and Michigan, on the public elementary schools, conducted by the state and mainly subject to Protestant influence. She has attempted, though thus far without the least success, to destroy them, in order (and one can hardly blame her

185

for it) to rid her own youth of the contaminating influence of schools, in which either no religion at all is taught, or the Protestant Bible is read, and a Protestant tone pervades the whole system of teaching, as well as the personal character of the great majority of teachers and pupils.

From all this it is plain, that the Roman Church is awake, and seeking in every way to make herself felt. Nay, the confident and not seldom most arrogant tone of her press clearly shows, that she entertains the highest hopes of her future in the United States, and contemplates yet most brilliant triumphs there.

It seems to me, many of the most educated and discerning Catholics cannot help feeling, that the Romanic nations of southern Europe and central and South America have so far outlived themselves, as to afford, at least in their present condition, no hopes of any new spiritual movement from Italy, Spain, or Portugal, Mexico or Brazil; that the Pope in Rome itself sits on a volcano, and will probably be driven away by a new eruption of radicalism, when the French bayonets are withdrawn. On fickle, revolutionary France, where there has been nothing but revolution and reaction since 1789, where infidelity rules to-day, and ultramontanism to-morrow, and where the church of St. Genevieve can as easily become again in a few years a pantheon of Voltaire and Rousseau, who still sleep in its vaults, as it could already be twice transformed from an idol temple into a church; — on France, no dependence can be placed, though just now, under the favor of Napoleon III, Catholicism in its most extravagant forms is in full sway there, and seems even to have extinguished Gallicanism for the present. In the East and North of Europe the Roman Church comes upon her old hereditary and arch-enemy, the Greek, and upon the colossal domain of the Emperor-Pope of St. Petersburg, who hates in the Pope of Rome his most dangerous rival. Hence she turns her eye to the heart and the West of

Europe, to the solid, vigorous Germanic nationality, to Germany, particularly Prussia, and above all to the world-ruling Anglo-Saxon race, to Great Britain, which spans almost every sea, and to its teeming rival, North America. Could she once conquer England and the New World, and re-assimilate the Germanic nationality, she would gain a victory more mighty and important than even her first Christianizing of the Germans, and her triumph over the universal empire of heathen Rome. "Give us the West," said the Catholic Bishop England, of South Carolina, "and we shall soon take care of the East." He referred, indeed, immediately only to the Western States of America in their relation to the Atlantic coast; but this significant word can be as properly applied in a wider sense.

But such a re-conquest of the Germanic nationality, and assimilation of the German, English, and Anglo-American Protestantism, would be at the same time a complete regeneration and rejuvenation of Catholicism itself. For the many living elements of Germanism and Protestantism, thus absorbed, would sooner or later inevitably revive and transform the old system, if not produce in it a fundamental reformation.

From some such point of view, which perhaps many Catholics hold, though they do not avow it, we can understand the high hopes which they have for their future in the western countries, and the enormous efforts which, to the shame of European Protestants be it said, they are making in North America for the advancement and permanent establishment of their interests.

What tends more than all else, to encourage and strengthen these hopes, is the Romanizing movements which have been for some twenty or thirty years spreading through many portions of Protestantism itself. The transitions of prominent German writers, from Stolberg and Haller to Huster and Gfrörer, are well-known. That the tide towards strictly confessional Lutheranism, of late so rapidly swelling, and the growing disposition to insist on outward visible unity and historical continuity of the church, on altar-service, on the idea of sacrifice, on a more compact form of Government, and many other things, tend, though unknown to most persons, towards Catholicism, can hardly be denied. Yet this is by no means saying they must necessarily end in Rome; they may possibly, on the contrary, form a strong barrier against this extreme, as well as against infidelity. On this we are not here called to decide. Still more striking and remarkable is the great Puseyite movement in the English Episcopal church, which began in 1833, and has resulted in the transition of some of her greatest divines, as Newman, and of her worthiest clergymen, as Manning. So the system of Irvingism, of almost contemporaneous origin, and likewise very worthy of attention, is far more Catholic than Protestant in doctrine, government, and worship, while it draws its strength in England and Germany almost entirely from the Protestant ranks.

These catholicizing tendencies have made their appearance within some twenty years past, at least have feebly begun to do so, even in America, in spite of its decided Protestant character, and in fact, to some extent, as a natural reaction against it. In the American Episcopal church, so closely connected with the Anglican, the Puseyite movement found an immediate response, and has already brought many offerings from this quarter to the Roman church, among which are some twenty or thirty clergymen, and even one bishop, though one of no great weight either of intellect or character. It is an interesting fact, that in America, as in England, the most learned and gifted champions of modern Catholicism, as Brownson and Newman, as well as the editors of most of the Catholic church periodicals, the "Freeman's Journal" of New-York, the "Catholic Herald," of Philadelphia, the "Shepherd of the Valley," of St. Louis (now defunct), and

"Brownson's Review," of Boston, are apostate Protestants. This fact argues, however, as much against as for the Roman church. It shows, indeed, that she has power to draw even talented and accomplished minds to herself; but it also shows that she has to depend on Protestantism for her most effective forces and her most skillful advocates. Most of these editors are laymen, and married, who could not well make themselves useful to the church of their adoption in any other line. This growing theological influence of laymen, which appears also in Europe (think of the editors of the "Rambler," the "Univers," the "Historisch-Politische Blätter," etc.), is quite a new and interesting phenomenon in the history of the papacy, and may prepare the way for some important change.

Orestes Brownson, of Boston, a consummate logician and controversialist, who crossed the Rubicon in 1844, and went right into the heart of the Italian territory, is in regard to talent, undoubtedly the most important convert the Roman church has yet made in America; though in character he has far less weight than Newman, Manning, or Wilberforce. He now defends extreme ultramontanism with the same unrivalled dialectic skill, brilliant eloquence, and unscrupulous sophistry, though always in decent and pure language, with which he formerly vindicated radical democracy and all possible phases of negative Protestantism (its positive evangelical life he probably never tasted), even to downright pantheistic infidelity. This itself will account for his enjoying so little confidence and exerting far less influence upon the Protestant reading community, than his rare talents would lead one to suppose. A man, who can prove everything, in a moral point of view proves nothing. In spite of all his asseverations (noticeably repeated, and for this reason rather suspicious) of absolute submission to the infallible authority of the pope and even of his diocesan bishop, Brownson has still in the bottom of his heart a whole mass of Protestant principles and impulses of independence and private judgment, and remains a restless agitator and democrat. Only he now thinks the Roman church alone can save American liberty and the American Republic, while he has the shameless effrontery to reproach Protestantism with favoring everywhere civil and religious despotism and barbarism.*

The Catholics, however, look further than these isolated cases of conversion. They believe that especially in America, where it has not the benefit of state support and protection, and is left to its own centrifugal tendencies, Protestantism will continue to dissolve into sects and parties, till it reduces itself to atoms, and thus, wearied with the endless fluctuation of subjectivity, and longing for repose in some tangible

* How he can reconcile this bold assertion, often repeated in his Review and public lectures with his recent admission that the Roman Catholic church enjoys more freedom in the predominantly Protestant United States, the Know-Nothing movement notwithstanding, than in any Roman Catholic country of the globe, we must leave to his logic, which never fails him. "There is no cause," he says in his Review for July, 1855, page 408, in an article against Know-Nothingism (which, by the by, he most ably defended to the great indignation of the Irish, about a year ago, when he vainly hoped to be able to control the anti-Catholic fanaticism of this party), — "there is no cause for our Catholic friends abroad to feel any alarm for American Catholics. Annoyances, vexations, and petty persecutions we have always suffered, and shall continue to suffer; but nothing can justify the desponding tone of those who are advising Catholics to emigrate to Canada, to South America, or to some other country. There is no country where the church is freer than she is here, and no country, Protestant or even Catholic, where, after all, ecclesiastical property is safer than with us. Look at Mexico, New Granada, Central America, Spain, Portugal, Sardinia, the Kingdom of the Two Sicilies, Baden, Bavaria, and Austria, and tell us if Catholics are freer, or their church property safer, than in our Republic? We can speak as freely in our Review on political and religious topics as we please, and yet the *Civiltà Cattolica*, published at Rome, an eminently Catholic periodical, is prohibited in the Catholic Kingdom of the Two Sicilies (we add, by the special protector, a friend of Pius IX., when in exile), and has lost, we are told, four thousand subscribers by the prohibition. The *Correspondance*, a truly Catholic periodical published in French at Rome, was suppressed, in order not to offend French sensibilities. Nothing of the sort has taken or is likely to take place here, and this is probably the only country where the Catholic press is absolutely free. Let us not be insensible to the advantages we enjoy, nor tolerate without rebuke those misguided journalists, who, under pretence of defending Catholic, but more especially Irish, interests in America, traduce the country abroad."

190

infallible authority, negatively prepares itself to return into the bosom of the one unchangeable Catholic church.

It is unquestionably very probable, that the ultimate fate of the Reformation will be decided in America; that it will there be proven, whether the work was of God or of man; and this gives that country, according to human calculation, which it is true may deceive, its extraordinary prospective importance for church-history. Both the great parties of Christendom are assembling there from all quarters of the Old World, and arming themselves for one of the most earnest and decisive battles, which the pages of history will record. The sagacious Cardinal Archbishop Wiseman is reported to have said once, in the sweet dream of England's being already in principle won over to Rome, that the Catholic church would strike her last blow of conquest on the sands of Brandenburg; probably on the "Köpeniker Felde" near Berlin, where, close to the magnificent evangelical deaconess house of Bethany, she is now erecting a splendid cathedral, and in a great measure with funds willingly furnished by a Protestant King, who also liberally aided the building of the Cologne Cathedral as a symbol of future union. We have not the slightest doubt, that on the sandy plains of Prussia's Capital great and momentous things will yet take place, especially in the empire of thought, which after all rules the world. But we think the last decisive engagement between Romanism and Protestantism will fall not in Europe, not even in the world's emporium of London and the learned halls of venerable, mediæval Oxford, but on the banks of the Hudson, the Susquehannah, the Mississippi, and the Sacramento; and that it will result in favor not, as the sanguine Papists think, of the Roman, but of an evangelical Catholicism. What is true and great and good and beautiful in the hoary but still vigorous Catholic church, should, must, and will be preserved; but its temporary form, the papacy, must perish, and with it saint and relic worship, the spirit of persecution, tyranny over conscience, and everything which makes believing Protestants, with all their longing for church unity, and all their grief over the weaknesses and faults of their own system, still stand apart from the Roman church for conscience' sake, and for the sake of the dearest blessings of the holy Gospel, and immediate communion with Christ, our all-sufficient Saviour.

Meantime, however, in America, as in England and Germany, Protestantism must be expected to lose many more noble spirits, repelled by the growing sectarian confusion, and unduly attracted by the idea of unity and catholicity, by the truly imposing organization of the Roman church, her rich and fascinating worship, her monkish asceticism, or her supernatural halo of miracles and saints. And Romanism, on her part, will have still to suffer mighty convulsions and deep humiliations, before she will consent to abate anything from her measureless claims, to bow in simplicity before the Gospel and to give Christ all the honor due to his name.

Our view here of the prospects of the two confessions in America, is based chiefly on the vital energy of Protestantism, which has already survived so many storms, and thrown off so much morbid matter; and on the conviction that the evangelical truth, which was brought out from the inexhaustible mines of Holy Scripture by the spirit of God in the times of the Reformation, as well as the evangelical freedom, which springs from this truth, can never perish, but, in spite of all hindrances, must spread in ever enlarging circles. But with this, we have also other reasons, why we think the ultimate triumph of Romanism in America impossible.

In the first place, we must remark the fact, that the Roman church in the United States, though it has considerably grown, as facts previously stated show, still has not kept pace with the number of Roman Catholic emigrants and the increase of the leading Protestant denominations. To estimate its progress fairly, we must not take it by itself, but in its relation to the whole country, where almost everything grows with unheard-of rapidity. The Presbyterian, Methodist, Baptist, Episcopal, Lutheran, German Reformed churches, have doubled within a few decades; and this growth will continue as long as emigration continues. Nay, more. The Roman church has even lost in proportion. Several of her own sheets bemoan, from time to time, the apostasy of so many immigrant Irish, Germans, and French from their mother church. Within the last five and twenty years, according to reliable Roman Catholic accounts, she has lost about two millions of Irish; so that the present numerical strength of Romanism is hardly as great as its loss in this quarter alone. Add to this, that in a country, where every one is free to choose his own religion, the religion of the minority is always at a disadvantage. And this may be said with double force of the Roman church, on account of its peculiar character as related to the genius of the American nation.

For the Roman church — and this is the second argument against her progress — is extremely unpopular in America. She has, indeed, as much freedom before the law, as any Protestant denomination, and more than she has in most Roman Catholic countries; for the Constitution of the United States forbids Congress to interfere in any way, positively or negatively, with matters of religious conviction, handing these over to the exclusive care of the churches and sects. But the ruling spirit of the nation, and its institutions, and the power of public opinion, are most thoroughly Protestant, more so than in any German State, or even in England.* If

* Even Brownson admits this in opposition to certain Irish Catholic assertions to the contrary. "The undeniable fact is," he says, in his "Review" for Jan., 1855, p. 140 — "that the United States, as to the dominant sentiment of the people, are more decidedly anti-Catholic than any other civilized country of the globe."

the framers of the Constitution could have foreseen the future growth and importance of Romanism in the States, it is not unlikely, that they would have inserted some disqualifying clause, and if the Know-Nothing party should ever get the control of central legislation, they would, in all probability, make an effort to do it yet, at least as far as the new Catholic emigration is concerned. But it is too late now for any organic change of the constitutional provisions for full civil and religious liberty and equality of all Christian denominations. The great battle between Romanism and Protestantism in North America must be fought on this basis.

In Germany, where the two confessions live rather quietly together on the basis of the Westphalian peace, and are often united under one government, you can hardly form any idea of the deep-rooted horror, which Puritanism and Presbyterianism have for Popery. Only think of the fact that so dignified and considerate a body, as the General Assembly of the Old School Presbyterian church, at its session in Cincinnati in 1845, solemnly and almost unanimously unchurched the Church of Rome altogether, and outpoping the Pope, declared all its ordinances, even baptism, null and void! The popular Protestantism of North America sees in Romanism the bodily Antichrist; the Man of Sin predicted by Paul, who exalts himself above all that is called God, or that is worshipped; the Synagogue of Satan; the Beast of the Apocalypse; the Babylonian whore; an enemy of all freedom of thought and faith; a fearful power of persecution and of tyranny over the conscience; a spiritual tyranny, which, if it rule, must also lead to political despotism. They can hardly conceive of the Roman clergy as embracing any honorable and pious men; but only as a horde of slaves under a foreign despot, the Pope; a band of avaricious priests, hypocrites, and rascals. This spirit pervades the religious press of America, with a few exceptions, from the "New York Observer" to the most obscure sheet of the smaller sects,

194

which happens to sail under the Protestant flag; and many of the political organs, especially those conducted by the Native American party, share in the same prejudices. The Roman Church is bemired from day to day with all possible accusations and calumnies, and combated with Scripture quotations, arguments, mockery, witticisms, horrible stories and absurd misrepresentations. The burning of the Catholic Convent at Charlestown in 1834, and of St. Augustine's Church in Philadelphia in 1844, and the public insults to the archbishop and papal nuncio, Bedini, in 1853, not to speak of the more recent committees and enactments of Know Nothing legislatures, are the natural fruit of this fanatical hatred, which at once meets even those Protestants, who have the courage to express and vindicate more liberal and favorable views of the Catholic Church.

And the Catholic press, it is true, does no better, making allowance, of course, for some honorable exceptions. Brownson lately wrote in cold blood, that the Reformers, after leaving the church of Rome, had not a single natural virtue, to say nothing of supernatural, and asserts again and again that Protestantism is no religion at all; but a sheer negation, a destroyer, a rebellion against divine and human authority, a diabolical movement which must end in absolute infidelity. The "Freeman's Journal," of New York, is full of bitter mockery and malicious exultation over every dispute and every difficulty in the Protestant camp, and shows towards us the same loveless, I might almost say Mephistophelian spirit, as the Munich "Historisch-Politische Blätter," and the Paris "Univers."

I have observed the Catholic and Protestant presses in America for years, and could hardly say which exceeds in injustice, deception, misrepresentation, and passion. But it is pretty clear that such illiberality and bigotry is far more inconsistent with Protestantism than with Romanism. This *rabies theologorum* in America, which, however, shows itself of late in Europe also, so far as religious interest and freedom of the press prevail, is one of those most unfortunate things, which might disgust many a man with the calling of a theologian. It must be considered, however, that religion is the matter of deepest and most universal interest to man, and therefore enlists his deepest sympathies and antipathies, awakens his warmest love and his bitterest hatred. I have no doubt there are many Protestants in America, who would vote on the spot for the banishment of every Catholic priest, and would justify this act by their very theory of universal freedom of faith and conscience, in the honest conviction, that the priests, especially the Jesuits, are the sworn enemies of this freedom, and are secretly working to destroy it.

Thus, while the Roman Church unquestionably has in America free play, full civil qualification, and unrestrained intercourse with her centre, in which she has often been in various ways, and still is in some instances, embarrassed even by many Catholic princes, jealous of their sovereign rights, in Spain, France, Austria; she has on the other hand a hard lot. She has to swim against the stream of public opinion, which in republican North America is more nearly almighty than anywhere else in the world; and which sees in Romanism not the pure, simple Gospel with the branch of peace, but an enslaving politico-ecclesiastical organization and an ambitious and intolerant hierarchy.

But finally; the American-born generation of Catholics cannot possibly remain entirely uninfluenced by the free political institutions, and the thoroughly Protestant spirit of the country. Their bishops, it is true, so far as I know, belong without exception to the ultramontane school, and were amongst the most earnest to urge upon the Pope the propriety of solemnly declaring the dogma of the Immaculate Conception; but they are mostly foreigners by birth and education. The laity cannot be judged of by them. The majority of these, especially the Irish and Germans, in political matters, go with even the Democratic party, the left wing of the Republic; and the longer they live in America, the more they become familiarized with political and social views quite foreign to the genius of Romanism. I know only one theological sheet, which has ventured there to advocate, for example, the principle of the persecution of heretics by civil punishments; while Archbishops Kenrick and Hughes, and several other organs have publicly disavowed it, the first from personal mildness, the others at least from prudent regard to public opinion. But the public schools especially, which, even where religion is not directly taught, are still Protestant in the general character of the pupils and teachers, will gradually free the Catholic youth from the exclusive influence of the priesthood, and put them on a more liberal track. This may, indeed, drive them to skepticism and unbelief; but it may also lead them to positive evangelical Protestantism. Hence the vigorous efforts of the hierarchy against these schools, in which it justly sees its life in danger. I doubt, however, whether it will ever succeed in overthrowing them; though we ourselves regard them as very defective in the matter of religious education, and as needing the addition of special denominational instruction.

Catholicism, therefore, must in process of time assume a more liberal character in America, than in Europe. It must more or less approach evangelical Protestantism. The Pope, it is true, will never yield as Pope. But we know not what events may take place in his communion in spite of him. The Reformation of the sixteenth century, and Jansenism and Gallicanism of the seventeenth; proceeded from its bosom and may be followed by similar or still greater movements. On the other hand the jejune and contracted theology of popular American Protestantism must likewise, and will no doubt, undergo in course of time a considerable revolution, especially since the best, most learned Protestant historians, both secular and ecclesiastical, English and German, have taught us to view the history of the church before the Reformation, in a very different light from that in which Puritanism used to regard it. Such changes in theological opinion would no doubt also affect the religious sentiment, and greatly contribute towards removing the bigoted prejudices of the two confessions, until the present relation of bitter enmity be exchanged for one of mutual respect and love.

(j) THE MORMONS

I confess, I would fain pass over this sect in silence. It really lies out of the pale of Christianity and the church; for as to single corrupted elements of Christianity, these may be found even in Manicheism and Mohammedanism. Nor has it exerted the slightest influence on the general character and religious life of the American people, but has rather been repelled by it, even by force, as an element altogether foreign and infernal. Besides, I fear I can say nothing at all satisfactory about this phenomenon, owing to want of accurate knowledge from the proper sources on our own part, and to the general immaturity of the phenomenon itself. But by such silence I should disappoint expectations. For concerning nothing have I been more frequently asked in Germany, than concerning the primeval forests and the Mormons — the oldest and the newest products of America — as if it had nothing of greater interest and importance than these.

Unquestionably a remarkable appearance in the history of the religious vagrancy of the human mind is this Mormonism. And the most remarkable thing about it is perhaps the fact, that this worst product of America should so rapidly spread in old experienced Europe, and seem to elicit, even in cultivated Germany, much more curiosity and interest, than the most important political and ecclesiastical matters in the New World. Something similar is true of table-turning and spirit-rapping. If America is so prolific of all sorts of "humbugs," Europe was the honor of immediately imitating them.

The principal points in the external history of this sect are these: — The Book of Mormon, the last prophet of the Indians, was miraculously discovered, it is pretended, near Palmyra, N. Y., written on golden plates, abounding in Scripture passages and gross grammatical errors, and consisting of a very tedious romance about the ten tribes of Israel driven away to America and converted by Christ in person. The discoverer, Joe Smith, an uneducated but cunning Yankee, was assisted by an angel to translate into English and publish this new bible, the original of which, full of Egyptian hieroglyphics, has since disappeared.* He was ordained to the "Melchisedekian priesthood," and made an effort, at first not very successful, to gather from the corrupt Babel of nominal Christendom, on the basis of this new revelation, a distinct sect, styled: — The Church of Jesus Christ of Latter-Day Saints, and to prepare them for the approaching return of Christ, (A.D., 1830). This sect moved to the states of Ohio and Missouri; and not thriving there, and encountering violent persecution, they went to Illinois, where they built a city and a splendid temple at Nauvoo on the bank of the Mississippi, in 1839. There they were attacked by a violent outbreak of popular indignation against them, as a gang of shameless imposters and robbers; their

* He furnished himself a history of his life and sect, for Rupp's work on the Denominations of the U. S., which begins in the following characteristic manner: "The Church of Jesus Christ of Latter Day Saints, was founded upon direct revelation, as the true church of God has ever been, according to the Scriptures (Amos iii. 7, and Acts i. 2). And through the will and blessing of God I have been an instrument in his hands, thus far, to move forward the cause of Zion. Therefore, in order to fulfill the solicitation of your letter of July last, I shall commence with my life. I was born in the town of Sharon, Windsor County, Vermont, on the 23d of Dec., A.D., 1805. When ten years old, my parents removed to Palmyra, New York," etc.

temple was destroyed, and their prophet Joe Smith, since venerated by his successors as a holy martyr, was killed, (A.D., 1844). The remnant of the Mormons then made a toilsome pilgrimage over the Rocky Mountains to the Great Salt Lake, surrounded by high mountains, in the fertile and mineral territory of Utah, on the overland route to California (A.D., 1846). There they founded the city of the Great Salt Lake, also called the City of the Desert; a second Solomon's Temple, which, when finished, is intended to surpass everything the world has yet seen in this line; and a theocratic community under the direction of the inspired prophet and priest-king, Brigham Young. In this remote high-land of the Far West, almost cut off from all communication, they have made rapid material progress. They have sent missionaries into almost all parts of the world, and have successfully propagated themselves in England (especially in Wales, where they are said to have made thousands of converts), as well as in Denmark and Norway. Thus, almost like a second edition of Mohammedanism, has this sect risen in the extreme West, to the astonishment of the world; and just at the time, too, when the old Mohammedanism in the East is decaying and lying as a carcass, around which the Russian, French, and English eagles are gathering together.

Their crisis, however, is yet to come, when they shall have reached the lawful number of sixty thousand (they now number perhaps half this at Salt Lake), and Utah, one of the territories of the United States, shall come to be erected into an independent state. They may possibly give Congress great trouble, and require its armed interference. For it is very questionable, whether it will admit into its confederacy a state on such a theocratic and despotic basis, and with such moral or rather immoral principles and institutions. American toleration, as we have before remarked, has its limits; the separation of church and state by no means involves a separation of the nation from Christianity and

Christian morality. The uncommon regard of the American people for the female sex absolutely requires monogamy; and for this reason alone they can never make terms with the Mormons. Their missionaries in Europe, it is said, indeed, commonly deny polygamy; but in the United States it is universally believed, that they practice it; and it has been recently stated in many journals, that their governor, Young, the successor of Smith, appeared in public with thirty wives, sixteen of whom had children at the breast. This would make the system a much enlarged and improved edition of Mohammedanism, with the best prospect of a numerous posterity. But, though this fact be not credited, we must still believe the American captain and engineer, Stansbury, who in his account of his expedition to the Salt Lake, states that he himself heard Governor Young say in the church, he had a right to take a thousand wives, if he thought good; and he challenged any one to contradict him from the Bible. The professed religious motive for polygamy is chiefly to raise up as fast as possible a "holy generation for the Lord."

Thus much is certain, that the Mormons and the Americans, or the proper people of the United States, do not fit together, but have a deadly hatred of each other. Hence the former, presecuted and driven away by their own countrymen, have tried their fortune in the Old World; and have already enticed hundreds and thousands to travel over sea and land to their New Zion beyond the Rocky Mountains, near the gold country of California; where a Mormon, in 1848, first discovered gold-dust in a brook. Declamations against their actual and supposed corruption of Christianity, and their high claims of new revelations and visions, always find ready access with a certain class. But at the same time the Mormons appeal to the spirit of emigration so widely diffused, and meet it with the most flattering promises. Their emigrant ships are said to be very cleanly, and in general excellently furnished. They have a special emigrant fund, to which every member is bound to contribute, to provide for the removal of indigent converts. They are even seriously thinking of opening an easier passage to the "State of the West," from the isthmus of Panama.

Mormonism, as a system of religion, strikingly resembles Irvingism. The Irvingites, in fact, see in it a diabolical caricature of their own figure; as the Roman Catholic missionaries thought the striking resemblances of some heathen religions of the East to the doctrines and usages of their church could be accounted for only as satanic imitations. Mormonism and Irvinigism are about contemporaneous in origin with each other and with Puseyism. Both look for the speedy return of Christ, and make it a leading object of faith and hope. Both consider all present Christendom, Protestant as well as Catholic, an apostate and hopeless Babel; only Irvingism is much more moderate and cautious on this point, having a high regard for church antiquity, and really seeking to combine the truth of Catholicism and Protestantism. Both believe, that the only remedy is to be found in a direct revelation and a supernatural new creation; nay, in a divine restoration of all the offices and miraculous powers of the apostolic church. Both have a hierarchy modelled on the apostolic constitution, with apostles, prophets, and evangelists. Both lay claim to the gift of tongues, prophecy, and the power of miraculous healing by prayer and laying on of hands; and indeed the Irvingites are inclined, with their rivals, to admit the agency of supernatural powers, but refer them to a satanic origin. Both regard the Jewish tithe-paying as a sacred Christian duty. Both send into all the world, where they are allowed access, apostles and evangelists to collect the "latter-day saints" into the true Zion, and to prepare for receiving the Lord in his glory.

But the Mormons lack the solemn liturgical worship of the Irvingites; and above all the fine culture, the deep moral and religious earnestness, the humility and mildness, the honest effort after holiness, and the Christian loveliness, for which the Irvingites, so far as I personally know, and can gather from the writings of Carlyle, Thiersch, Böhm, Rothe, and others, are highly distinguished, and by which they prove themselves true disciples and followers of Jesus, in spite of all their singular views. Nay, if only the half be true of what is reported in the public prints respecting the horrible "spiritual-wife system," as it is called, and other peculiarities of the Mormons, they are on a decidedly immoral and abominable track; so that the Americans cannot be particularly blamed for wishing to be rid of such a pest. But then the fact remains the more striking, which Captain Stansbury gives from his own observation, that among these "Latter-day Saints" peace, harmony, and happiness generally prevail. It is remarkable, too, that Mormonism has had far better outward success, than Irvingism, which, though less bold and energetic, is incomparably higher and more pure and earnest in an intellectual and moral point of view. The Irvingites have only two small congregations in America, so far as I know, in the State of New York; and even in England and Germany they seem of late to be rather stationary. Thus, however, the tares often grow much faster than the wheat; and error is not seldom more popular than truth.

But I readily grant, that Mormonism is, to me, still one of the unsolved riddles of the modern history of religion; and I therefore venture no final judgment upon it. I must only beg, in the name of my adopted fatherland, that you will not judge America in any way by this irregular growth. She has inherited from her mother Europe, and preserved, much that is infinitely better, and will undoubtedly produce in future far worthier fruits in the field of religious and ecclesiastical life.

We need no new sects; there are already too many. We need no new revelation; the old is sufficient. America, to ful-

203

fill her mission, has only to present in its unity and beauty the old and eternally young church of Christ, according to the word of God and the nearly two thousand years' experience of Christian history, whose results are there embodied in so many denominations and sects, yet united in a common national life. Whatever may be her immediate future, thus much is certain: that there, as everywhere, the Lord rules supreme over the wisdom and folly of men, and that all kingdoms must at last bow to him, "from the rising of the sun even unto the going down of the same."

PART III

Germany and America

GERMANY AND AMERICA

The Evangelical Church in Germany in its relation to the Daughter Churches in America, and its duty to the German Emigrants. Report of Prof. Dr. Schaff, of Mercersburg, Pennsylvania, read before the Seventh meeting of the German Evangelical Church Diet, at Frankfort on the Maine, on the 20th of September, 1854. *

HONORED FATHERS AND BELOVED BRETHREN: —

First I present to you, as the Representatives of the German Evangelical Churches of Europe, a benediction and fraternal salutation in the name of the German Evangelical Churches of America, which although separated from you by land and sea, are yet flesh of your flesh and bone of your bone; and as the two hemispheres are now brought nearer and nearer to each other through the power of steam and electricity, so she desires to become more and more closely united to you through the deeper power of faith and love.

Thousands of evangelical Christians in the New World, who still revere and love Germany as their natural and spiritual birth-place, and take the most heartfelt interest in the struggles and victories of the mother-church, hailed also with delight the rise of the German Church Diet in the year of 1848, as a bow of peace and promise, after the storms of the Revolution, and as the dawning light of a new day to German Christendom. They saw in it the fruit of the free

* This address, as printed in the official report of the Frankfort Church Diet was translated from the German, by the Rev. Prof. Thomas C. Porter, of Franklin and Marshall College, Lancaster, Penn., for the "New York Observer." It is here added as a third part, although it was not included in the author's book on America.

pastoral conferences, a beginning toward the concentration and consolidation of the noblest powers of the German Churches of the Reformation, a mighty engine for moral improvement, a living embodiment of "Inner Missions," a noble evangelist for the suggestion and furtherance of every good work. With the liveliest sympathy they followed its annual meetings from Wittenberg to Stuttgart, Elberfeld, and Berlin, were edified by the beautiful evidences of faith in the most sterling representatives of the Evangelical theology and piety from all parts of Germany; admired the remarkable unanimity and lofty enthusiasm, with which, in the year 1853, it replanted the standard of the venerable *Augustana* against infidelity and superstition in the city of Frederick II. and Nicolai, and hoped for the most complete success in its great work of a thorough inward regeneration of German Protestantism. And even at this hour, when you are holding your seventh session in the old imperial city, so renowned in the history of the nation, innumerable prayers on your behalf are ascending on the other side of the Atlantic Ocean, that the humiliating scenes of the Frankfort Parliament may not be repeated in the Frankfort Church Diet, but that a stream of blessing may issue thence, flow over all Germany, and even reach the far-off shores of the Mississippi, and that a deep foundation may be laid for spiritual unity and moral freedom, till the Lord himself, beyond our prayers and comprehension, shall crown our defective endeavors after union and confederation with the perfect exhibition of one flock, gathered out of all lands, nations and confessions under Him, the one Shepherd.

The Church Diet, on its side, has not forgotten its kindred in foreign countries and its large heart and true tact appear in this, that at Bremen it admitted into the compass of its transactions *the German emigration,* and at Berlin *the dispersions of Germans in Europe,* as an important department of Inner Missions. Hence it was very natural to take into view the much greater *dispersions of Germans in America and the entire relation of the German Evangelical mother-church to her American Daughter.*

This is the theme which the central committee of the "Congress of Inner Missions," handed over to me for an introductory report. Permit me, therefore, to direct your attention to the following three points:

1. The significance of America in general for the development of the kingdom of God.

2. The position and work of the German Evangelical Church in America.

3. The duty of the mother-church in Europe to her American-German Daughter.

In so doing, I will consider the German Church of America as a whole, embracing all the denominations, which the reformatory confessional basis of the Church Diet marks out; and I can do this the rather, because I was ordained in the Evangelical Church of Prussia, and in January, 1848, the year in which the Diet took its rise, established a periodical, the "German Church-Friend," as a "central organ for the common interests of the Lutheran Reformed and United Confessions, and the Moravian Brotherhood," the very same communions represented this assembly.

I. THE SIGNIFICANCE OF NORTH AMERICA FOR THE FUTURE
DEVELOPMENT OF THE KINGDOM OF GOD

The United States of North America — whose citizens are called *Americans* in an emphatic sense — because the bearers of the historical life and progress of the whole Western Hemisphere — are a wonder in the annals of the human race. Their development, in its rapidity and gigantic proportions, far outstrip all former experience, and their significance for the future mocks the boldest calculation. Though not an hundred years old, they have become already, by natural force of expansion, one of the mightiest empires of the civilized world, with the control of one entire continent and two oceans, and spread, in the most peaceful manner, the meshes of their influence over Europe, Asia and Africa. And yet their history up to this time is only a faint prelude of what is to come, and the Americans of the twentieth century will look upon the present age of their country, with feelings akin to those with which modern Europeans regard the exodus of the threshold of the Middle Ages. The "Young Giant," has not yet, so to speak, sown all his wild oats, and along with many heroic deeds, commits also some wanton and extravagant pranks, which prove, however, the exuberant vigor of his youthful powers. Providence, who creates nothing in vain, has there made physical preparations on the grandest scale, and formed an immeasurable territory, containing the most fruitful soil, the most valuable mineral treasures and the most favorable means of commercial intercourse, as a tempting asylum for all European nations, churches and sects, who, there freed from the fetters of antiquated institutions, amid circumstances and conditions altogether new, and with renovated energies, swarm, and jostle each other, and yet, in an incredibly short space of time, are moulded by the process into one powerful nationality. Whilst Europe had first to work her way up out of heathenbarbarism, America, without earning it, has appropriated the civilization and church-history of two thousand years, as an inheritance, and already put out at the highest rate of interest for the benefit of after generations.

For, these Americans have not the least desire to rest on the laurels of the past and comfortably enjoy the present; they are full of ambition and national pride, and firmly resolved to soar above the Old World. They are a people of the boldest enterprise and untiring progress — Restlessness and Agitation personified. Even when seated, they push themselves to and fro on their rockingchairs; they live in a state of perpetual excitement in their business, their politics and their religion, and remind one of the storm-lashed sea, which here

"Seethes and bubbles and hisses and roars,
As when fire with water is commixed and contending"
"— it never will rest, nor from travail be free,
Like a sea that is laboring the birth of a sea."

They are excellently characterized by the expressions, "Help yourself" and "Go ahead," which are never out of their mouths. It is also a very significant fact, that they have invented the magnetic telegraph, or at least perfected it, and are far advanced in the useful arts. For there the car of the world's history moves swifter on the pinions of steam and electricity, and "the days become shortened."

The grandest destiny is evidently reserved for such a people. We can and must, it is true, find fault with many things in them and their institutions — slavery, the lust of conquest, the worship of Mammon, the rage for speculation, political and religious fanaticism and party-spirit, boundless temerity, boasting, quackery, and — to use the American word for it — humbug, as well as other weaknesses and dangers, that are moreover wanting to no country in Europe. But we must not overlook the healthy, vital energies, that continually re-act against these diseases: the moral, yea Puritanical earnestness of the American character, its patriotism and noble love of liberty in connection with deep-rooted reverence for the law of God and authority, its clear, practical understanding, its talent for organization, its inclination for improvement in every sphere, its fresh enthusiasm for great plans and schemes of moral reform, and its willingness to make sacrifices for the promotion of God's kingdom and every good work. The acquisition of riches is to them only a help toward higher spiritual and moral ends; the grain derived from the inexhaustible physical resources of their glorious country only the material ground-work toward the furtherance of civilization. They wrestle with the most colossal projects. The deepest meaning and aim of their political institutions are to actualize the idea of *universal* sovereignty, the education of every individual for intellectual and moral self-government and thus for true freedom. They wish to make culture, which in Europe is everywhere aristocratic and confined to a comparatively small portion of society, the common property of the people, and train up if possible every youth as a gentleman and every girl as a lady; and in the six States of New England at least, they have attained this object in a higher degree than any country in the Old World, England and Scotland not even excepted.

In short, if anywhere in the wide world a new page of universal history has been unfolded and a new fountain opened, fraught with incalculable curses or blessings for future generations, it is in the Republic of the United States with her starspangled banner. Either humanity has no earthly future and everything is tending to destruction, or this future lies — I say not exclusively, but mainly — in America, according to the victorious march of history, with the sun from east to west.

But America has also equally as great a prospective significance and mission for the internal and external development of *the kingdom of God.* The history of the world is only the vestibule to the history of the church, the voice of one crying in the wilderness, preparing the way for Him, who shall come. All political events and revolutions, all discoveries and inventions, all advances in art and science; in fine, all that belongs to the kingdom of the Father and is under the guidance of his general providence, must serve the Son and spread abroad his name, until the whole world is filled with his glory, and all nations walk in the light of eternal truth and love. For the Father draws all men to the Son, and "they shall honor the Son, even as they honor the Father."

American church-history is still in the storm-and-pressure-period. Its roots, with all their living fibres, are in Europe, especially in England. It draws its life from the past, most of all from the conquests of the Reformation of the sixteenth century, and the principles then established exert there an enormous power, and find the freest scope of action and influence upon the entire national life. Meanwhile it is all merely the labor of preparation, the heaping up of materials and plans, the chaotic fermentation that precedes the act of creation. But the prolegomena are laid out on the most comprehensive scale; the cosmos lies in the chaos, as man in embryo, and He who in the beginning said: "Let there be light!" lives and rules with his Divine Spirit, brooding over the ecclesiastical *Thohuvavohu* of the New World.

The history of the kingdom of God in America has already entered upon the dawn of a new era, and will unfold itself, under circumstances and conditions altogether peculiar, not indeed beyond Christ — for He is Alpha and Omega of church-history, and before Him the Americans bow with the deepest reverence as before the highest and holiest name in the universe — but beyond all that has hitherto existed in the ecclesiasticism of Europe. I can only touch briefly upon the new circumstances and conditions, which aid *the internal progress* of the church. To these belong the Protestant, or rather Puritan starting-point of North American Christianity, its complete deliverance from Mediæval Catholic and feudal institutions, its independence of the State, the universal religious freedom and liberty of conscience, and the meeting of all European confessions and sects on the basis of the voluntary system and political equality. In America the most interesting experiments in church-history are now made. There the idea is, to found a church, which, without any direct support from the government, and having for this very reason a stronger hold on the sympathies of the people, shall be the expression of all their untrammeled convictions, the bearer and guardian of their highest spiritual and moral interests. There the idea is, to actualize the genuine Protestant principle of a congregation, independent and yet bound to an organic whole, in a far greater degree than has heretofore been the case in the Old World; and to make each Christian a priest and a king in the service of the universal High Priest and King of Kings. There the idea is, to settle the conflict between the greatest diversity and essential unity, between freedom and authority in religion. There the whole controversy between Romanism and Protestantism has been taken up anew, and is rapidly drawing towards a most earnest, perhaps even a bloody issue. For North America is a land thoroughly Protestant, almost to an extreme, since Protestantism embraces not merely the large majority of the population, but is the source, at the same time, of all its social and political principles; in fine, is interwoven most intimately with the entire national life, and goes hand in hand with all the nobler struggles after freedom and ideas of progress. The public opinion, formed under the influence of Puritanism, regards Romanism, whether justly or unjustly, as the veritable Antichrist, Intolerance and Persecution personified, a system of the most terrible spiritual despotism, which, if successfully established, would also annihilate all political freedom and arrest the progress of history. Hence the more this church grows — although its growth does not keep pace with the immigration from Ireland, Germany and France, so that in fact much more material is lost than gained by the transition to America — the more do national jealousy and hatred, which have already found vent in manifold riotous proceedings, increase also. Here it will be seen, whether the Papacy, under conditions and circumstances like these, can maintain herself unaltered, or whether she will rush to ruin, or undergo a fundamental change.

In North America, moreover, the fate of the Reformation

is to be decided. There Protestantism, along with its enormous vital energies, its devotion to liberty, its ability to make sacrifices and its bold enterprising spirit, exhibits also its faults and weaknesses much more plainly than in Europe, where its free development is still checked by the fetters of ecclesiastical and civil forms and regulations, the growth of ages. There it will be seen, whether it, as its enemies prophecy, being left to its centrifugal and unchurchly tendencies, will at last break up into atoms, and prepare a greater triumph for Catholicism than even the victory over the Old Roman and Germanic heathenism; or whether, as we believe and hope, following its positive Christian principles, with the Word of God in hand and heart, it will come together, consolidate, concentrate itself, and out of the phœnix-ashes of all Christian denominations and sects, rise glorified, as the truly universal, evangelical Catholic Bride of the Lord, adorned with the fairest flowers of the church-history of all centuries.

Such a mighty mission appears to lie before the church-history of the country, of which we speak; not indeed as isolated from the rest of the world, but in connection with the other Christian nations, who are brought nearer every year, the barriers of space and time being broken down. To such a mission even the rude beginnings of their labor point, and thus much, according to human view, is at all events certain, that North America, along with England and Germany, furnishes the most important contributions toward solving the vast problems touching Christ and his Church, which now press upon Christendom with a mighty weight, and which will yet be determined to the honor of the God-man and Saviour of the world, and His Bride.

Not only upon the internal development of the Church but also upon the *external spread* of the Gospel, in all heathen lands, America, from its geographical position and by its rapidly increasing commerce, must exert an incalculable influence. The Sandwich Islands, that halfway station upon the route over the Pacific Ocean, have, by Puritan missionaries of New England, been already won over to the Gospel, and will soon become an integral part of the great Anglo-Saxon Republic. The ports of Japan have been lately opened to American trade, and the various Missionary, Bible and Tract Societies, with their fresh, energetic powers, will certainly follow up this advantage at the earliest favorable opportunity. The railroad and canal, soon to be made over the Isthmus of Panama, indicate, that the whole commerce between Europe and Further Asia, as well as the Missionary operations, for which it has thus providentially furnished a path, will, in a short time, take up their march through America, as the real centre of the world. Already a direct line of steam ships between San Francisco and Canton has been projected, and through this channel, Christianizing and civilizing influences beyond number will stream towards China; and already these Divine preparations are met, without their knowledge or wish, by the inhabitants of the "Celestial Empire" crowding by thousands into California, who, lured thither by gold and the high wages of labor, will yet find there and carry back to their native land, where just now events occur that will fill the whole world with astonishment, something infinitely better than all the treasure of the Sacramento, the precious pearl of the Gospel. For the Colossus of three hundred and sixty millions, after a long stagnation, amid dim forebodings of what should come, has at last set itself in motion, and rolls, like a tremendous avalanche of nations, toward a speedy political revolution, which, in the end, must certainly pave the way for a much more important one, in the sphere of the Spirit.

Similar stars of hope for the approaching triumph of the peaceful kingdom of Christ have risen above the African horizon. In the negro colony of Liberia, founded by American philanthropists, we not only see the first step toward the solution of the fearful riddle of negro-slavery, but the dawn also of a new day for the dark night of Africa, which will be yet conquered for the Gospel and civilization by her own sons and daughters, exported as rude heathen and now returning as Christian men and women.

But finally, North America will also take part in Inner Missions among the nominal Christians of the Old World, in order to restore the candlestick of the pure Word of God, where it has been obscured, or thrust aside, by various human ordinances and inventions. If Mexico, with its boundless sources of wealth, is ever to be delivered from the fetters of Romish ignorance and superstition, and raised out of the whirlpool of an eternal revolution to a state of rational freedom and order; if "the pearl of the Antilles" is yet to be transformed into a pearl in the diadem of the Evangelical Church and become an intellectual and spiritual paradise, — then it is evident, that this must be accomplished chiefly by the nationality and Protestantism of the United States. It is known, moreover, that the Americans have already established flourishing missions among the schismatical sects of the Greek Church; especially among the Armenians in European and Asiatic Turkey, and that they afford aid to the modern movements of the Waldenses in Piedmont, and to the Evangelical Societies of Geneva and Paris in the work of evangelizing France and Italy, through their political and religious institutions and their new-born literature.

I need only remind you of the fact, that the book, which has been most read during the last few years, is a religious novel, written by a New England lady, the daughter of a preacher and the wife of a professor. The United States exert already a very considerable influence, partly destructive, but partly regenerative also, on public opinion in England, Germany and France; an influence which must increase every year either as a curse or a blessing to old mother Europe.

217

I do not say all this in vain-glorious laudation of America, still less of the Americans, who, as men and Christians, are not one whit better than their European forefathers. Their vast mission and significance in the future history of the Church and the world can just as little be ascribed to any special merit on their part, as the choice of the people of Israel, who, in spite of their stubbornness and ingratitude, were called to be the bearers of the Law and the Prophets, and the stock from whence the Saviour of the world should spring. There is the hidden purpose of God, alike in both cases, and each time bound to a corresponding measure of enormous responsibility.

And just as little do I wish to depreciate Europe and the Europeans by the above remarks. For America is indeed the daughter of Europe and operates with European forces, of which a fuller stream flows thither every year. And the signs of the times appear to indicate, that, as the powers of darkness deepen and concentrate, so likewise all the positive elements of Christendom, in all parts of the world, should draw nearer, and become more closely joined together, so that they may achieve a more certain victory in the last decisive conflict. America and Europe ought to understand more clearly, prize more highly, and seek to know and love each other more fully in the common service of the one Lord, to whom all the parts of the globe belong, and must at last submit in free, blessed obedience.

II. THE POSITION AND WORK OF THE GERMAN EVANGELICAL CHURCH IN AMERICA

Into this American chaos of nations, creeds and sects big with the destinies of the future, the German element was cast, more than a hundred years ago, like leaven into a process of formation, out of which will grow a universal church-cosmos. Next to the English, which is plainly the original stock of the North American nation, it is the strongest in numbers and much more important than the Spanish, the Dutch, the French, or even the Irish element. The number of Germans in the United States, including their English descendants, is computed at four millions, constituting thus almost the sixth part of the collective population. And in this we find nearly all the races and religious denominations of our tongue represented: the Lutheran Reformed and United Confessions, the Moravian fraternity, the older sects of German Protestantism, along with several new ones, which have sprung up there, mostly of a Methodistical order; but, at the same time also, the very worst forces of irreligion and infidelity, which, as far as their influence extends, cover the German name in the New World with shame and disgrace, and, next to the Roman Catholic Irish, give the most nourishment to that bitter hatred of foreigners, which characterizes a strong American party, the Native Americans, or as they now call themselves, the Know-Nothings.

This German-American population will become stronger every year, by an *emigration*, which has almost swollen to a national exodus. I will refer to but one fact, that in the year 1852, in the single port of New York, one hundred and eighteen thousand six hundred and seventy-four Germans landed; the next year, one hundred and nineteen thousand four hundred and ninety-eight, and that this year the number will greatly increase; * for the German Society of that city mentions the arrival of thirty-two thousand five hundred and ninety-nine for the month of May alone. Like a contagious fever, the rage for emigration spreads through all parts of Germany and all the Cantons of Switzerland. Agencies for emigrants are to be met with in every city, works in every book-store, and advertisements in every newspaper; and the name of America has now become as familiar to

* The German emigration to the port of New York alone amounted for 1854, to 170,648.

every German peasant and laborer, yea to every child in the street, as that of the nearest neighboring country, whilst to thousands and hundreds of thousands, it is the goal of their warmest wishes and boldest hopes. In all probability, this movement from the East to the West will rather increase than slacken for many years to come, as long indeed as its causes and incentives continue, which are the diminishing prospect of obtaining a livelihood or wealth in Germany with its superabundant population, and, on the other hand, the brightening promise of material prosperity in America, together with the fact that the passage thither and settlement there, are becoming easier from year to year. No power on earth is able to check this movement, because *a law of historical development and the will of Providence are thereby fulfilled.*

This emigration has two sides. For Germany, under present circumstances, it is an absolute necessity, and in general a blessing, a relief from an excess of population with whose growth the products of the earth and the means of living cannot keep pace; a beneficial letting of blood and a drain for poverty as well as political and religious disaffection. At the same time, it opens new markets for German industry, so that the loss from money carried out of the country is amply repaired by the amounts, which are ultimately returned. But for America, this phenomenon has the same significance, as the emigration of the Celtic, Germanic and Sclavonic races from Asia to Europe, the Greeks into the West, and the dispersion of the Jews into all parts of the world. Emigrants, in general, are the pioneers of secular and ecclesiastical history, the scions of civilization grafted upon a wild stock in its luxuriant vigor.

Since, then, Providence has imparted to the German people so great an impulse toward emigration, and directed it principally to the United States, he must have designed for them a mission in the New World answering to their cosmopolitan character. That the Germans, by their industry, perseverance and skill, can aid and have aided very largely in rendering the inexhaustible natural resources of that country available, and furthering its material prosperity, is clearly visible and generally acknowledged. But this must serve only as means for the solution of a *spiritual and moral religious problem*, which is incomparably higher and more important.

This higher problem consists in preserving, applying, independently unfolding and elaborating the peculiar gifts of the German mind and spirit as well as German theology and piety, partly for their own wants and partly for the advancement and modification of the entire process of development in Anglo-American Christianity and its Churches. The design is, to transplant the treasures of German literature, the results of thorough investigation in the departments of exegesis, church-history, dogmatics and ethics, which the most distinguished English scholars are learning to prize more and more, into the fruitful soil of the Western Hemisphere; the design is, to impart to the Anglo-Saxon race and thereby complete it, a spirit of depth and inwardness, a tendency towards the ideal and eternal, a disposition to dig and burrow into principles, an enthusiastic love for truth and knowledge for their own sake, a will to rank the spiritual far above the material interests; in short, that which makes up the peculiar *charisma* of the German nation and Church in their noblest representatives; finally, the design is, to deliver the German mind itself from its own one-sidedness, to enlarge and enrich it by a living appropriation of the great excellences of the English character, and to fit it for new achievements in the sphere of science and of life.

The German nationality, in its pure form, bears a similar relation to the English, as the Old Greek to the Old Roman. The former is predominantly idealistic and speculative, the latter realistic and practical; the former has the deepest mind, the latter the strongest character; the former rules the world in that it fathoms and comprehends it in thought, the latter in that it subjects it to its own will and makes it serve its own ends; the former labors in the quarry and brings the rough material to light, the latter builds it up into a stately dwelling-house. Whilst the Germans, perhaps more than any nation ever did, prepare thoughts and ideas, which are the real life-blood of profane and ecclesiastical history — look only at the Reformation of the sixteenth century, substantially the work of the German mind! — the English and the Americans immediately convert thoughts into resolutions, and resolutions into deeds. With the one, everything runs into theory, and indeed so radically, that they are oftentimes in danger thereby of losing all they aim at: with the other, everything runs into practice, and it is quite possible, that many of the best and worst German ideas will yet attain in practical America a much greater importance than in the land of their birth, and first become flesh and blood on the other side of the ocean, like certain plants, which need transplanting to a foreign soil, in order to bear flowers and fruit.

If America, as many suppose, is to become the theatre of the last decisive conflict between faith and infidelity, between Christ and Antichrist; of the greatest collision between the various Christian nations and confessions and also of their final reconciliation; then surely the earnest and deep thinking of the German mind, especially through the medium of the English language, which is already and will always be the ruling language of the whole Northern part of the Western Continent, has no insignificant part to play therein.

At all events, if German science, the German Church and German piety, have yet a future anywhere in the world beyond Germany, that future lies in America, a new, vast, yea, immeasurable field of action. But it does not consist — for I must protest against a shallow over-rating of our language and nationality — in self-sufficient exclusiveness, or in hostile opposition to, but in friendly intercourse and union with the sterling and earnest English nationality, so nearly allied to ours. For surely God has brought together these two nations, branches of the same original Teutonic stock, upon American soil, not for hatred, but mutual completion and gradual intermingling, so that as one people they should promote the kingdom of God and Christian civilization. And since America is spreading her net further and further over the globe, and exerts upon public opinion, especially in Great Britain and Germany, a growing influence, the American-German Church, as soon as it lives to see its blooming-period, as we hope it will, and produces an Anglo-German literature of its own, can adapt the treasures of the German mind to the wants and tastes of the entire English nation, since indeed all important Anglo-American works are re-printed in England. Thus, to cite only one example, the fifth edition of Torrey's translation of Neander's Church History has already appeared in Boston and a double reprint of it in Edinburgh and London, whilst the German original has only reached the second. On the other hand, such an Anglo-American literature would bring the peculiar excellences of the English and American mind nearer to Germany, and thereby arouse even her to renewed activity.

O amiable enthusiast! So perhaps many will inwardly exclaim at this statement of the mission of the German nation and Church for America and the whole Anglo-Saxon world. But I know as well as any one, that the *present condition* of the Germans in the United States is still very far removed from this aim; yea, partly in flat contradiction to it. I know it, and would here utter in sharp tones, that in general it is not at all calculated to give the least nourishment to the pride of culture of our old German Adam, but much rather, to cover it with deep shame and humiliation. The great mass of the German emigrants have from the beginning belonged to the lower and uneducated classes, and, therefore, they are still far behind the Anglo-American population. But the so-called educated emigrants, many of whom were floated over by the unsuccessful revolutions of the years 1848 and 1849, are, alas! for the most part, not only estranged, in a painful degree, from all Christianity and the Church, but even from all higher morality, and deserve rather to be called the pioneers of heathenism and a new barbarism than of civilization. Such persons naturally bring only reproach and shame upon the German race in the congress of nations in the New World, and expose it to indignation and horror, or to the pity and contempt of all sober and respectable Americans.

Excuse me from the unpleasant task of giving a minute description of this godless German-American pest, as it shows itself daily in the rudest and most insolent fashion, especially in so many scurrilous political newspapers and tippling-houses in all the larger cities of the Union. Only allow me respectfully to remind you, that the guilt of it rests on Germany herself, who sends over, or permits to go, to America, as though it were merely a general house of correction for all European scamps and vagabonds, thousands, yea, hundreds of thousands, and among them a large portion of its very worst and most incorrigible population, without caring for their spiritual and moral wants, although they are flesh of her flesh and bone of her bone. On the night-side of German-American affairs are seen the fearful consequences of German rationalism and infidelity, of political and ecclesiastical mismanagement and of that modern philosophy, or rather pseudo-philosophy and mis-education, which makes fallen man, instead of the living God, the centre and end of all things; which exchanges the Bible-doctrine that man was created in the image of God, for the blasphemous notion that God is no more than the likeness of man, and, from the dizzy height of self-deification sinks down into the abyss of brutality and devilishness.

Yes, these swarms of emigrants, in their sad state of spiritual decay, constitute a powerful call on the German governments and German nation to tremble and repent. Would that this misery were recognized as a common sin and a common guilt! O that it would penetrate our very bones and marrow! O that the entire German Church, along with the abhorrence of the sin, would at the same time feel a Saviour's love, which led him to seek and to save the sinner, and neither slumber nor sleep till her lost sons and daughters, with penitent hearts, return again into their father's house from the beggarly husks of vice and impiety.

Notwithstanding all this, thanks be to God! there is no reason to despair. Paul was not cast down, when solitary and alone he wandered amid the numberless temples of the gods in Athens and Corinth, and preached the Divine foolishness of the cross to light-minded Epicureans, self-righteous Stoics and immoral worldlings; and God blessed his word with the most abundant success. The Jews were certainly, in the time of Christ, a degenerate race, and yet the Saviour came out of their midst, and his Apostles, the teachers of all centuries — and the synagogues of the dispersion of the cities of the Roman empire formed green oases in the wilderness of Heathenism and nuclei for Christian congregations. The Greeks had long sunk down from their eminence under the iron arm of the imperial Romans, and yet their literature educated the latter in humane studies, and the conquered gave laws to the conquerors.

But not this alone. The circumstances mentioned present only one aspect of the picture. Besides the many unworthy representatives of the German race, there are also in America thousands of our countrymen, who, as workmen, farmers and merchants, as clergymen and scholars, belong to the most useful and esteemed citizens of the United States, and a sufficient host also of believing souls as salt to preserve the mass from corruption. The German Churches of the Reformation with the Augsburg Confession, the Lutheran and Heidelberg Catechisms, and the rich treasures of the German hymns and liturgies, have been in existence there for a hundred years, and everywhere offer to the new immigrant a spiritual home.

It is, of course, impossible to give here a detailed description of the state of the *German-American Churches*, and I can the rather pass on, because I have attempted to do so in a book of mine, just about leaving the press. I will only say thus much: The German Evangelical Churches of the United States are yet in the first chaotic stages of development, and have to contend with innumerable troubles and difficulties, inasmuch as they are deprived of the support of religious institutions and traditions, which are the growth of ages, and are obliged to create new regulations, and govern and administer their own affairs; because there everything rests on the voluntary principle, to which the Germans, spoiled by the habit of receiving maintenance and protection from an established church, can only become reconciled by degrees. But notwithstanding all this, their advance is steady and even very rapid. Out of their long-continued lethargy and ignorance, they have awakened at last to self-consciousness and activity. They have not only doubled their numbers within the last twenty years, but have also grown in knowledge, piety and zeal, and assume already no mean position beside their English neighbors, although certainly in many things still behind the leading denominations. They now possess independent scientific institutions of their own, and can thus develope their resources and multiply their intellectual and ecclesiastical powers every year. Indeed, they can already point to the beginnings, even if they be small, of an independent theological literature and earnest ecclesiastical movements. In spite of countless discouragements and difficulties, they present one of the most promising fields of missionary labor, and have as much prospect of external and internal growth, as any Anglo-American denomination, or any established church in Europe. The more they expand and are built up in piety and true culture, the more will they exert a determining influence upon the course of development in the whole American Church; work in it like a beneficial leaven, bring honor to the German name, and become a real blessing to the New World.

But just in proportion to this advancement, the consciousness of the greatness and responsibility of their work and their distance from that, which they should and might be, increases also; especially in view of the immigration, which every year only enlarges their material and missionary field, without, at the same time, supplying the necessary spiritual force for its cultivation. They, therefore, still louder and louder cause to resound over the waves of the Atlantic, the Macedonian cry: — "Come over and help us."

III. THE DUTY OF THE GERMAN EVANGELICAL MOTHER-CHURCH
TOWARDS HER DAUGHTER IN AMERICA

In this great and difficult mission of German Christianity in the New World of freedom and the future, it is clear that the German mother-church ought to take an active and joyful part, prompted, if not by the higher motives of duty, at least by a certain Christian ambition and her own prospective advantage. I do not speak here of the native American-German population; for these the churches there ought themselves to provide; but of the new emigrants, who, like flocks without shepherds, have left their fatherland, and cannot possibly be cared for by them; hence the church in which they were born, baptized and confirmed, must lose a large portion of them unless a corresponding number of ministers emigrate along with the people.

We Protestants, and especially we Germans, are lacking in *esprit de corps* and a conscious feeling of unity. The interests of the Church, the Body of Christ, and thus of Protestantism also, are fundamentally the same everywhere, and become more and more so in an age, when the most distant regions of the globe are brought so near together by means of communication that mock at time and space. If one member suffers, the others suffer with it; if one member rejoices, the others rejoice with it. England will continue to live in America and Australia, and from thence rule the world, when St. Paul's cathedral has long crumbled into ruins and but a single pier of Westminster bridge is left standing as a witness to the departed glory of the city of Two Millions. And shall German Christianity not be concerned to have itself worthily and honorably represented on the chief theatre of future history in the world and the Church; to have its peculiar charisms, its profound ideas, its glorious hymns, its inwardness and genial spirit maintained and made a blessing to the whole Anglo-American people?

Here, if anywhere, a rich missionary field is opened, and a favorable opportunity afforded for the erection of enduring monuments of honor and victory. And then, do we not know, that the giving of aid in the kingdom of the Spirit is reciprocal, and that every gift, sooner or later, comes back, directly or indirectly, to the giver, laden with blessings? It is known, that the most flourishing Anglo-American Churches begin already to pay back the debt of gratitude which they owe to Europe; that during the terrible famine of the year 1846, they sent large supplies to Roman Catholic Ireland, even in spite of religious differences. Such a time of thankful repayment will also come for the German Church in America. Remember, that what you do for her, is done, if not directly for yourselves, perchance for your own, or your children's children. For the emigration continues and will go on, and who knows if it may not yet become a necessity, yea, a Divine command to the faithful, like the exodus of the children of Israel from Egypt. No one, who has the interests of

Germany at heart, can wish for such a result; but Europe rests upon a volcano, which can at any moment break out into a new eruption, and no bayonets, no political wisdom is able to stand security for the present order of things for the space of two years to come.

It is true, indeed, that matters are not so desperate in America, as is sometimes represented, that the German emigrants, if they fail to carry their own ministers with them, necessarily fall back into heathenism. On the contrary, America has become to many the birth-place of the new life. The Bible, Tract and Home Missionary societies stretch over the Germans also an arm of love, and several Anglo-American Churches, especially the Methodists, have for some years labored among them with considerable success, and established a fair number of missionary congregations. We rejoice with the Apostle, if only Christ is preached. It is infinitely better that the German emigrants should become pious Methodists, or Presbyterians, or Baptist Christians, than that they should sink into indifferentism and unbelief. But the praiseworthy zeal of Anglo-American Churches in behalf of the spiritual welfare of our countrymen, does, of course, not relieve us from our own duty; it ought rather to spur us on to renewed efforts, so that the material, that justly belongs to us, may be, if possible, retained, and contribute its part to the accomplishment of the great work, which directly belongs to the German Evangelical Church and can be performed adequately by her alone.

Yet, why should I bring further proofs for what is as clear as the light of the sun, the duty of a faithful mother, who can never forget her own child, but follows it everywhere with a heart full of love, sends up to heaven prayers and supplications for its welfare at all seasons, and beholds in it the continuation of her own life, her joy and her crown!

The sense of duty in this matter needs not to be awakened for the first time. Philanthropic societies in Germany, actuated by motives purely humane, have already taken care to provide moral regulations for the emigrants and safeguards against extortion and cheatery of every kind, especially in the sea-ports of both countries. The need also of ecclesiastical and religious regulations in behalf of the emigrants, so that they may become a blessing to Germany and America, has long been felt, and for supplying this need, several societies have reared up ministers and school-teachers for sending out to America, and thus effected much good. It is, therefore, only required to render this sense of duty already existing, and the religious interest felt in the affairs of German emigration, more intense, deep and universal, and provide ways and means, by which this want may be best met, and profitable results attained in the surest way.

We see little to hope from grand schemes for founding colonies of German churches; for their success is more than doubtful, because of the divisions that reign both in Europe and America. It is far better for the Germans themselves to become amalgamated with the Anglo-Saxon race, and to coalesce with them into one American nation, than to be isolated and form a state in the state and an ecclesiola in ecclesia. For the present we must be content with doing good to individuals and multiplying the amount of intellectual and spiritual resources, by which the cause of the Gospel may be best aided to a final triumph among the Germans in the United States. Organization in mass, the formation of a church-cosmos out of the American chaos of sects, we must leave to the creative activity of God and the progress of events. But the following can, and ought, to be done by Germany, in order that the emigration to America, which actually exists and continually goes on, may be made an honor to our church and a blessing to the Old and New Worlds.

1. *The introduction of a farewell service for emigrants*, in which, in the presence of the interceding congregation,

they will be warned by their pastor of the dangers and temptations of the journey, exhorted to remain true to the faith of their fathers and their own vows of baptism and confirmation, and provided with Bibles and other good books and tracts. Such a service has already been introduced in several places in the kingdom of Würtemberg and with good effect both for those remaining behind and those departing, since the heart is peculiarly sensible to religious impressions in moments of separation.

2. *The appointment of missionaries for emigrants in places of embarkation*, especially Bremen, Hamburg, Havre and Antwerp. There are indeed in all these places agents for their material interests. Why should there not also be agents of the Church, whose special duty it shall be to keep a moral guard over the swarms of emigrants, and labor among them by all lawful means — by private conversation, by public preaching in the church, in the streets and on shipboard, and by the distribution of Bibles, hymn-books, works on practical religion, and useful directions for new settlers? The beginnings of such an enterprise already exist.

3. *The sending out of well qualified ministers to those who have emigrated*, and especially, if possible, such as possess, along with the necessary theological culture, sound evangelical and churchly principles, energetic faith, a talent for popular speaking, practical wisdom and a tact for ruling well and organizing congregations, but above all a self-denying missionary zeal. The notion, that what is no longer fit for Europe may be good enough for America, is radically wrong. He who is not able to help himself here will fail completely yonder, where every man is thrown upon his individual exertions and measured by his personal merits; and if the German Church would assume an honorable position over against the Anglo-American Churches, and do credit to her mother, she must be represented by a faithful ministry, well qualified, theoretically and practically, for their work.

The venerable Orphan House of Halle has won great credit by having sent out the Fathers of the American Lutheran Church, and those for the most part, worthy, able men of blessed memory, such as Muehlenberg, Kunze and Helmuth; and, in our times, special societies have been formed for this purpose at Langenberg, Bremen, Stade and Berlin. I am personally acquainted with several, who have gone from the Langenberg Society, the Rough House of Dr. Wichern, the Basel Missionary Institute and the Swiss Pastoral Aid Society, and here cheerfully bear testimony to the fact, that they labor, amid manifold difficulties, with great success, and have founded many flourishing congregations. How much even one man may do for America is seen in the examples of Pastor Lœhe, who, in a certain measure, can be called the founder of the Old Lutheran Synod of Missouri, and Pastor Spittler, from whose Missionary Institute at the Crischona near Basel a Synod has gone forth for the Germans in Texas. These Societies might be revived, strengthened and enlarged, and, if possible, other similar ones besides established, say in Frankfort, Stuttgart, Hamburg and Bremen.

The chief difficulty appears to lie in the lack of means, since enough can scarcely be obtained for the growing practical wants of Germany herself. But every new want, if only felt aright, creates also its supply, and the sending out of missionaries to the heathen-world has done no injury to our list of candidates; nay rather, the zeal for Foreign Missions has awakened new zeal for Inner Missions, and *vice versa*. Perhaps, by negotiation with the German Church Governments, there might be brought about a *temporary transfer of candidates*, who, enriched by an experience of five or ten years in America, could afterwards return home, and thus, at the same time, form so many personal links of union between the German Churches in both hemispheres.

4. *The special training of pious and gifted young men for the service of the German Church in America*, with full

regard to her peculiar circumstances and wants. This can be done, either by the establishment of a particular theological school in some seaport, like Bremen or Hamburg; or in connection with institutions for foreign missions, like those of Basel and Barmen; or finally — the most simple and practicable method — by founding and supporting professorships and scholarships in the American-German Colleges and Theological Seminaries already existing, which are obliged, for want of funds, to turn away many indigent applicants. By assistance of this kind, permanent fountains of life and blessing would be opened in these institutions, and infinitely more be done for the great mass, than by the contributions of single congregations towards the building of a church or similar local ends, which should rest altogether on local sympathies and be supported by them.

5. The easiest method to obtain the necessary means for the various undertakings, especially the latter, would be by raising a *voluntary collection in all the churches* which, of course, would not exclude particular efforts in certain cases. Such a collection should, however, be repeated, from time to time, especially in countries where the emigration is the greatest. The money received might be distributed by a responsible central committee, partly to American societies of this kind, which already exist in various cities of Germany, and partly to the Education Boards of the Lutheran, German Reformed and United Evangelical Churches, in proportion to the numbers of their students, for the purpose of training up preachers for the German emigrants in the Eastern seaports and in the Western States. If a church-diet similar to the German, is formed among these American Churches — a thing not at all impossible — the whole business can be carried on by the central committees of these two bodies. But as matters now stand, it can be accomplished with no great difficulty, through the trustees of the seminaries and the presidents of the Synods.

This proposition is not altogether new. The Established

233

Church of Mecklenburg, by the efforts of Dr. Kliefoth, sent out some years ago a general collection to the Lutheran Concord College in St. Louis, and the Evangelical Church of Prussia has done the same this very month, for the United Evangelical Seminary of Marthasville in the State of Missouri. These are noble deeds of love, which will hold an honorable place in the annals of church-history, and bring down the blessing of God on both parties. O that the entire Evangelical Church of Germany would imitate these beautiful examples, rear for herself a glorious monument of helping love, exhibit to the world a proof of the unity of the German Protestant churches, and lay her numberless emigrants, with their children and children's children, under a perpetual debt of gratitude!

I leave it altogether to the Diet, whether to adopt these or similar propositions, whose practicability is partly at least guaranteed by experience, or to hand them over to the Central Committee of Inner Mission for closer consideration and carrying out in due time.

6. But, finally, it is a matter of great importance, to bring about *a more intimate connection between the German mother-Church of Europe and her German and Anglo-German daughter in America,* for their mutual strengthening and encouragement in every good work. This can be best done by an occasional correspondence, introduced by a letter of fraternal salutation from the Church Diet to the German Evangelical Churches of America, as well as by an occasional exchange of delegates; and in regard to the latter, I can promise any representative of the German Church a most cordial reception from all our American German Synods.

The greatest misery and the deepest wound of the Protestant Church, next to the wide-spread apostacy from living faith, is her dismemberment into so many confessions, sects and parties. It is the devil, who sows the seeds of discord and employs against us so successfully the cunning policy of *divide et impera.* These divisions, it is true, must, in the hand of God, who knows how to bring good out of evil, contribute to the greater increase of Christian powers and activities, and will at last, as negative conditions, lead to the highest unity, just as the fall of Adam was the occasion of the resurrection of Christ. But in spite of this, we must condemn them in principle, and bewail them as a common sin. Melanchthon, the "teacher of Germany," esteemed the water of the Elbe insufficient, as a stream of tears, to give a complete expression to his grief over the distractions of the Evangelical Church. Now, it is very questionable, whether Protestantism as such and with its present resources, has the capacity and the mission, to produce an external church-organism, possessed of complete unity; or whether the Lord himself has not rather reserved this till his second advent. At all events, however, it is the sacred duty of Evangelical Protestantism, as the voice of one crying in the wilderness, as a Church bearing witness by the pure word and sacraments, as the representative and guardian of personal Christianity, of direct living intercourse between the individual soul and its Saviour, to pave the way for his glorious second coming, and promote, in the most zealous manner, the free inward communion of faith and love, the unity of the spirit in the bond of peace, according to the earnest exhortation of the Apostle, till the Lord, by a new reformation, or by his personal appearing in the clouds of heaven, gather his people from all the ends of the earth and create a body of such inward unity, that the colossal theocratic organism of Church and State in the Middle Ages — that fleshly anticipation of the *regnum gloriæ* — and all our boldest ideals of union and confederation will be thrown far into the shade. Thus much stands immovably firm, as sure as Christ is the truth: The day will come, when there will be but one Shepherd and one flock, when all believers will be perfectly one, as He and the Father are one.

Do not the signs of the times, the present discoveries and means of communication, point out typically and prophetically the approaching fulfillment of the precious promise and intercessory prayer of our Great High Priest? Europe and America are brought nearer together every year in the way of commerce and multifarious intercourse, and the Atlantic ocean forms now a barrier of separation scarcely greater than the Alps did formerly between Germany and Italy. The more pressing, therefore, does the exhortation of the Apostle come to us, to cherish and promote the communion of faith and love in the Lord, who is the fountain and centre of life to all believers; the exhortation, which one of the most noble and pious Germans has so beautifully clothed in poetic language:

> Let us so united be,
> As Thou with the Father art,
> Till no more on earth we see
> Sundered members dwell apart,
> And alone from thy bright glow
> Drink our glory like a star;
> Then the world shall see and know
> That we thy disciples are.

With this wish and prayer, I turn back again, from the dear land for my birth and home of my spirit, to severe labors for the German Church in America; and indeed in great sadness of heart, but, at the same time, in the certain expectation of a reunion, if not at a European or an American church-diet, yet in the general assembly and Church of the First-Born, amid an innumerable company of angels, at the grand festival of reconciliation for all nations and confessions in the holy city of God on high, the heavenly Jerusalem, the mother and final home of us all, I bid you an affectionate, brotherly farewell!

INDEX

THE JOHN HARVARD LIBRARY

The intent of
Waldron Phoenix Belknap, Jr.,
as expressed in an early will, was for
Harvard College to use the income from a
permanent trust fund he set up, for "editing and
publishing rare, inaccessible, or hitherto unpublished
source material of interest in connection with the
history, literature, art (including minor and useful
art), commerce, customs, and manners or way of
life of the Colonial and Federal Periods of the United
States . . . In all cases the emphasis shall be on the
presentation of the basic material." A later testament
broadened this statement, but Mr. Belknap's inter-
ests remained constant until his death.

In linking the name of the first benefactor of
Harvard College with the purpose of this later,
generous-minded believer in American culture the
John Harvard Library seeks to emphasize the impor-
tance of Mr. Belknap's purpose. The John Harvard
Library of the Belknap Press of Harvard University
Press exists to make books and documents
about the American past more readily
available to scholars and the
general reader.